Contingent Meanings

Contingent Meanings

Postmodern Fiction,
Mimesis, and the Reader

Jerry A. Varsava

The Florida State University Press / Tallahassee

Permission to reprint the portions of chapter 4 that originally appeared as "Walter Abish and the Topographies of Desire," in *Thought* has been graciously granted by the publisher. Reprinted by permission of the publisher from *Thought* 62, no. 246 (New York: Fordham University Press, 1987), copyright © 1987 by Fordham University, pp. 295–310.

Florida State University Press
© 1990 by the Board of Regents of the State of Florida
⊗Printed in the U.S.A. on acid-free paper.

The Florida State University Press is a member of University Presses of Florida, the scholarly publishing agency of the State University System of Florida. Books are selected for publication by faculty editorial committees at each of Florida's nine public universities: Florida A&M University (Tallahassee), Florida Atlantic University (Boca Raton), Florida International University (Miami), Florida State University (Tallahassee), University of Central Florida (Orlando), University of Florida (Gainesville), University of North Florida (Jacksonville), University of South Florida (Tampa), University of West Florida (Pensacola).

Orders for books published by all member presses should be addressed to University Presses of Florida, 15 NW 15th Street, Gainesville, Florida 32611.

Library of Congress Cataloging-in-Publication Data

Varsava, Jerry A.
    Contingent meanings : postmodern fiction, mimesis, and the reader / Jerry A. Varsave.
        p.   cm.
    Includes bibliographical references.
    ISBN 0-8130-1004-7 (alk. paper)
    1. Fiction—20th century—History and criticism—Theory, etc. 2. Postmodernism (Literature). 3. Mimesis in literature. 4. Reader-response criticism.   I. Title.
PN3503.V35   1990
801'.953'0904—dc20   90-33551
                                                                CIP

for Hans

CONTENTS

Preface

MANY VIEW CONTEMPORARY POSTMODERN FICTION as having no
meaning, no "world reference," no "relevance" to fundamental moral
concerns in the late twentieth century. Such critics see in its manipu-
lations of narrative form a purely literary enterprise with a purely
literary-aesthetic appeal. Accordingly, socially-minded readers like
Gerald Graff and John Aldridge criticize postmodernists for their re-
lentless pessimism and self-preoccupation, while formalists like William Gass and Richard Kostelanetz admire postmodernists for the purity of their aesthetic vision. Both critic and apologist have neglected
the positive mimetic function of postmodern fiction. *Contingent Meanings* seeks to redress this situation in some measure. As I will demonstrate, it is wrongheaded to suggest that postmodern fiction is unmimetic because it displaces certain narrative conventions and, in so
doing, unsettles many of our own attitudes on literature and life. Further, it is untenable to declare that postmodern fiction is unmimetic
simply because authors themselves declare for their work such a bias.
In making my case for a mimetic function in postmodern fiction, I
evaluate the reception of postmodern fiction and, before going on to
interpret selected texts, I advance a contingent, reader-centered view
of mimesis.

In chapter 1, as a preamble to the discussion of the reception of
postmodern fiction, I analyze Aristotle's views on literary representation. At the level of production, Aristotle, promoting the superiority

of literature over history, allowing for both *poiesis* (inspiration) and *mimesis* (imitation/reflection), espouses a conception of representation essentially nonnormative. However, at the level of reception, he maintains a substantialist view of interpretive validity. Through catharsis, the beholder/reader apprehends emotionally the significance of the text. In Aristotle, interpretive validity rests on a successful recuperation of an authorially intended meaning and effect. Later critics, acknowledging the centrality of the mimesis issue in criticism, have applied Aristotle's ideas dogmatically, particularly his production-oriented view of mimetic adequacy.

In the twentieth century, the reception of innovative literature has been primarily concerned with the shaping vision of the author rather than with the reader's appropriation of a text. Critics have legislated private standards of mimetic adequacy which, in view of much postmodern fiction, appear arbitrary. They have evaluated literature on the basis of the author's supposed fidelity to these standards. Though in various respects an Aristotelian, Lukács, unlike Aristotle, emphasizes mimesis over poiesis and finds the modernism of Joyce and Kafka unpalatable because it fails to emulate the values and intentions of High Realism. In like fashion, many readers of postmodern fiction have praised or denigrated it while paying scant regard to the operation of readerly bias in their interpretations. In chapter 1, I consider what are in my view disabling weaknesses in the readings of postmodern fiction put forward by cultural historians like John Aldridge, Gerald Graff, and Charles Newman. Further, in chapter 1, I investigate the reception of postmodern fiction tendered by formalist critics like Jerome Klinkowitz and Richard Kostelanetz and author-aesthetes such as William Gass and Ronald Sukenick who have all offered enthusiastic defenses of contemporary innovative fiction that have celebrated, what is for them, the latter's healthy disregard of the real world. In my view, both critic and apologist have neglected to establish the salutary mimetic function of postmodern works because of normative views that disregard the phenomenology of reading.

In chapter 2, citing as a constructive example the nonnormative, reception-biased theory of mimesis applied (though not formally developed) by Auerbach in *Mimesis*, I consider mimesis from the point of view of the reader, discussing how the reader makes mimetic sense of innovative literature, how he or she establishes (or fails to establish) a relationship between the literary artifact and the reader's own *Le-*

benswelt (lived-world), that nexus of codes, processes, and values which structures his or her world view. Drawing primarily from Gadamer, Jauss, and Ricoeur, and their appropriation of Heideggerian phenomenology, I develop a distinction between a *private mimetic response* and a *significant mimetic response*. A private mimetic response is always "one-sided" and takes one of two forms. It can overemphasize purely formal or textual phenomena or it can indulge in the affective fallacy, using the text as an inducement to self-analysis. In each instance, the dialectical relationship between text and reader has been sacrificed through the valorization of one or another of the two elements involved. In contrast to the private mimetic response, the significant mimetic response is always "two-sided"; it is able to establish an intimate relationship between text and reader. Herein, the *mutual implication of each* in the interpretive process allows for an intersection of the *Lebenswelt* of the text and that of the reader. In this intersection, the mimetic or world referential significance that the text holds for the reader comes to the fore, and the reader recognizes elements of his or her world in the world of the text.

Chapter 3 serves as a conceptual bridge between the general and theoretical discussions in chapters 1 and 2 and the interpretive illustrations that make up the later chapters. In it, I elaborate on the issue of the mimetic significance of postmodern fiction, a significance that, in my view, is clearly not politically revolutionary—contrary to the desires of contemporary Marxists like Fredric Jameson, Terry Eagleton, and Jürgen Habermas—but rather, I would argue, morally reformative. In chapters 4 to 7, I postulate a significant mimetic function for a number of representative postmodern works. Rather than choosing fictions that deal with the same subject(s), I have elected to look at a body of thematically disparate works, a strategy that should yield a more forceful justification of the general claims I make in the early chapters. Other factors have also governed my selection of texts. All of the works I consider were published in the seventies or eighties, and hence they have not yet received the critical attention that they merit. Further, because of their unconventionality, the respective works are open to the charge of being nonmimetic, or mimetic in an unhelpful way; consequently, these fictions test certain assertions I make in chapter 2. Finally, I freely admit that I find the various works challenging and entertaining hermeneutic puzzles to confront, if not to solve once and for all.

It is only fair that I also outline what this study is not. *Contingent Meanings* is not an attempt to define the essence of postmodern fiction or postmodernity generally. Indebted to the phenomenological tradition, it does not offer an original theory of reading, nor does it offer more than simple postulations of a salutary mimetic significance for postmodern fiction. As my discussion of reading in chapter 2 suggests, individual readers must decide for themselves what constitutes significance and moral exemplarity. *Contingent Meanings* is both traditional and untraditional. In seeking to assert for a body of literature a positive world-referential function, it is securely tied to historical precedent. However, in attempting to assert such a function for postmodern fiction, it is something of a departure from critical practice, though not isolated in its efforts as early work by Robert Alter, Robert Scholes, and Ihab Hassan, as well as more recent studies by Theo D'haen, Linda Hutcheon, Dina Sherzer, Alan Singer, and Allen Thiher document.

This book is based on the premise that the professional reader should resist the separation of literature from life. There is a considerable burden of responsibility on the literary scholar in that he or she is not only a researcher but citizen and teacher as well. If we overlook these various roles in the pursuit of our research interests, if we fail to consider the existential import of that which we study, we as well as literature will be poorer for it. As he does so often, Bakhtin provides insight through a commonsensical observation, an insight from which literary scholars, and excessively specialized professionals, can obviously benefit:

> The author when creating his work does not intend it for a literary scholar and does not presuppose a specific scholarly *understanding.* He does not aim to create a collective of literary scholars. He does not invite literary scholars to his banquet table. (*Speech Genres,* 165)

Through an orchestration of general assertions and detailed analyses, *Contingent Meanings* seeks to provide an alternative reception for postmodern fiction. If persuasive, this counterexample will encourage academics to discuss postmodern fiction as an awareness of world, as a mode of knowledge that is in itself as valuable as other, more obviously discursive narrative forms, whether fictional or nonfictional.

Were *Contingent Meanings* to have such an influence, it would advance, however modestly, a very worthwhile project, the overcoming of the very strong technocentric impulses that propel our profession, like others, in the late twentieth century.

Portions of this book have appeared elsewhere and I wish therefore to thank a number of editors for their generous permission to reuse material here: Craig Barrow and Reed Sanderlin (*Politics, Society, and the Humanities*); Robert Canary, Henry Kozicki, and Clark Butler (*CLIO*); G. Richard Dimler (*Thought*); S. Elkhadem (*International Fiction Review*); and Steen Spove (*Studies in Short Fiction*). I am also grateful to my dean, Michael Staveley, for a travel grant that allowed me to participate in the 1985 Writers' Reunion in Lahti, Finland. Vereen Bell, Roy Gottfried, Jürgen Pelzer, and Charles Scott all contributed patient, insightful readings of major portions of the book, and I thank them. To the students in my contemporary fiction course, English 4813, and my critical theory courses, English 410A/B and 7020, I am grateful to you for helping to clarify my thoughts sometimes, for sometimes helping to cloud them profitably. Special thanks are due my friend and colleague Larry Mathews whose interpretation of this book helped me with my interpretation of other books. I have been the fortunate recipient of both the goodwill and good advice of three Press readers, Gregory Ulmer, Alan Singer, and an anonymous third party. The book has also benefited from the care of my editor, Teresa Saul. Jeanne Ruppert, director of the Florida State University Press, has been encouraging from the very outset. I am indebted to you all. I would also like to thank Julian Schnabel for permission to use on the dustjacket his fine "Portrait of Joseph Ramaseder," from *CVJ*, a painting, like many of his, that exemplifies the contingency that I see as a key element of postmodernity. And, finally, I acknowledge the invaluable help of Hans Schulz, *Doktorvater* and friend; to him, my favorite Prussian, I dedicate this book, inadequate recompense though it be.

1

Mimesis: The Problem
but also the Solution

"THE HISTORY OF CRITICISM," writes René Wellek, "is rather like a long drawn-out debate about a few contested concepts" (33). *Contingent Meanings* centers on precisely one of these major contested concepts, that of *mimesis* and its relevance to an understanding of postmodern fiction. Many readers rebuke postmodern fiction for what they feel to be its essentially *antimimetic* quality. In this view, self-indulgent formal play supplants what is otherwise the primary function of literature—to say something about life, reality, the "out there," that is salutary and *meaningful*. As I will demonstrate later in the chapter, the "meaningful" comes to be contained within quite restrictive ideological limits. Others, its apparent apologists, cling to a similarly narrow antimimetic view of postmodern fiction but claim that therein lies the latter's achievement, its meaning, its progressive feature. Such proponents impute to it a purity of aesthetic purpose that allows it to transcend (however indeterminately) our status as social beings. This attitude harkens back to the possibly apocryphal statement (attributed to certain of the Victorian aristocracy) that *life* is something best attended to by doormen and domestics. Postmodern fiction is, then, not about life but about something else, imaginative genius, for example, or, perhaps, aesthetic transcendence. As I will illustrate, such a reading artificially separates the text and the world, sundering what are the essentially indivisible.

Both its detractors and its champions have failed to develop the

1

kind of conceptual frame required to restore to postmodern fiction its legitimate and, in most instances, inevitable status as an instructive life-referential literary form. This referentiality will, naturally, have to be seen in quite other terms than those illustrated, for example, by Stendhal's muddy-road-in-the-mirror image or modernist mytho-poeticism or traditional Marxist aesthetics. That, indeed, is the object of this study—to transvalue the notion of mimesis, to free it from naive optic metaphors and insupportable totalizing visions, and to in-still in it a vigor, a phenomenological fullness that more completely describes the postmodernist's relationship to the world. In the present chapter, I maintain a polemical tenor in order to distance my analysis of postmodern fiction as quickly and as firmly as possible from most that have preceded it. Before considering the various receptions of postmodern fiction, and the theories of representation that seek to legitimize them, it will prove useful to consider briefly Aristotle's ger-minal views on mimesis.

Aristotle

The term *mimesis* surfaces several times in the *Poetics*. Aristotle sees mimesis in terms of production, assigning to it three components: the medium employed, the objects represented, and the manner of rep-resenting (*Aristotle*, 291). *Medium* refers, variously, to *rhythm* and *melody* as in the musical mimesis of the flute and lyre, *rhythm* as in dance, and *language* as in written mimetic forms. Mimesis is given here, at the outset of Aristotle's discussion of it, a general quality that is often de-nied it in subsequent criticism. Further, Aristotle is quick to criticize formalists who, solely concerned with meter and its operation, apply the epithet "poet" merely on the basis of technical considerations rather than on that of a work's representational efficacy (291). As for the *objects* of this mimetic representation, it is again important to note that Aristotle establishes a very broad category of appropriateness, that, simply and inclusively, of "human beings in actions" (292). Simi-larly, he defines the *manner* in which the *objects* of mimesis "may be represented" in unprescriptive terms. He very clearly assigns to the poet the responsibility—indeed, the right and privilege—to deter-mine the manner of mimesis. It is the poet, for example, who discerns the mix of dialogue and narrative most fitting to his or her mimetic representation of humans in action. Likewise, it is the poet who is en-

titled to "use the various modifications of which language is susceptible" (322). Ricoeur is correct in seeing a conflation of mimesis and
poiesis in Aristotelian aesthetics:

> On the one hand, it [Aristotle's concept of *mimesis*] expresses a
> world of human actions which is already there; tragedy is des-
> tined to express human reality, to express the tragedy of life. But
> on the other hand, *mimesis* does not mean the duplication of re-
> ality; *mimesis* is not a copy: *mimesis* is *poiesis*, that is construction,
> creation. (*Hermeneutics and the Human Sciences,* 179–80)

Many receptions of postmodern fiction fail to see this union of reflection and performance in the literary creative act.

While Aristotle defines *mimesis* in inclusive terms, his structure-
oriented discussion of tragedy with its requisite unities and plot form
leaves him open to the charge of "formalism" and prescriptive criticism. In general, Aristotle's method is inductive; aware of the Attic
literary tradition, he describes the latter as he moves toward the formulation of his aesthetic theory. If his notion of tragedy is "classical"
and prescriptive, his definition of mimesis is not. It endows the poet
with a good deal of creative latitude. As Milton Nahm writes, "Too
literal interpretations of mimesis have obscured the significance of the
naturalist [i.e., Aristotelian] effort to sketch boundaries of a free
world of art" (4). In his discussion of mimesis, Aristotle's is, then, not
a prescriptive bias but a descriptive one. His occasional inclination toward prescription might be attributable to the scientist's need for con-
clusiveness and totality or, perhaps, to the fact that sociohistorical
change was, in Aristotle's society, measured over generations, not over
months and years as it is in the postmodern era. Given the tremen-
dous acceleration of change, both material and intellectual, over the
last century and a half, and particularly since World War Two, a prescriptive definition of mimesis can only lead to anachronistic critical
criteria. Unfortunately, many readers of postmodern fiction have not
learned from Aristotle's nonlegislative bias. Where he speaks of *possible* "manners" or modes of mimetic representation, others talk of
modes *necessary* for "truly" mimetic depiction.

While one can reasonably demonstrate that Aristotle sees mimetic
efficacy in nonprescriptive terms, his view of the reception of aesthetic
representation admits no such relativism. The *Poetics* addresses liter-

ary mimesis primarily from the point of view of production. The allusion to the cathartic role of tragedy is an isolated reference to
reader/beholder response.[1] Tragedy is replete with incidents arousing
pity and fear in such a way as to accomplish a purgation (*catharsis*) of
such emotions (296). In assigning to tragedy a cathartic agency, Aristotle implies the reader's recognition of the six formal elements of
tragedy, i.e., staging, song, diction, plot, character, and thought (297).
Extrapolating from the highly structured, inductive analysis of *Poetics*
and Aristotelian epistemology in general, we may assume for Aristotle's "ideal reader" a capacity to *reconstruct* a fixed, stable "meaning,"
one that the author has invested in his or her work through, what
Aristotle calls in *The Nicomachean Ethics*, technique (*techne*), "a trained
disposition to make in accordance with correct calculation" (*Aristotle*,
227).[2]

The experiencing of catharsis confirms the "correctness" of the beholder's response. However, to interpolate from the *The Nicomachean
Ethics*, catharsis can only occur where the beholder has practiced the
art (*techne*) of assaying mimetic objects.[3] Aristotle implies that the beholder may not be consciously aware of the structural elements of
tragedy and the manipulation of these the author may work. These
elements and their manipulation do, in any event, have a definite and
determinate meaning, operating within a nexus of stable relationships. In *On the Soul*, Aristotle points out that "actual knowledge is
identical with the known object" (*Aristotle*, 149). Catharsis becomes the
emotional manifestation or, as was cited above, the confirmation of an
actual knowledge of the *known mimetic object*. Given certain formal pa-
rameters, the Aristotelian view of production allows the "tragic poet"
"either a natural talent or an enthusiasm that verges on madness" (*Poetics, Aristotle*, 313). In contrast, the reception of the mimetic object is
akin to the analysis of a natural phenomenon wherein correct understanding is based on the beholder's transposition from his own world
to that of the mimetic object, a project founded epistemologically on
what Paul Feyerabend calls a "sophisticated version of naive realism"
(148).

The reception of postmodern fiction has been largely based on
theories of mimesis earmarked by the narrow ethical and epistemological prejudices of their formulators, prejudices in many instances
far more constraining than those of Aristotle, particularly with regard
to production. As Darko Suvin points out, Brecht called his theater

"non-Aristotelian" not out of a lack of deference for Aristotle himself but out of opposition to bourgeois codifications of the latter's theories:

> Art is not a *mirror* which reflects the truth existing outside the artist; art is not a static presentation of a given Nature in order to gain the audience's empathy; Brecht sees art as a *dynamo,* an artistic and scenic vision which penetrates Nature's possibilities, which finds out the 'co-variant' laws of its processes, and makes it possible for critical understanding to intervene into them. (173)

All doctrinaire theories of mimesis, whatever their nuance, posit an essentially static history. Truth lies in the consistent application of a few formal requisites. Through surface description, through dialogue, through "omniscient" commentary, through exemplary characters, the novelist can effectively "freeze" reality between the covers of his or her text. The reader of Balzac need not long for time-travel in order to experience Restoration France; the price of one's admission into Rastignac's world is not so inflated—one need only buy *Père Goriot.*

To those embracing de-historicized notions of human being there may appear to be no need for a continuous redefinition of the human condition. Traditional Christian metaphysics sees the present as yet another exemplification of fundamental, predefined moral oppositions. Doctrinaire Marxists simply assign the present a predefined status within a teleological world view. Formalism regards literature as nothing more than an aestheticized melodrama wherein writer-as-protagonist grapples yet again with the great suprahistorical questions of artistic truth and beauty. Art-as-making is reduced to art-as-repetition where innovation is preempted in the face of an apparently unchanging *Lebenswelt.* In the history of literature, literary forms have often proved to be as insensitive to historical contingency as the dogmatized world views mentioned above (though as Bakhtin has pointed out, perhaps even overstated, the novel has been the most protean of genres). Where communication is posited on strong similarity, if not identity, of author/reader codes, deviation from generic conventions always jeopardizes literature's goal of communication. Until relatively recently, say the last century, few writers have radically deconstructed accepted forms. The persistence of formalisms, whether *classical,* for example, until the late eighteenth century, or *bourgeois,* for example, from the mid-eighteenth century until the present, implies a transhistorical adequacy for values and concepts formulated in and particularly relevant to unique cultural milieus. As a preamble to reviewing the reception of postmodern fiction, let us consider the precedent set by one of the century's greatest critical minds in his reaction to literary innovation in his own time, a response homologous with many readings of contemporary experimental fiction.

Beyond mimesis: Postmodernism's failure

i) The Lukácsian precedent

Lukács's attack on German Expressionism, Brecht notably, highlights some of the basic tenets of his theory of representation. Lukács identifies a fundamental opposition between mimetic/realistic aesthetics and intuitive/expressionistic aesthetics. The latter, in Lukács's view, conceives of reality as unbounded by laws, as chaotic, as "unknowable." Marxist mimesis posits the operation of certain historical laws (determined primarily by class antagonisms) and a teleological world view. Second, expressionist aesthetics attempts to capture the essence of phenomena by abstracting them from the sociohistorical continuum; Marxist aesthetics locates essential properties of social phenomena not through abstraction but through their contextualization within the broad fabric of history. Third, whereas for the Marxist, aesthetic creativity is the product of a sober, rational contemplation, for expressionist aesthetics creativity comes from intuition, passion, and irrationality (*Essays on Realism,* 102–3). In its inability to confront concrete social situations in a methodical, rational manner, expressionist aesthetics yields ultimately to solipsism and caprice: "the purely subjective 'expression,' empty of content and separated from the objective reality, can only produce in its totality an empty series of 'eruptions,' a rigid combination of sham movements" (109). The solipsism of expressionism turns on self-indulgence and an empty formalism. Symbolism and verbal play take the place of true content (110). The expressionist work can have no social effectiveness as it has no referentiality to its historical context.[4]

Theories of artistic production that fail to see as meaningful the inevitable interaction of the personal and the social confine themselves to a myopic formalism. Theories such as that of Lukács come to reflect dogma, not the vital circumstances of human life. Lukács's inability to respond favorably to twentieth-century fiction (that of Thomas Mann a noteworthy exception) is based on his reluctance to see post–World War One society as essentially different from that of the early Industrial Revolution years of the nineteenth century. Fredric Jameson has noted that genre is a "social institution," a "social contract" ("Beyond the Cave," 158). Like society itself that gives shape to the laws of genre, genre remains dynamic and protean. The Lukács who sees the need for "effective artistic forms which are commensurate with the requirements of the age" stands in sharp contrast to the man who disparages the extended representational ranges afforded by such developments as the literary montage and interior monologue as "subjective distortions and travesties" (*Studies in European Realism*, 18).[5] Lukács, despite the basic premise of Marxist epistemology that the world stands in a state of flux (attributable to the dialectical interplay of contending phenomena), does not posit time in correctly dialectical terms, as a current alteration of pastness, of history, through its absorption into an everchanging present.

Karl Faber, a German historian, attributes the need for a continual rewriting of history to the ongoing "quantitative increase" in time, that is, of history itself (quoted in Fokkema and Kunne-Ibsch, 139). This brings to mind Gestalt psychology which holds that the *whole* is substantially altered through even minor changes in a *part* or *parts*. The genuinely creative novelist, context notwithstanding, does, like Faber's historian, confront a constantly changing reality which, while conditioned by the past, has an essentially unique stamp. A priori creative codes as expounded by Lukács restrict artistic insights into contemporary phenomena to artificial formal-conceptual boundaries. Art becomes ideology rather than freedom.

ii) Postmodernism's failure

Lukács's views have of course been analyzed at length elsewhere and would not otherwise require brief elucidation here except that a kind of neo-Lukácsian critique of postmodern fiction's existential relevance has been put forward by a number of critics in the United States. Important essay collections by John Aldridge, Gerald Graff, Charles Newman, and Andreas Huyssen have all called into question the usefulness of a burgeoning tradition that, as Newman puts it, insists that "objective reference is not merely impossible, but irrelevant" (91).[6]

Philosophically, these critics can be characterized as either traditional liberals, moderate Marxists, or some amalgam of the two. Identifying tags aside, they are linked by their respect for literary modernism and avant-gardism, particularly of the interwar period, and by their disparagement of postmodern fiction for failing to emulate the aesthetic resolutions and philosophical concerns of the recent past. These readers criticize postmodernists for not conforming to the standards of their predecessors and reflect a bias pervasive among students of twentieth-century literature. Of this bias Ihab Hassan writes, "The assumptions of Modernism elaborated by formalist and mythopoeic critics especially, by the intellectual culture of the first half of the century as a whole, still define the dominant perspective on the study of literature" (*Paracriticisms*, 44).[7] Hassan himself, an early and articulate student of postmodernity, has correctly seen the need to contextualize major twentieth-century trends within a broad continuum of literary experimentation: "Modernism does not suddenly cease so Postmodernism can begin: they now *coexist*. New lines emerge from the past because our eyes every morning open anew" (44). Hassan's emphasis on the dialectical interplay of tradition and contemporaneity, at once honoring the past and legitimizing the present, is exemplary.

John Aldridge's *The American Novel and the Way We Live Now*, a collection of highly readable, often cantankerous essays, evaluates the relevance—really the irrelevance—that contemporary experimental fiction has for late twentieth-century people. Disabled by preoccupations with apocalypse, entropy, meaninglessness, much postwar fiction has lost its resonance, its vitality, its capacity to engage and instruct. Writes Aldridge, "The novel has not only lost its authority but is failing, perhaps for just that reason, to attract the kind of new talent that might ultimately reconstitute its authority" (3). Alas, opines Aldridge, contemporary writers—Bellow, Barth, Pynchon, Roth, Heller, Updike, Hawkes, for example—no longer provide the "intellectual and imaginative leadership" that the major novelists of the twenties and thirties did, that Fitzgerald and Hemingway provided, to name two from Aldridge's pantheon. The latter, in fact, as Aldridge points out, were so esteemed by the media and masses as to merit dockside lionizing when they returned triumphant from their European adventures. Aldridge notes regretfully that reporters no longer rush to meet the belletrist as he or she disembarks at the local jetport. Yes, the times are indeed a changin'. We, today, live in an unheroic era—

though of course, *People* magazine and *The National Inquirer* still attempt the myth-making exercises of their predecessors, informing us of the dolls and brawls that preoccupy our lettered great. The Algonquin round table has yielded pride of place to Studio 54. Yet, notwithstanding the sociology of celebrity—Aldridge's, mine—what of the former's assertion that contemporary writers no longer provide leadership—intellectual *or* moral?

Though I believe that contemporary writers, especially innovative postmodernists, exercise a kind of leadership, the nature of their authority is very different from that engendered by the writings of the great American modernists—Fitzgerald, Hemingway, Faulkner, Dos Passos. The lives of Gatsby, Frederic Henry, the young Bayard Sartoris, and Jimmy Herf are all reducible to moral allegory wherein the reader learns that one wins by maintaining the purity of an ideal— even when oneself or one's loved ones perish. Even when the rest of humankind is hellbound on a fast train (as it is in many modernist novels dealing with war and economic struggle), the modernist hero maintains moral stature, moral authority. (Due both to the protagonist's unheroic idiom and his intransigent amorality, a modernist work like Céline's *Voyage au bout de la nuit* is the exception that proves the rule.) In much modernist fiction, a kind of positive hero prevails. Aldridge is right. Ambiguity, indeterminacy, self-doubt in no way characterize Nick Carraway's claim that Gatsby is better than "the whole damn bunch of them." (Unless, of course, we impeach our source and consider Nick's sexual preferences and capacities, as some impious readers have done. But this is not the place.) Similarly, Frederic Henry's candor and stoicism may appear heroic (though of course lately Henry has been indicted by some for narcissism and misogyny). No. There is a genuine dearth of characters in postmodern fiction who can claim to be exemplary in any but the most minimal terms. But, I would venture, there is a certain exemplariness on the part of the postmodern novelist that is quite as real—if not more so—as that which Aldridge sees in certain earlier writers, people who led lives, he writes, "that might in various ways instruct us in the possibilities of freedom, adventure or individual integrity" (2). This exemplariness is not, however, due to an ability to generate journalistic memorials to antics on the playgrounds of the French Riviera and in the *corridas* of Castile as in the cases of Fitzgerald and Hemingway. It is attributable rather to the integrity the postmodernist brings to fiction-making, to a reluctance to find easy paradigmatic "codes" for effective moral action.[8]

At his or her best, the postmodernist exercises a sort of moral authority but of a kind and in a manner dissimilar to the writer of the twenties. The postmodernist's moral authority is devoid of bravado and self-congratulation. Much has been made of the postmodern preoccupation with formal innovation and too little of the latter's philosophical import. Predictably, critics have responded differently to what we might call—borrowing from the German *Thematisierung*—the thematization of the act of writing. Aldridge, for example, admonishes Gilbert Sorrentino's highly imaginative parody of parody, *Mulligan Stew,* for its absence of meaning, for its nihilism (120). Gerald Graff is similarly unsympathetic with this apparent formalism—whether evident in fiction or in its reception:

> Knowing and naming itself as fiction, literature becomes a vehicle for a nihilistic metaphysics . . . In a world in which nobody can look outside the walls of the prison house of language, literature, with its built-in confession of its self-imprisonment, becomes once again the great oracle of truth, but now the truth is that there is no truth. (*Literature Against Itself,* 179; hereafter *LAI*)

Graff regrets this thoroughgoing skepticism. It was more fun when we could pin things down. He and Aldridge prescribe one standard of mimesis and proscribe another. Ultimately, their readings of postmodern fiction express their impatience with indeterminacy. In this respect, their interpretive projects appeal to the standards of a dated humanism, one that holds that man, the measure of all things, is also the mender of all things.[9]

Gerald Graff has identified two postmodernisms—one salutary, the other vapid and self-indulgent. Of Borges's work Graff writes that "even in presenting solipsistic distortion as the only possible perspective, it nevertheless presents this distortion as distortion—that is, it implicitly affirms a concept of the normal, if only as a concept that has been tragically lost" (56). In Graff's view, other postmodernists such as Pynchon, Federman, and William Gass claim the death of an intersubjectively meaningful "reality" and assert fiction's nonreferentiality. Here, resignation to solipsism becomes a "form of heroism" (*LAI,* 62).[10] Though generally a perceptive reader, Graff succumbs nonetheless to the critical temptation to legislate what is and is not appropriate to fiction and, implicitly, what one may or may not think about the contingency of late twentieth-century existence. The postmodernist is cast out of the Republic. For Graff, modernism and (what he perceives to be) its intrinsic humanism are being eclipsed by contemporary solipsism of form, by the "normalization of alienation" (*LAI*, 60–62). Graff is misguided on two accounts: the purported humanism of modernism and the solipsism he imputes to current literary avant-gardism.

Modernism, particularly in its more experimental forms, was perceived as "humanistic," that is, supportive of the notions of human worth and dignity, only after the informed reader had come to terms with its conventions and clearly elitist aesthetics. It may be that readers have been slow to attribute a *humanistic vision* to postmodern literature because of a couple of allied difficulties: the initial conceptual problems posed by new forms and the challenge of redefining humanism in a radically changed, and radically changing, postmodern world. Is not the postmodern concern for the intellectual involvement of the reader suggestive of a democratic bias that is humanistic in its own way? In its parodies of literary conventions and satires of contemporary life doesn't postmodern fiction encourage the reader to attend closely to the structures and values that construct the warp and woof of contemporary life? Don't its self-parodies inspire in us, through example, self-criticism? Isn't the ludic impulse in postmodern fiction—an impulse not confined to it obviously—inspiriting to the reader? Are not "authorial power and playfulness," as John O'Neil writes (albeit referring to literary innovation in another period), "signs that the author function is not subordinated to the schema of received tradition and society ... and consequently exemplary" (705)?

Modernist humanism too took advantage of formal innovation and consequently complicated its own reception. It rebelled against the effete conventions of realistic narrative which it saw as the mirror image of out-of-date epistemologies, for example, empiricism and positivism. Through the debunking of worn conventions, literary modernism made literature an expression of contemporaneity rather than of pastness. Thus Virginia Woolf claims that such prominent Edwardians as H. G. Wells, Galsworthy, and Bennett are too "materialistic," not "spiritual enough" ("Modern Fiction," 116–23). Woolf, from her self-professed "high-brow" vantage point, unveils the "little daily miracle, illuminations, matches struck unexpectedly in the dark" (*To the Lighthouse*, 240). Yet, Woolf's manner was so profoundly unsettling that even a professional reader like Leavis can dismiss her art as mere "sophisticated aestheticism" ("After *To the Lighthouse*," 99). Similarly, the humanizing potential of Joyce's compassionate rendering of Dublin's lower middle class could only be felt after his innovative conventions had been assimilated, or "conventionalized," by his readers. And, as with Woolf, Joyce's reception fell victim to dogmatic formalisms. Lukács, deeply misguided by his classicizing of bourgeois realism, could assert that "the broad mass of the people can learn nothing from avant-garde literature. . . . the latter is devoid of reality and life" ("Realism in the Balance," 57).

Graff, in denying the aesthetic achievement of many postmodernists, in denying them moral and philosophical relevance, perpetuates the intolerance of innovative contemporary writers that has found expression in tiresome Ancients-versus-Moderns debates throughout the history of modern literary criticism. Formal experimentation makes onerous demands that many—whether due to the covert dynamics of vested interests or intellectual inertia—refuse to meet. The problem is not, of course, peculiar to literary criticism. Montaigne takes up the issue in his "On Custom" essay. He relates the following parable and explanation thereof:

> There is a story of a village woman who, having gotten into the habit of petting a calf and carrying it in her arms from the hour of its birth, continued to do so long after the calf grew into a great ox. . . . Custom is indeed a violent and treacherous schoolmistress. Little by little, and by stealth, it gains a foothold in us; and after such gentle and humble beginnings, and after having made good use of time, custom suddenly throws away the mask and reveals those wild and tyrannical traits that almost paralyze us. At every turn we see custom forcing the rules of nature. (48)

Difference, change, historicity all become problematic when interpretation is the mere reiteration of views no longer timely. The critic who persists in inveighing against alternative theories of representation does so under the considerable burden of personal axiological oxen.

Graff sees, quite correctly, the need for critics to move away from crude theories of mimesis that hold literature (and language) to be simple mirror reflections of an incontrovertible "reality." He does, at the same time, maintain that literature refers to something beyond itself. These propositions are, in themselves, sound. The community of literary conventions is subsumed by a larger community, that of human being in all its completeness. To the extent that literature responds to being in a manner uniquely determined by its own conventions, it can be said to be *relatively autonomous.* These conventions are themselves, however, determined by the ongoing interactions between the author and the world. In this way, literature is *relatively determined.* Literary production is best seen in such dialectical terms, as the intersection between the specialized codes of genre and the general codes of social being, as the meeting of "private" and "public" horizons, as the integration of the past into a living tradition of the present. Graff bases his critique of "bad" postmodernists on the claim that the latter have somehow superseded the dialectical relationship between *self* and *world* that is necessary for "good" literature and have placed the literary work in an excessively subjective realm. "Bad" postmodernists have not succeeded in reaching a "state of balance between unchecked fabulation and objective social realism" and hence literature becomes "a trivial playing with the infinity of imaginative possibilities" (*LAI,* 238). Graff's aesthetic, like that of Lukács and other normative critics, values only those fictions that address a narrow range of issues: typicality of characters, totality of social representation, and problem resolution. Though valorizing the works of different periods, both Lukács and Graff have a more or less static model against which to measure the relative efficacy of a fiction's response to these issues.[11]

Typicality, totality, and problem resolution are issues of incontestable importance. Literature that remains oblivious to their importance degenerates into kitsch and/or genuine solipsism. The former devitalizes life by representing it as a formulaic abstraction as we see in many popular literary genres and in most film today; the latter remains inaccessible, a genuinely "private vision" that has rejected the contractual nature of communication. Postmodern fiction concerns itself with the problems of intersubjectivity, but its approach is essentially different from that of modernism. Typicality, totality, and resolution of problem are all there but frequently only in their negative dimensions, in counterexamples, as false totalities, as problems and not solutions. As noted above, there is, for example, a strongly satirical sensibility in much postmodern fiction that privileges, notably, black humor and the mock heroic. The indirection of highly current, strongly topical satire requires an interpretive stance that is often hard-won. Indeed, the genius of satire is its ability to call our attention to negative phenomena that have all but eluded our attention. We will return to this later. The essential point here remains that postmodernism is communicative in its own vital way. The problem with Graff's critique of certain postmodernists lies in his imposition of purportedly objective standards of evaluation. The primary condition of any objective notion of "correctness" or "truth" is of course *timelessness*, a supratemporal state for the *observer* and the *observed*. The scientist *feels* he or she has achieved this when method allows him or her to repeat, experimentally, cause and effect. Literature affords no possibilities of a timeless stance for either the imaginative or critical writer. Literature, whether from the production or reception point of view, should not engage in a Quixotic search for it. One can ignore temporality, but one can never escape its reach. The production and reception of literature are historical phenomena.

One major problem in Graff's outlook lies in the utilitarian bias that he, like Lukács (and Arnold in the last century), brings to the study of literature. We know the circumstances under which Lukács worked in the thirties and forties when political expediency (and not for the worse in every instance) helped mold, to a very great extent, a theory of artistic production that defined the artwork as an instrument of ideology. Graff, for whatever reasons, retains the liberal's faith in objective knowledge and human ability to design panaceas for the most obdurate problems. It is in this context that he scorns "novels which reject conventional novelistic typology in favor of privately cooked-up language and personal voodoo" (*LAI*, 217). He directs these remarks at the novels of Norman Mailer, but they are meant to apply to a broad body of innovative fiction, including, for example, the work of Kerouac, Burroughs, and Pynchon.[12] The stasis of his critical criteria, in this case "typology," is unmistakable. What is a *conventional typology* and what is not? Notions of conventionality are only significant within a broader frame of normative and largely arbitrary criteria. Clearly, the "typical" and "conventional" are held in esteem while departures from tradition are exposed to vague metaphorical polemic, e.g., "personal voodoo." The critical pantheon is likely to remain a cavernous tomb for a few "classics" if readers cannot get beyond a model concept of literary appreciation. Graff's interpretive practice remains locked within the labyrinth of immutable *opinions*. Of the latter Gadamer writes: "Opinion has a serious tendency to propagate itself. It would always like to be the general opinion, just as the word that the Greeks have for opinion, doxa, also means the decision made by the majority in the council assembly" (*Truth and Method*, 329). Where critics merely propagate personal views in their reception of literature, do they not interfere with the dialectical link between reader and text that allows literary communication to take place?

Graff's prescriptive mimetic theory maintains that "observational neutrality is relatively approachable as an ideal. . . . the technique of methodological detachment is something that can be acquired and improved by training" (*LAI*, 86–87).[13] Here the primary task of the novelist remains a cognitive one, that is, to abstract essential objective truths about human reality. The primary task of the critic is also cognitive—to describe these truths from a position of methodology and objectivity and then to evaluate them. Description is objective; evaluation is necessarily value-charged, but "value itself is objective in that it rests on prior objective understanding" (*LAI*, 87). Effectively, then, description and evaluation become aspects of an objective reception of literature. With proper application, one develops an acumen for faultless, objective judgments. Kuhn has of course gone to some length to disprove the existence of an objective language of pure instrumentality and, despite certain revisions, his thesis remains that we have not "yet come close to a generally applicable language of pure percepts" (127).

In his provocative *Against Method*, Paul Feyerabend writes:

> It is possible to create a tradition that is held together by strict rules, and that is also successful to some extent. But is it *desirable* to support such a tradition to the exclusion of everything else? Should we transfer to it the sole rights for dealing in knowledge, so that any result that has been obtained by other methods is at once ruled out of court? (19–20)

Feyerabend rejects "method" for two reasons: first, epistemological prescriptions may look good compared with other such prescriptions but there is no guarantee that they can move beyond mere factual

information to an understanding of "some deep-lying secrets of nature"; and, second, citing Mill's *On Liberty,* he believes scientific procedure tends to reduce the freedom of those who apply it (19–20). Like
Heidegger, Feyerabend locates truth and understanding in freedom,
in temporality.[14] Graff, on the other hand, finds truth in the internal
coherence of a rational critical method. His theory of mimesis is primarily epistemological in that mimetic efficacy can only be achieved
through methodical, nonheuristic means. From a position of heroic
stasis, Graff claims the following:

> The rejection of objectivity in the name of "situated" knowl-
> edge is the epistemological equivalent of anti-mimetic aesthetics.
> The first severs the knower, the second the work of art, from the
> possibility of understanding the world. It is this chronic episte-
> mological weakness that makes the anti-mimetic position self-
> defeating when used as an aesthetic of radical intransigence.
> (87–88)

Like all normative theories of art, Graff's ultimately reverts to an application of a few criteria in an effort to separate the wheat from the
chaff. In fact, criticism becomes an utterly predictable exercise in the
confirmation of one's own methodology.

In fairness, Graff occasionally moves beyond the prescriptive confines of his method in his practical criticism. He offers two conflicting
readings of Donald Barthelme's *Snow White,* one that disparages it for
its nonreferentiality and another that recognizes the work's mimetic
function. In "The Myth of the Postmodern Breakthrough," Graff
writes of *Snow White* that "the novel's inability to transcend the solipsism of subjectivity and language becomes the novel's chief subject
and the principle of its form" (*LAI,* 53).[15] In this reading, the novel is
for Graff merely autotelic. Language merely expresses its incapacity
to explain or reflect anything other than the author's own obscure vision. The novel becomes a prolix discussion of a literary problem, that
is, the communicative range of language, and, therein, a retreat from
objective reality. *Snow White* is a tale of estrangement "from significant
external reality, from *all* reality" (*LAI,* 55). For Graff, "estrangement"
is apparently something that is nonrepresentative and hence his dismissal of its representation as a *solipsistic* rather than mimetic act. The
same goes for the problem of language, although the prominence of

the theme, especially in the twentieth century (as in the work of Musil, Rilke, Hemingway, Beckett, not to mention any number of philosophers of language), would seem to make language more than the purely private concern of Donald Barthelme. *Snow White* becomes an instance of "bad" postmodernism.

This, however, is not Graff's last word on Barthelme's incisive satire of pop culture. "Babbitt at the Abyss" develops an evaluative scheme similar to that of the "Breakthrough" essay. Graff has, though, extended the limiting factors of "good" postmodernism, a category that now comes to include Barthelme and Barth yet excludes Mailer. Indeed, Barthelme and Barth are now seen to have avoided "some of the pitfalls of postmodern subjectivism" (*LAI*, 225). Although recognizing that it is not easy to see socially critical attitudes at work in Barthelme's fiction, Graff goes on to illustrate these in a perceptive way— the parody of the pop intelligentsia, the exhaustion of language through colloquial overkill, the trivialization of ideals, the crisis in consumer society. Here Graff has not confused the depiction of the sad, often vicious realities of contemporary life with an authorial endorsement of these. He has become attuned, in effect, to the parodic intentions of the work. He has granted this depiction of the purely negative its correct status as life-referential.

As Graff realized, it is not always easy to locate the *typical* and the *relevant* in fictions that radically displace our readerly expectations— no more easy than to locate "value, pattern, and rationally intelligible meaning" in today's postindustrial society (*LAI*, 55). In the second reading, Graff's *openness* allows a dialogical relationship between reader and text to flourish. The reader refrains from injecting irrelevant "opinion" into his or her reception of the work.[16] While in general not suggestive of Graff's approach to postmodernism, this strategy marks a necessary precondition for establishing the mimetic force of any text, particularly the innovative one.

Graff's critique of postmodernism has been dealt with at such length because it puts forth a number of characteristic arguments that are inimical to the basic thesis being outlined here—that postmodern fiction, the expressed intentions of its major shapers notwithstanding (as we will presently see), "may well bear a useful and quite direct relationship to certain aspects of our human situation" (Scholes, *Structural Fabulation*, 10). Postmodernism's mimetic force is sometimes direct and assertive, sometimes indirect and muted. Its ongoing attempt to destroy the paradigms of fiction, its own included, destabilizes the once fixed relationship between *reader and word,* between *text and world.* Or, in more positive terms, the postmodernist attempts to embody the ever-changing circumstances of life by "creating" fictions that are expressive of authorial and readerly historicity. Hugh Kenner notes that "the real history of one's own time is invisible, being composed of events too diffuse or too abstract to be visible to the people who live through them" ("The Next Hundred Years," 205). Indeed the hallmark of the great writer is the ability to diagnose the "timeliness" peculiar to the contemporary epoch in a manner that genuinely communicates its history. In Richard Kostelanetz's view, the "radical critic" is interested in works that are unlike others that he has encountered ("An ABC of Contemporary Reading," 365). Given the range of paradigmatic deviation within postmodernism (or perhaps its very "non-paradigmatic" nature), every reader is faced, in a sense, with a choice between interpretive radicality and mere obsolescence.

In *The Post-Modern Aura,* Charles Newman, friend and intellectual confrere of Graff (who, incidentally, provides the preface for the book), finds postmodern fiction guilty of aesthetic, and hence moral, entropy.[17] Newman draws from economics his ordering metaphor, supporting it through a selective econometrics, e.g., GNP figures, rates of inflation, investment patterns, etc. Throughout the present century, and particularly over the last forty years, we have witnessed, in his view, ongoing economic instability that has led to, variously, unemployment, inflation, moral indifference, and, finally now, cultural anomie. Fiscal inflation, with its mockery of standard notions of value, has brought with it "inflation of discourse." In literature, discursive inflation manifests itself as a preoccupation with form and a repudiation of objective reality, i.e., History; in criticism, it appears as cant and conceptual hermeticism (10). In our era we have printed money profligately and brought on it impotence, i.e., reduced purchasing power; similarly, we have become short-term traders of ideas, intent on quick profits, i.e., money, promotion, celebrity, intellectual *frisson,* while paying scant regard to long-term intellectual and moral solvency.

Many of the specific criticisms Newman makes of contemporary literature and its reception are valid for *certain* writers and *certain* readers during *certain* times since 1946, his threshold year for postmodern fiction. Formalism, excessive theorizing, the substitution of terminology for thought, the dichotomization of language and life, the cult of creativity—these are all abundantly present in postmodern fiction but not in all postmodern fiction and certainly not in the best of it. The sixties and early seventies witnessed an innovation hysteria which promoted the bizarre and the banal as important. However, contemporary literature has moved on, making of its former fetishes—narcissism and originality—artifacts to perplex cultural historians of the period. Newman maintains that postmodern fiction must reach beyond the realism of Bellow and the formalism of Gass.[18] It *has*, though Newman contests the claim. For him, as for kindred spirits like Gerald Graff and John Aldridge, the contemporary experimental tradition has fled the historical and ethical for the literary and onanistic. It has shaped neither corrective nor alternative; it has offered plurality, not panacea. In short, contemporary fiction has not cured the common cold.

Newman longs for an age dominated by common sense. That "common sense" has long served as a euphemism for exclusion and autocracy he does not consider. "Common sense" in this context refers, of course, to *his* way. Newman claims postmodern fiction overlooks the ethical. His rejection of multiplicity and his suspicion of change illustrate, rather, that he has simply overlooked a primary moral implication of this literature: tolerance. What Newman calls moral indifference is simply a different morality, not a wrong one. Newman appears to be calling for a return to the epic with its integrative vision and naive teleology. An unnostalgic, pre-Marxist Lukács noted the impossibility of epicality in a non-epic age. The novel *is* the (makeshift) epic of our age. The prescription by socialist realism for a Positive Hero resulted in formulaic farce; Newman wisely concentrates on the *pro*scriptive. To his ideal (post-?)postmodern fiction he devotes two full sentences on his next to last page. Such a fiction would involve the "recombinancy of 19th century emotional generosity with the technical virtuosity of the 20th" (202). As for exemplars— he cites Nabokov, Grass, and "many of the Latin Americans" as "the most astonishing writers of his time" (202). But what about contemporary American writers? What about Coover, Barth, Pynchon, Hawkes, Gaddis, McElroy? Do these writers not deal compellingly with important contemporary themes, with, for example, war, bigotry, deception, sexuality, imperialism, even "emotional generosity"? Nope. Sorry. Newman informs us that "no age has been less sure about what

a novel is" (9). What for many will pass as tribute is for Newman indictment. Charles Newman is sure about what the novel *is*, and sure
what it *should be*.

Newman not only writes about the "post-modern" aura, he positively basks in it (his repudiation of multiplicity notwithstanding). If
postmodern fiction, particularly in the United States, suffers from malaise, *The Post-Modern Aura* illustrates that the illness is highly conta-
gious. Newman's "inflation" conceit is highly idiosyncratic, "eccentric"
in his own words, postmodernly so (187). Though critical of the contemporary "rhetoric of crisis," Newman serves up here a paean to the
(perceived) problems of his age. In his capacity to at once derogate
and exploit jargon, Newman illustrates a "recombinancy" (*sic*) much
in evidence today. And, of course, his essayistic format presents a col-
lage of (often warring) thoughts, emulating an age shaped by fragmentation, change, and an often unsuspended dialectic. If, as a
genre, the novel possesses "no inherent equilibrium" (143), why is the
absence of "internal coherence" a problem (38)? Why, if the melding
of nineteenth-century themes and twentieth-century techniques is an
exemplary practice, are Doctorow's *Ragtime,* Irving's *Hotel New Hamp-
shire,* and Thomas's *The White Hotel* criticized as "nostalgic" for doing
exactly this (93)? How, if the revisionist history of Grass and "many"
(unnamed) Latin American writers is exemplary, do *The Public Burning, JR,* and *Gravity's Rainbow* fail in exemplarity (90–91)? As these few
examples indicate (and there are others), the polemic of *The Post-
Modern Aura* is certainly ambitious, but it is also ambivalent. This "en-
cyclopedic" mode of argumentation is also, of course, postmodern
(though the postmodern aims at *conscious* self-parody).

For Charles Newman literature and criticism are in crisis. The time
is sorely out of joint. These claims form the refrain of a critic/scholar
from Newman's "golden age" of fiction, the nineteenth century. Matthew Arnold too engages in cultural critique. Like Newman, he posits
the need for a "high seriousness"; like Newman, he proffers a motley
of golden eras and "great" authors. Arnold sees in the Romantics no
"thorough interpretation of the world," no "national glow of life and
thought" (Adams, 585); Newman says much the same thing of the
postmoderns. And, there is the suspicion of method and theory in
both, with the concomitant incapacity to state clearly and intelligibly
what constitutes "good" literature. For Arnold the halcyon epochs of
Aeschylus and Shakespeare were inaccessible "promised lands." New-

man is likely to find passage to the nineteenth century equally difficult, even with the benefit of a pocket calculator and a subscription to
The Wall Street Journal.

Andreas Huyssen, a student of European-American cultural exchange, also questions whether postmodernism can have a meaningful social praxis or mimetic status. In "The Search for Tradition:
Avantgarde and Postmodernism in the 1970s," the first of two essays
dealing with the social significance of postmodernism, Huyssen ex-
pounds a thesis similar to Graff's—"the myth of the postmodern
breakthrough"—seeing in postmodernism an abandonment of the
traditional avant-garde's historical ideals of integrating life and art, of
subverting "art's autonomy, its artificial separation from life, and its
institutionalization as 'high art'" (in *After the Great Divide,* 163; here-
after *AGD*).[19] Rather than establishing forms genuinely authentic and
antithetical to tradition (and by mid-century "tradition" has come to
mean *modernism*), postmodernism has merely engaged in a rearrang-
ing and reassembling of essential modernist strategies, e.g., ". . . ex-
periments in visual perspective, narrative structure and temporal
logic" (170).[20] The paradox of postmodernism is, then, that its "search
for cultural tradition and continuity, which underlies all the radical
rhetoric of rupture, discontinuity and epistemological breaks, has
turned to that tradition [the avant-garde of the early twentieth cen-
tury] which fundamentally and on principle despised and denied all
traditions" (169).

One can, I think, question Huyssen's paradox thesis. Postmodernism aims at a conditional rupture, at a qualified originality, through a
selective appropriation and calculated dismissal of the modernist tradition. On the one hand, postmodernists are very much aware that art
and literature do not emerge out of a cultural vacuum, a point my
critical readings will not overlook. There are very few postmodern
"primitives" sitting isolated in their studies, working out their literary
puzzles beyond the reach of external literary influences. Huyssen's
imputation of modernist influence is correct. Indeed, intertextuality—nothing more than an awareness of the historicity of literary
forms and themes—has become a major theme in postmodern fiction.
Literary and philosophical echoes resound in such contemporary
works as *Ada,* Plenzdorf's *Die neuen Leiden des jungen W.,* Handke's *Der
kurze Brief zum langen Abschied,* and Sorrentino's *Mulligan Stew.* Certainly, many of the initiatives undertaken in postmodern fiction are

prefigured in modernist works. Yet, one can claim identity only through brute generalization. Yes, both *Manhattan Transfer* and *How German Is It* experiment with visual perspective, as do *Ulysses* and *Slaughterhouse-Five* with structure, as do *Light in August* and Coover's *Gerald's Party* with temporality. However, differences between these modernist novels and their postmodern epigones seem more noteworthy than do similarities. (One can of course push the identity issue farther. Notwithstanding suggestions of the bildungsroman tradition in each, would many see substantial commonalities in, say, *David Copperfield* and Hawkes's *The Passion Artist?*) The relationship of postmodern fiction to its antecedents is not of course founded simply on either repetition or repudiation but on the dynamic interplay of the two.

In "The Search for Tradition" Huyssen disparages postmodernism because it has "lost confidence in the future" (*AGD*, 166).[21] Postmodernism is not based upon an unrelieved pessimism although its vision is certainly a negative one. One might agree with Sartre and Adorno, who, each in his own way, see negation as fundamentally progressive in that it affronts, in large and small degrees, the reigning injustices of the moment. Huyssen, with some justification, attacks the pretensions of an aesthetic that locates itself in the future—"post"-contemporary, "post"-modern. Postmodernism's inclination toward grandiose rhetoric and exaggeration notwithstanding, the effect of contemporary literary innovation has not been to rocket humanity into the futurity of utopian fantasy but rather to establish its contemporaneity. Where the epistemological and aesthetic concerns of much current fiction look to the past for old approaches to new problems, the postmodernist *looks around* for models and heuristic designs to render the present more intelligible. The postmodern outlook is neither *retro-spective* nor future-oriented but rather *circum-spective*. Like the classical avant-garde, postmodernism—or certain of its manifestations—is "a genuinely critical and adversary culture," but it is so in terms of its own history (169). It remains the task of the critical reader to avoid implicit demands for identicality of perspective and purpose between past and present cultural phenomena if the essential nonidenticality of contemporary literary modes and styles is to be appreciated. Postmodernism should be judged neither a social nor an aesthetic failure, i.e., bereft of substantial cognitive import, "meaning," and "real world" referentiality, because its initiatives are dissimilar in intention and significance to those of a bygone era. Here, once again, we find custom and its attendant autocracy blinding us to *difference* as a possibly positive phenomenon. As in the case of such prominent critics as Lukács and Leavis, the arbitrary "classicizing" of certain forms and themes here can only lead to the derogation of legitimate alternative approaches.[22]

In describing postmodernism as the "endgame of the avantgarde," Huyssen again posits failed identity between the two (*AGD*, 168). Within this frame of comparison, postmodernism can only appear self-indulgently preoccupied with the realization of purely personal aesthetic goals, an obvious social failure. Certainly, Brecht's Epic Theatre and the socially concerned *Die Brücke* group self-consciously linked innovation and social praxis, whatever the success of their respective efforts. Further, Italian Futurists, the Bauhaus group, and Russian Constructivists saw their art play a meaningful pedagogical role through its formal experimentation. One looks in vain for anything resembling a postmodern manifesto on the order of those issued by the expressionists and surrealists, for example. Beyond its emphasis upon experimentation, postmodernism lacks a stable program, social or aesthetic. It is this that Huyssen finds reproachable. There is in his view no positive or constructive voice in postmodernism. Handke's work, for instance, "defies the notion of a unitary style"; the films of Herzog and Fassbinder "lack one of the basic prerequisites of avantgarde art, a sense of the future" (166). One can concur with these readings (as I indeed do) without characterizing the respective artists as either socially irrelevant or bound to reactionary politics. Postmodernism has remained surprisingly free from the visionary fantasies that marked early twentieth-century avant-gardism. Fassbinder's pessimism keeps him firmly rooted in the present, focused on the barren materialism of the age. "A sense of future" is merely utopian where it preoccupies itself with an unlikely futurity, ignorant of a dire present.

Huyssen expresses understandable concern that postmodernism continues to run the risk of becoming affirmative culture (170). Bourgeois society has of course ignored or trivialized much of the liberating power of radical art. The plastic arts have become an anti-inflation buffer in investment portfolios. Literary critics have frequently treated innovative texts as their own hermeneutical playgrounds, thereby relegating literature to ethical irrelevance. Huyssen's concerns are legitimate, but the problems related to the co-option of the radical work of art are not determined in every instance by anything intrinsic to art itself but rather by the current politics of reception, both professional and popular. For instance, *A Clockwork Orange*, Burgess's dystopian novella, could become *affirmative culture* where reception centers on, for example, linguistic play (as it might in critical or philological circles) or on sensual excitement (as it might in the milieu of the adolescent). Co-option remains quite as much determined by interpretive stance as by any perceived "essence" of the artwork. Furthermore, one should not automatically assume, as Huyssen and Enzensberger seem to, that co-option invariably follows the commercial marketing of experimental works. A network of distribution is an obvious prerequisite for artworks, and clearly distribution needs to be highly rationalized today for works to achieve broad visibility. It is a tribute perhaps to their short-sightedness, if not avarice, that businessmen frequently promote and sell cultural artifacts that encourage the collapse of the very system that permits them their self-aggrandizement. The marketing of activist music of the sixties and early seventies is an obvious example of the complex, often paradoxical, relationship between adversarial cultural forms and capitalism.

The fragmentary style of Handke, of Barthelme, of the later Frisch, can have social and philosophical import when readers seize upon the implications of an insecure, probing style and, where deemed appropriate, translate authorial distrust of literary conventions into a personal distrust of social and political custom. The stylistic profusion that one encounters not only among a writer's various works but even within the covers of a single text suggests the play of a critical temperament consumed by a need to question. Where postmodern fiction instills or reinforces a critical attitude in the reader, it has the potential to influence attitudes on a variety of subjects, though literary critics will usually find it difficult to prove incontrovertibly that "influence" is the case. It is probably too early to know if and to what extent postmodernism can effect the "cultural rejuvenation" that Huyssen regards as its unrealized goal (*AGD*, 170). Certainly, one might argue that the very notion of "cultural rejuvenation," with its presumption of a moral and epistemological center, has a decidedly un-postmodern ring to it. It is unclear to me that any single phenomenon, short of world war or perhaps the collapse of the international banking system, can profoundly and pervasively affect Western culture. Certainly, I do not believe that anyone other than an aesthetician or literary scholar could make such a claim, whether explicitly or otherwise, for contemporary experimental literature. I think it appropriate to interject the McLuhanesque platitude that today, in broad social terms, the print medium is no longer primary. Such an observation does not trivialize the contemporary importance of literature, past or present, traditional or vanguardist, so much as acknowledge, soberly, its social place. In any event, I suspect that postmodernism will go the way of the classical avant-garde of the early twentieth century, having achieved local, rather than widespread, social influence. And, as has been the case in the past, this failure will be attributable in some degree to the critical community's failure to explicate innovation in socially relevant terms.

It is interesting that in his later essay, "Mapping the Postmodern," Huyssen moderates his critique of postmodern art forms, bringing his reading of postmodernism into closer orbit with my own.[23] Although he regards the second essay an elaboration of the first, important differences separate the two. A wide-ranging essay that draws from architecture, the plastic arts, and critical theory as well as imaginative literature, "Mapping the Postmodern" offers an instructive overview of postmodernity and the problem of its reception. Huyssen criticizes the "dead-end dichotomy of politics and aesthetics" fashioned by scholars and cultural critics (*AGD*, 221). He rejects the blanket association of postmodernism with neo-conservativism that Habermas makes in the "Modernity versus Postmodernity" essay. Postmodernism cannot, in Huyssen's view, be profitably considered in terms of simple oppositions—"progress vs. reaction, left vs. right, present vs. past" (217). Aware of Lukács's reductive reading of modernism, Huyssen proposes that we consider the "productive contradictions" of postmodernism (200), a project for which I have considerable sympathy. Huyssen's call for an analysis of the relationship between history and the text is perceptive and marks a significant shift in his own response to postmodernism. Certainly, as Huyssen suggests, and the following section documents, the life–art dichotomy burdens the reception of postmodern fiction.

Beyond mimesis: Postmodernism's success

Many apologists for postmodernism, particularly American critics, have emphasized its nonmimetic quality. Such literature is not about *life* or *reality* or, at least, not primarily. Literature speaks to aesthetico-formal issues of a highly specialized, that is to say obscure, nature. Perhaps because so many contemporary American critics are active writers of fiction, critical discussion often appears to be more an apologetic for personal aesthetics than a comprehensive textual interpretation. As various metafictions have amply illustrated, such criticism can, in itself, be of considerable interest, but it runs the risk of becoming a vapid, inbred kind of "shop-talk" that effectively alienates the discussion of literature from a consideration of broader moral concerns. This tendency is observable, for instance, in the response to literary experimentalism put forward by apologists/critics like Richard Kostelanetz and Jerome Klinkowitz as well as in the critical prose of such writers as William Gass and such Fiction Collective figures as Ronald Sukenick and, arguably, Raymond Federman. Let us consider the various justifications put forward to support the formalistic view that the success of postmodern fiction lies in its ability to supersede the lived-world, to exist on a purely aesthetic plane. Curiously, as I will presently highlight, their formalism lapses upon occasion, allowing each to acknowledge, however covertly, the mimetic function of literature that they otherwise seek to deny.

Richard Kostelanetz makes the following two unsettling statements in an essay entitled "An ABC of Contemporary Reading":

Modern art exists in a domain apart from human life, just as scholarship inhabits yet another autonomous domain.

. . . each work is primarily about matters that belong exclusively to art. It is only incidentally about life, just as Life is primarily about Life and only incidentally about Art. "Feelings" belong to Life; "forms" to Art. (346)

Such claims reflect the ongoing dissection of human existence at the hands of professional specialists in the post-Renaissance world: art versus science, literature versus history, form versus content. Their surgery, where effective, conceptually displaces fundamental parts or aspects of being into private autonomous worlds. Yet, the apparent radicality of his formalism notwithstanding, Kostelanetz assigns a rather traditional function to innovative art:

Constant change in art restimulates perception in a constantly transforming world, for art best influences society precisely by enhancing the understandings of its audience. People who are blinded by innovative art (or allow themselves to be) are liable to be similarly ignorant about what is most original in contemporary life. (375)

Innovative literature, then, must depict facets of life, must in fact be *mimetic* to a greater or lesser degree if it is to fulfill the cognitive-emotive functions necessary in "preparing the perceptual faculties for the puzzling forms in the changing scene around us" (375). With Kostelanetz, as with many other "radical" critics, art's autonomy dissolves into a dependence upon *life-forms*. This shift defines their paradoxical attitude toward art which always returns from the fringes of radical formalistic criticism to the center of human reality, that is, experience. Finally, one encounters not an absolute demarcation between *art and life* and *form and content* but rather an unsteady focus upon the former of each juxtaposition.

What accounts for this preoccupation with Form and Art at the expense of a more integrative approach to innovation? As seen earlier with Lukács, Graff, and Huyssen, a departure from the preferred model, or what I would call *aesthetic difference*, veiled fundamental mimetic properties in the work of Joyce, Barthelme, and Handke. The attempt of Joyce and Barthelme to invest in the novel form some of the energies of urban life involves, of course, the introduction of certain "formal imperatives," really something like novelistic "objective correlatives," that convey the vision of the author. The "formal" mannerisms of *Ulysses*, of *Snow White*, momentarily distract one from the *Lebenswelt* that engenders these fictions, for example, turn-of-the-century Dublin and New York of the sixties. The mock epic of urban life, in both its modernist and postmodern versions, directs the possibilities of montage, parody, and parataxis with such singularity that it is only with time that one discerns the overlap of form and content that constitutes the mimesis of literature. One wonders with what difficulty viewers of, say, Duchamp's "Nude Descending a Staircase" (1912) were able to move from an awareness of its perspectival novelty to the genuinely mimetic force of the work, that is, its ability to capture the fourth dimension of time within the limited purview of the canvas. The work masterfully captures the essential insight of the

twentieth century that *truth* is time-conditioned, not absolute. Kostelanetz, contradicting the practical functions he assigns "unprecedented art," notes that "when Marcel Duchamp 'abandoned art for
life,' his decision had meaning only within the traditions of visual art;
life went merrily along, unaffected" (347). While I acknowledge the
unavailability of an "influence meter" by which to measure accurately
the impact that Duchamp has had on the public, it is not difficult to
posit for him and his work a general "relevance." Whether informing
us of our historicity or detailing the beauty of the *found-object* and the
readymade (and the pretensions of traditional "high art"), Duchamp
thematizes, however expressively or intuitively, aspects of contemporary life.

One should separate form and content only as an expedient of
analysis, an expedient openly admitted and temporarily employed.
Kostelanetz perpetrates the fiction of a form–content dichotomy in
order to assign, arbitrarily, the one a privileged status over the other.
The following illustrates the problem: "When content is more important than mediumistic qualities, then the reader is perceiving the work
not as literature but as something else—as history, as sociology, as psychology, or as reportage" (347). The clear implication is that only a
formalistic priority in interpretation will guarantee the "literariness"
of literature. I would contend that such a bias would in fact reduce
literature to an excuse for one to indulge oneself in intellectual
gamesmanship. The problem of understanding literature is considerably reduced when one eliminates its mimetic function. Kostelanetz
merely repeats the error of those who see literature solely as sociology,
for example, or as psychology. While the latter may be fairly said to
de-aestheticize literature, Kostelanetz commits an equally serious oversight. He *de-temporalizes* literature by placing its production and reception in a realm of aesthetic solipsism. Literature is certainly more than
sociology, but it is also more than a purely self-referential, aesthetic (in
his narrow sense) phenomenon. The common sense view of art as
the optimal balancing of form and content frequently gets lost in the
radical rhetoric. It is only from the de-temporalized position of formalism that literature can be viewed as an *alternative* to history or sociology. Perhaps this unfortunate compartmentalization of life is
symptomatic of the fragmentation of late bourgeois society into the
petty egos of lobbies, chauvinisms, and disciplines. "Those who really
wish to work on the frontiers of knowledge," writes Walter Kaufmann,

"must cross the frontiers of their departments" (quoted in Hassan, *The Right Promethean Fire*, 124).

Kostelanetz contrasts the experimentation of Stein, Joyce, e.e. cummings, of Lewis Carroll's *Alice in Wonderland* with the work of Faulkner, Frost, Lawrence, George Eliot. In the face of the novel's subsequent development, Eliot's *Middlemarch* is "by now sociology or history" ("ABC," 356). Perhaps the finest of nineteenth-century English fiction is thus dismissed with the wave of a hand. Again we find the radical critic's arbitrary determination of value, the need for neatness. An arbitrary "experimentation index" serves as the sole arbiter of achievement—Stein not Faulkner, Wyndham Lewis not Lawrence or Eliot. And what of the protean, vital relevance of *Oedipus Rex* and *Hamlet?*—archeology perhaps, artifacts of purely antiquarian interest in light of the theater of the absurd and "happenings." The autonomy Kostelanetz assigns art leaves it hermetic and self-referential and only "incidentally" mimetic of life. Such is the rhetoric of contemporary radical criticism. Kostelanetz does not always tender this view, however, with consistency when he departs the theoretical plane for that of exegesis. For example, he attributes a supra-aesthetic cognitive function to the inveterate punning of *Finnegans Wake,* that of reflecting the circularity and repetition of history, and cites, approvingly, the words of Beckett—"'Here form *is* content, content *is* form'" ("ABC," 356). More than ever, literary mimesis must be posited in dialectical terms. While emphasis may in fact waver, flattering here the "autonomy" of the work, there its referential qualities, criticism must finally conflate the two if it is to indeed elucidate literature and not merely its own polemic.

It is difficult to discern if Kostelanetz's views are representative of "autonomist" readings of postmodernism. He expresses his opinions perhaps more stridently than some others. Yet, we find similar tendencies in academic critics such as Jerome Klinkowitz and in novelist-critics like Ronald Sukenick, Raymond Federman, and William Gass. Let us consider for a moment the views of Jerome Klinkowitz, particularly as expressed in his *The Self-Apparent Word.*

Among American academics Klinkowitz has done perhaps the most over the last ten or fifteen years to publicize and promote the accomplishments of postmodern fiction, particularly American works. Two of his earlier studies, *Literary Disruptions* (1975; rev. 1980), a survey of selected experimental American fiction from the mid-60s

to 1980, and *The American 1960s* (1980), an overview of countercultural aesthetics and politics, are generally accomplished. In introducing innovative, little known fiction, *Literary Disruptions* makes an
important contribution to literary history and continues to be useful.
(Its emphasis on form and its reading of "post-contemporary" fiction
as effecting a radical rupture with past literature, that is, the "breakthrough" thesis, distract one without undermining the validity of individual analyses.) In ranging widely over a number of cultural forms,
for example, poetry, film, fiction, and pop music, in connecting the
aesthetic and the political, the essays of *The American 1960s* provide an
insightful cultural history of the decade. As Klinkowitz notes in his
preface, *The Self-Apparent Word* seeks to illuminate the theoretical
foundations of the earlier exegetical studies. In designating it "theoretical," Klinkowitz suggests that *The Self-Apparent Word* is a different
kind of undertaking, at once more foundational and more synthetic,
and seemingly more ambitious.

   The Self-Apparent Word is, as the title implies, about language. Klinkowitz resists the temptation to buttress his study with an extensive
personal lexicon. Rather, he coins only two expressions to characterize
two fundamental attitudes toward language and its operation in fiction. "Self-effacing words," reflective of realism and its traditional emphasis on the *signified,* are unobtrusive and transparent. They serve as
mere conduits which fade away after having conjured up a fictive
world in the readerly mind. Alternatively, "self-apparent words" are
egotistical; they call attention to themselves through, primarily, norm
violation and its consequent unsettling of readerly expectations. Self-
apparency is, for Klinkowitz, characteristic only of contemporary
experimental fiction and, in fact, establishes the latter's superior aesthetic value. His view of literary history is, then, teleological, with self-
apparency the most recent crowning achievement of fiction, part of
"our century's aesthetic progress" (*The Self-Apparent Word,* 122; here-
after *SAW*). Curiously, Klinkowitz makes little effort to consolidate his
own theory of language through reference to contemporary debates
on the philosophy of language. There is little sustained philosophical
discussion. Derrida's attack on logocentrism is briefly considered. Beyond the repetition of a single, fundamental tenet of his thought—
that all human concerns are inextricably bound up with language—
Wittgenstein is neglected.

   The Self-Apparent Word unfolds like a traditional detective novel.

The exegete goes in search of "pure" self-apparency in contemporary experimental fiction. And, after tracking down a number of false leads—incomplete self-apparency in William S. Burroughs and Robbe-Grillet, reflexivity in Sorrentino's *Mulligan Stew*, Barthelme, and Coover's *The Public Burning*—he finally "gets his man." The last two chapters discuss two modes of self-apparency—an earlier metafictional one and its successor, "experimental realism"—each of which moves beyond "one-shot revolutionary gestures of novelistic self-reflection" (*SAW*, 85). In paying particular attention to Abish, Stephen Dixon, and Clarence Major, Klinkowitz surveys writers at once significant and often overlooked. His readings, as commonly the case, are sensitive and enthusiastic. The weaknesses of *The Self-Apparent Word* lie elsewhere, in its reluctance to move beyond critical readings of fiction to explore, variously, the philosophical presuppositions behind self-apparency, fiction's status as a "social discourse," and obvious commonalities between contemporary experimentalism and the innovations of certain modernist and, even, certain premodernist writers. *In fine,* the "theoretical" component of this theoretical study proves to be rather slight.

The distinction between self-effacing and self-apparent fiction is hardly problematic or, even, surprising. Difficulty arises, however, through terminological confusion. "Self-apparency," both as a theoretical tenet and as an interpretive concept, loses some of its incisiveness through contradictory definition and uneven application. On occasion, as noted above, "self-apparency" denotes a pure textuality that mesmerizes the reader, keeping one from moving beyond the text to one's own world or a fictive one (or to the intervening space where, for example, Gadamerian hermeneutics locates correct interpretation). In concluding his introduction, Klinkowitz describes self-apparency as a privileging of the signifier over the signified. Therein, "readers may attend to the ultimate realism [*sic*] of words on the page and signs at play" (*SAW*, 16). This view of the self-apparent text as autonomous form is not consistent with one tendered a few pages earlier in a discussion of Barthelme and Steve Katz where self-effacement is viewed as a constituent of self-apparency: "Self-effacing and self-apparent fiction provide the extremes of reading experience, but they are not polar opposites, for the latter includes the former (while not vice versa). The dual vision that self-apparency allows is a key to the form's fascination" (*SAW*, 14). Offering no further terminological refinement, the critical analyses of self-apparent fiction that follow valorize either "pure textuality" or the "dual vision" thesis as suits local purpose. Klinkowitz appears undecided as to the ontological status of contemporary experimental American fiction. Is it, *purely* and simply, an aesthetic object? Or, is it an aesthetic object with existential relevance? As a consequence of this indecision, he can, on the one hand, appeal to Mallarmé for support—"Poetry is made of words, not ideas" (*SAW*, 18)—and, on the other, to Steve Katz: "The most informed and exhilarating moments occur when quotidian reality and my inventions intersect or have a mutual resonance" (*SAW*, 13). In *The Self-Apparent Word*, we see the interesting case of a literary critic poised on the divide separating formalist and life-referential modes of reception without apparently being aware of the precariousness of his critical posture.

The same unresolved tension occurs in Ronald Sukenick's ontology of the literary work, a position that Klinkowitz draws upon in *The Self-Apparent Word*. Sukenick has presented his "theory" of literary production in pointillistic fashion over the last decade and a half in his many essays, reviews, and "digressions." His most notable critical writings are conveniently collected in *In Form: Digressions on the Art of Fiction*, from which I will draw. Sukenick wears many hats in his criticism—those of critic, cultural historian, apologist for the American avant-garde, and, after a fashion, aesthetician—though not that of the literary theorist. In his introduction, Sukenick makes a pitch for authorial vision and intention as privileged criteria in interpreting literary works, though the general implications of genetic criticism go unexamined. In his view, we should think about art "based on the way it is composed rather than on the way it is interpreted" (xix). Until the former strategy is realized, the artist, "who knows the most about his work," will always be viewed by the "analytic interpreter" as a poor expositor of his own work (xix–xx). Though implying the novelty of genetic criticism, Sukenick pleads here for a return to a long-entrenched critical position—the Romantic cult of genius. The point seems to be that interpretive truth will come to the reader who attends long enough to the author, who carefully culls the latter's letters, memoirs, and essays. In confirmation of his *traditional* romantic leanings, Sukenick appeals to the views of Emerson and Wallace Stevens on artistic genius and literary composition.[24] Predictably enough, the author is presented as the moral superior of, and oracle to, the rest of the race (xviii–xxi).

The claim that authors "know the most" about their work is no more valid than Dilthey's that interpreters do.[25] Authors and interpreters know different things, when they know at all. This is borne out in Sukenick's lengthy essay on Stevens in which he points out, very perceptively, that inconsistencies exist in Stevens's poetry and essays that the author does not himself acknowledge (187). Sukenick's understanding of Stevens is determined ultimately not by what Stevens says but by what Sukenick thinks his work means. Clearly, given the frequent unreliability of self-explication and divergences of interest between author and reader, the author's explanation of his or her work is simply one explanation among many and often not a superior one.

In other respects too, the views of Sukenick are, like those of Stevens, inconsistent. Though by admission not a formalist, Sukenick voices a radical rhetoric that often inadvertently suggests as much. He asserts, for example, variously, that language is "self-contained" (11), the primacy of the "nonrepresentational novel" (211), and the importance of "essential form" (95). Such commentary contradicts his notion of art as experience, experience that takes place in the world. In continually straining to discredit the mimetic theory behind nineteenth-century realism, he often obscures the referential bias of his own theory of representation. While one admits the difficulty, perhaps even impossibility, of dealing with literary aesthetics in a systematic, "consistent" way, metacritical awareness of self-contradiction would make various of the essays of *In Form* more persuasive and establish the "order in disorder" Stevens talks about.[26]

Perhaps *In Form* is most interesting as an apology for the radical cultural politics of the sixties and seventies. Sukenick tirelessly reiterates the virtues of originality and formal experimentation. But the world is, as he ways, "changing" and "there are new circumstances that demand new paradigms" (113). We no longer live in the sixties. The eighties have indicated nothing so clearly as the cyclical nature of politics and culture. Many avant-garde initiatives of the recent past appear to us now idle, even desperate—"one-shot insights" (as Sukenick says, however appropriately, of the *nouveau roman*) (77). Much of the shrill rhetoric and many of the metaphors of *In Form* seem dated.

We no longer think of the novel (or much of anything else) as "energy." The future of literature no longer seems to depend on adapting the tape recorder to literary production (143), on typographical manipulation (99–103), on substituting adding machine tape for bond paper or computer forms (206). While several of the brightest writers of the sixties and seventies found it necessary, philosophically and artistically, to break with the past, many gifted authors today—the likes of Handke, Coover, Sorrentino, Abish, and Calvino—move freely between traditional and experimental modes of fictional narrative. For better or worse, aesthetic compromise and pragmatism rule the eighties. We have realized, as Sukenick concedes at one point, that "novelty does not guarantee quality" (243). *In Form* is an articulate evocation not only of its author's views but also of the countercultural aesthetics of the recent past. Students of the period and, of course, those interested particularly in Sukenick and other Fiction Collective writers will find it most illuminating. Its value, however, as critical prescription or a portrait of literary exchange is less certain.[27]

In his discussion of the ontology of literature, William Gass—novelist, critic, essayist, and philosopher—reflects many of the inconsistencies of Kostelanetz, Klinkowitz, and Sukenick. Gass's essays manifest imagination and stylistic verve. William Gass joins his interest in the literariness of literature, in its linguisticality, to reflections on literature's ability to make meaningful statements about life. Quite obviously, scrupulous attention to empirical detail has little to do with the mimetic effectiveness of literature. This is not the "reality" of Gass's fictional or ontological world. In "Philosophy and the Form of Fiction," Gass, philosopher and novelist, compares the insights that philosophy and literature each may claim as the fruits of its activity:

> Novelist and philosopher are both obsessed with language, and make themselves up out of concepts. Both, in a way, create world. World? But the worlds of the novelist, I hear you say, do not exist. Indeed. . . . there is frequently more reality in fairy tales than in these magical constructions of the mind . . . which raise up into sense and feeling, as to life, acts of pure abstraction. (*Fiction and the Figures of Life,* 4; hereafter *FFL*)

For Gass, as for many postmodern thinkers, the object of imaginative discourse is not to serve up a vulgar reflection of the "real world" (though, in alluding to the superior verisimilitude often invested in the fairy tale, Gass's "reality" seems constrained by certain unidentified, yet identifiable, constants, what we might call "ontological benchmarks"). Gass contrasts this so-called *real world* with the world of the poet's making. Here, the traditional constructions of *poiesis* as poetic making and *mimesis* as unpoetic reflection crop up. The former is artistic and genuine, the latter a deceptive sham. The poet's "business" is to "make" a world of his or her own. And, to the separation of poiesis and mimesis, Gass adds the form–content split:

> Philosophers continue to interpret novels as if they were philosophers themselves, platforms to speak from, middens from which may be scratched important messages for mankind; they have predictably looked for content, not form; they have regarded fictions as ways of viewing reality and not as additions to it. (*FFL*, 25)

The above claims, taken from "Philosophy and the Form of Fiction," indicate the centrality of aesthetico-formal interests in Gass's theory of text.

"Philosophy and the Form of Fiction" is his attempt to redress the imbalance created by untold generations of thematic criticism. And yet, curiously, he undermines this enterprise. Despite his seemingly radical formalism, Gass never ceases to find rather conventional "meanings" in literature. "Metafiction," Gass's own coinage, provides an ontology of the writing experience, of the demiurgic will. Writing has become an increasingly self-conscious task for the contemporary novelist. Awash in a great sea of "influences" that obscure national and linguistic frontiers, the imaginative writer today comes to reflect on the issue of originality in his or her fictions. Metafiction portrays the writer responding to the stimuli of *his* or *her* world, ordered, as it is to a very large extent, by the literary heritage of his or her culture. This, it would seem, would represent a primary mimetic function of metafiction, one that transcends the purely formal. Notwithstanding the importance of Gass's critical priorities, and the "comprehensive aesthetic" of the novel form that he seeks, these can have no literary or critical significance if the reader is not able to integrate them into the context of his or her own world. In fact, Gass himself suggests the mimetic import of innovative fiction yet characterizes this import in

narrowly formal terms. As we will see, the relevance of much innovative fiction lies in the obvious epistemological revolutions that it effects
in its dissolution of form.

There has been an ongoing concern with epistemology throughout
the last century, the consequence of the failure of positivism and
Cartesianism to render the human condition more meaningfully explicable.[28] There is a close connection between conservative literary
forms and firmly entrenched epistemologies. Rigorously conventional
literature is the product of structured epistemology. Literary form is
the *way* the author understands his or her material just as epistemology or its absence (as in modern phenomenology) is the *way* we know
the world. Postmodern fiction, like its modernist antecedents, rebels
against write-by-numbers programs. It is decidedly antinomian.
Hence we find in postmodernism a de-structuring of conventions
within genres and between them. This de-structuring reflects the de-
epistemologized world view of postmodernism in which the horizons
of observation, dream, fantasy, logic all lose their traditional discreteness. "Truth" becomes less product than process; the process is of
course fiction in the act of writing itself out. What for Gass appears to
be formal concerns, for example the structure of language, the "rule
of chance and chaos," and "the forms of space and time," are in fact
matters of the broadest possible concern to life in a postmodern culture. That these concerns are depicted in postmodern fiction suggests
that the latter, far from being a manipulation of recondite forms, is
actually a mimesis of humankind in search of its world. New ways of
thinking, of postulating "world," manifest themselves in new forms.
Metafiction is such a form, a way of looking behind the mask of appearances, a way of avoiding the dreamlike trance into which a nonreflexive mode of expression may lull one.

In her *Beautiful Theories* Elizabeth Bruss offers an insightful critique of Gass's narrative theory and fiction:

> To inquire into the ontology of a literary construct or to explore
> the metaphysical preconceptions of a sentence by Beckett or
> Austen [as Gass proposes] is therefore to valorize literature by
> operating on it with the same philosophical instruments nor
> mally reserved for more prestigious subjects. . . . Yet one won
> ders occasionally if these particular interests were not seized
> upon for the sake of the domain, to constrain the issues and the

information that would be relevant and keep attention riveted on form and medium alone. (187)

Bruss regrets that Gass does not pay more attention to problems of epistemology, for epistemology (as I claim here) "brings in its wake all the trappings of social and psychological and historical context that Gass would clearly prefer to exclude from the literary study" (187). What Gass terms "the philosophical analysis of fiction" (really a philosophical analysis of the language of fiction) suffers when such analysis dwells on the traditional dualities of form–content and poiesis–mimesis. In the next chapter, I will outline a more integrative approach, one that will collapse traditional dichotomies by advancing a revised, more inclusive notion of mimesis and mimetic efficacy. If compelling, such a reconstruction of mimesis might help to bring the reception of postmodern fiction out of the academic ghetto where it largely resides today.

Gass's formalist aesthetics precludes for the work of art both social status and function. He seems to allow it a "social value" in "The Artist and Society" essay but this becomes asocial when it is the product of a socially de-contextualized interpretation:

> The aim of the artist ought to be to bring into the world objects which do not already exist there, and objects which are especially worthy of love. We meet people, grow to know them slowly, settle on some to companion our life. Do we value our friends for their social status, because they are burning in the public blaze? do we ask of our mistress her meaning? calculate the usefulness of our husband or wife? Only too often. Works of art are meant to be lived with and loved, and if we try to understand them, we should try to understand them as we try to understand anyone— in order to know *them* better, not in order to know something else. (*FFL,* 284)

Of course in this passage, Gass rehearses a familiar debate regarding intrinsic and extrinsic value. In his view, we should regard each phenomenon we encounter in life as a discrete, inimitable entity. We should ponder its identity, beyond the pale of any comparison or social context. To do otherwise is to make of things beautiful vulgar instrumentalities. Yet, I wonder, is such a course desirable or indeed

even possible? Should we view books or statues or people like the inscrutable Grecian urn of Keats embalmed in beautiful truths and
truthful beauties? Our interpretation of any phenomenon—a literary
work, an action of another, natural events—never understands solely
that phenomenon; our understanding occurs in the mutual implication of interpreter and the phenomenon of interpretation. Interpretation is always interpretation of one's self and, to some extent, of
one's historical place. Gass's ontology aestheticizes literature, divorcing it from life. He neglects literature's second order significance, its
capacity to generate both structural and thematic homologies of
worldly situations. In doing so, he suggests a *hermetic* rather than a
hermeneutic norm for interpretation. Aesthetic hermeticism brackets
out the formative qualities of time and place that enframe the interpreter; it is the aim of hermetic interpretation to recapture the beautiful voice with which a text speaks. Text-oriented criticism, while
often valuable for the close proximity it achieves to the text, is of scant
value if it cannot locate the text within the broader constellation of
cultural and social factors that condition the reader's world.[29] While
Culler's caution against moving too quickly from word to world
should be heeded, the trip should ultimately be taken (*Structuralist Poetics,* 130).[30]

Curiously, and a point brought out well by Bruss, Gass's aesthetic
returns again and again to a premise basic to all theories of representation—that literature ceases at some point to be simply self-referential (Bruss, 198–202). Literature cannot evade the lived-world. The
reader's self-projection into the world of the text effectively increases
his or her sensitivity to life and takes him or her well beyond the reality circumscribed in the literary work itself. Amid the discussion of the
nonmimetic purity of the fictional world, we find in Gass the following
prescription (made with an almost Jamesian candor):

> A dedicated storyteller, though—a true lie-minded man—
> will serve his history best, and guarantee its popularity, not by
> imitating nature, since nature's no source of verisimilitude, but
> by following as closely as he can our simplest, most direct and
> unaffected forms of daily talk, for we report real things. (32)[31]

Yet, the claim that the writer does depict "real things"—if not *nature,*
then *human nature*—undermines Gass's assertion that literature is au-

tonomous form. Thus, Gass exchanges the radical rhetoric of the aesthete for that of a closet phenomenologist. Gass, finally, despite the frequent hyperbole, is not merely attentive to the sound of words but also to their worldly allusions. As in the case of other critics considered here, Gass's earnest efforts to separate mimesis and poiesis succumb to an intuitive realization that literature is ever burdened with referential import.[32]

The reception of postmodern fiction has entered Stage 2. Stage 1 was marked (and marred) by a preoccupation with form. Encouraged by the apologetic manifestos and interview posturing of certain authors, scholars have long been preoccupied with the aesthetic dimension of contemporary innovative fiction. Though doubtless aware of intentionalism's foibles, we have, nonetheless, been content to privilege authorial readings with their nearly invariable emphasis on the problems of genesis. The tide has turned. The autonomist mania promoted by, among others, Sukenick, Kostelanetz, Sorrentino, and Gass finds increasingly fewer and fainter echoes in our scholarship. The autonomists have played their metafictionality card—"Hush, Writer At Work." Having taken note initially, scholarship now goes on to consider other elements of postmodern fiction. Language, trope, and generic convention shape our feelings and attitudes toward the world. There is an obvious need to confront in a forthright, consistent manner a challenging problem peculiar to contemporary experimental literature—the relevance of such literature to life.[33] In order to further this project, in order to consider the allied issues of representation and relevance, we as readers shift our focus from the weaver and the woven to the woven and the world.

THERE EXISTS A CLEAR NEED to rehabilitate "innovation," particularly postmodern innovation, as a positive force in aesthetic and moral terms, and to propose for it a possible social role, however modest. Postmodern innovation has ceased to be positive when both its detractors and its promoters deny it a place in the evolution of literature as an existentially responsive mode of communication. A social conscience and hence a social role are denied to a literature that is posited in solely formal terms. And, it must be emphasized, the issue is less an expressed social commitment on the part of the postmodernist than the reader's perception of such a commitment in the work itself. As Engels pointed out long ago, a writer can achieve in his or her writing something quite other than what the writer apparently intended or could be reasonably assumed to have intended (Baxandall and Morawski, 114–16). What remains, then, is a hermeneutic problem. To what extent can critical readings of innovative literature outline possible areas of moral significance, of "meaning," of real world referentiality, that are broadly available and broadly relevant? Do the new conceptual modes of postmodernism, its alternative phenomenologies, necessitate solipsism and nonreferentiality? Or, can a redefinition of the idea of mimesis, or even a "de-definition" of it, be established that will ensure innovative literature the very *raison d'être* of literature—communication?[34] We now turn to a discussion of the philosophical premises that might allow a rehabilitation of innovation. What has been cast here, in this chapter, as a problem of production will be seen in chapter 2 as a problem of reception and readerly competence.

2

Mimesis and the Reader:
A Reading

AS I DISCUSSED in the preceding chapter, the reception of postmodern fiction has historically suffered because many have founded their readings on unfruitful theories of representation that, in the main, emphasize authors and production rather than readers and reception. Appropriately enough, cultural critics and historians such as Aldridge, Graff, and Newman tie aesthetic achievement to moral import. However, inappropriately, they deny ethical significance to a body of literature that is *post*modern rather than modernist, that typically refuses to offer either positive character models or indeed general narratorial suggestions for the amelioration of problems. Yet, I maintain, the absence of an obvious, easily digestible exemplarity— whether related to character or narrator or plot resolution—does not vitiate postmodern fiction. This absence merely places a greater burden on individual readers upon whom the assertion of mimetic adequacy or moral relevance relies and, in my view, has always relied. On the other hand, the formalists and aesthetes simply and arbitrarily privilege one aspect of literature, suggesting that innovative literature is purely (and happily) autotelic. In so doing, they commandeer literature, making it the captive of professionalism and specialization.

Postmodern fiction, or at least the best of it, is both mimetic and instructive even if the theories of representation identified above are too prescriptive, too "hard," to allow the claim. Prescription, of course, takes different forms here. The traditional cultural critics demand

that postmodern fiction confidently project the dogma of classical liberalism that such "high" cultural forms as literature can save civiliza-
tion (even though the times in which we live hardly allow postmodern
fiction the comfort of this presumption). These readers go on to assume that pessimism and paralysis are inevitably aligned. The formalists, for their part, are too quick to indulge their parochial, specialized
interests, interests that are shared by very few readers and certainly
not by all professional ones. I think the entire issue of mimesis needs
to be cast in new terms. What will emerge in this chapter is a reconstruction of mimesis that will honor Aristotle's flexible model of mimetic competence, that is, representation as both a miming and a
making. Yet, in its emphasis on the phenomenology of reading, the
current·discussion will at the same time move mimesis from the context of production to that of reader-response. Before concerning ourselves with the philosophical grounding that would allow such a re-
reading of mimesis, Erich Auerbach's nonnormative view of *effective
textual representation* merits brief consideration.

Auerbach and the historicity of mimesis

In his famous study *Mimesis* Auerbach discusses the world-referential
function of Western literature over the two and half thousand years
of its history. Auerbach puts forward a "soft" nonprescriptive theory
of representation. Like Aristotle, he promotes a relativized view of
verisimilitude, allowing the individual to respond creatively to the ex-
igencies of his or her personal vision. The subtitle of *Mimesis* defines
the central concern and range of the text: "The Representation of
Reality in Western Literature." Auerbach sets for himself no mean
task. What is most likely to strike the reader as anomalous in *Mimesis*
is the absence of a prefatory statement or introduction. Auerbach
provides the reader no methodological overview and no justification
for the work. What Auerbach admits only later in his brief epilogue
becomes rapidly evident—that *Mimesis,* rather than a "systematic and
complete history of realism," an impossibility in Auerbach's view, is
guided by a descriptive, nontheoretical bias that "takes the reader directly into the subject and makes him sense what is at issue long before
he is expected to cope with anything theoretical" (556).

Auerbach eschews a practice common to positivistic historiography,
that of mapping out the "events" of history against the backdrop of
determinate and omnipotent laws. Auerbach's interpretive strategy is

influenced by his study of Vico (whose *Scienza Nuova* he translated in 1924).[1] Vico's considerable contribution to the philosophy of history is of course his assertion that human consciousness is temporally conditioned. Values and world views are dependent upon historical circumstance. Human history becomes meaningful to the historian only when he or she gives up absolute standards of significance and value. Freed of such a priori baggage, the historian can move on to the special genius of a given individual or era. The most obvious virtue of Vico's historical method is its *tolerance,* tolerance vis-à-vis disparate standards of verisimilitude, tolerance of disparate formal means of realizing such mimetic standards. "If we assume with Vico that every age has its characteristic unity," writes Auerbach, "every text must provide a partial view on the basis of which a synthesis is possible" (quoted in G. Green, 17). Auerbach refuses either to define "mimesis" or to involve himself in questions of periodization, both of which are "hopeless" tasks in his view (548). Guided by a single presupposition—that great literature is responsive to historical circumstance— Auerbach immerses himself in a concentrated study of twenty primary works that range from *The Odyssey* to Woolf's *To the Lighthouse.*[2]

In addition to philosophical good sense, another factor suggested to Auerbach the need to suspend absolutist judgments and to pursue the pluralistic strategy outlined above. As a German Jew, Auerbach fell victim to Nazi anti-Semitism. In 1935, yielding to external pressures, he gave up his chair in Romance philology at the University of Marburg. Indeed, Auerbach composed *Mimesis* in exile in Turkey during the last three war years. As many came to realize (and some continue to overlook today in critical circles), the consequences of intolerance can be considerably more serious than the misunderstanding of a work of literature. Auerbach stands in the tradition of classical Western humanism. *Mimesis,* composed as it was during wartime, responsive to generations of European anti-Semitism, is the author's paean to tolerance.

While seeking to understand Western humanity through the study of differing modes of literary representation, Auerbach does not arrogate to himself the interpretive objectivity he implicitly denies others. Just as literature is a product of its historicity, so also are critical analyses of literature:

> Historical research, indeed, has an exact side. . . . But where selection, interpretation (in the higher, more general sense), clas-

sification enter into the picture, the historian's activity is far more comparable to an art than to a modern science. It is an art that works with scholarly material. (Quoted in G. Green, 18)

"For," as Auerbach writes in *Mimesis,* "there is always going on within us a process of formulation and interpretation whose subject matter is our own self" (549). Critic and imaginative writer alike never reach more than a partial, temporary (and temporal) understanding.

Auerbach's assertion of "many realisms" has a theoretical under- pinning that has only been hinted at. In the first instance, "reality" is not for Auerbach an absolute concept. It is an interpretation that the imaginative writer seeks to capture in his or her work. Auerbach iden- tifies three primary imaginative approaches to the "representation of reality": the classical or Greco-Roman; the Judaic-Christian "figural"; and the modern. Classical mimesis is sensitive to a sensuous reality involving eating, loving, fighting, and so on—"Delight in physical ex- istence is everything to them, and their highest aim is to make that delight perceptible to us" (13). Classical mimesis finds no "antagonism between sensory appearance and meaning" (49). The figural mimesis of Judaic-Christian literature depicts discrete events as manifestations of "universal history" (16). Such events allegorize the world views of the Old and New Testaments. The classical mimesis of Homer brings readers immediately into the fictional world and affords them easy access to its significance. The Bible requires an interpretive effort: "Doctrine and promise are incarnate in them [biblical stories] and inseparable from them; for that very reason they are fraught with 'background' and mysterious, containing a second, concealed mean- ing" (15).

Modern mimesis embodies a key feature of each of these historical antecedents. It does, like classical mimesis, bring the reader into a sen- suously immediate realm, though modern mimesis does not promote the kind of conceptual categories that one finds in classical definitions of styles and genres. And, while Christian vertical transcendence, e.g., from the Augustinian city of man to the city of god, is no longer op- erative, modern mimesis, as we see in Dante's *The Divine Comedy,* rep- resents "reality" in the contemporary vernacular. In neither Judaic- Christian nor modern mimesis does genre or rhetorical trope stand in any necessary relation to subject matter. Yet, unlike both Greco- Roman mimesis and that of Judaic-Christian figural interpretation,

modern mimesis represents an unstable vision wherein "reality" dissolves "into multiple and multivalent reflections of consciousness"
(551)—an observation valid for both early and late twentieth-century
fiction. Unlike other theorists, Auerbach does not valorize a particular
mode of mimesis; he rejects all transhistorical standards of verisimilitude. His theory employs a *diachronic differentiation* that emphasizes
the historicity of imaginative literature. At the same time, Auerbach's
mimetic categories resist a fate common to much categorization in the
human sciences, that of excessive schematization. The modicum of
abstraction and reduction that all categorization requires can easily
become excessive. Auerbach's theory of mimesis avoids methodological rigidity.

The mimetic modes that Auerbach proposes are not monolithic.
The literature of subsequent periods represents an intersection of the
preceding mode(s). The various modes "compete" with one another,
at times reinforcing, at times tearing down, a notion of modal conflict
not unlike Bakhtin's. The various modes of mimesis exist simultaneously. They fashion our literary canon. This position complements
what we have called "diachronic differentiation." The critic not only
distinguishes between the primary mimetic modes on a diachronic
scale but also on a synchronic one. In his discussion of French Realism, for instance, Auerbach admits the manifest differences in modern mimesis across the canon of nineteenth-century fiction (512–23).
"Aesthetic realism" is evident in both *Madame Bovary* and the Gon-
courts' *Germinie Lacerteux* wherein the "art of style" is concerned with
"producing pleasing effects in the conventional sense of the term."
The incomparable richness of Balzac's *Comédie Humaine* and Zola's
Rougon-Macquart series excites the righteous indignation of the reader
and encourages social reform. Due, perhaps, to Germany's political
fragmentation before 1871 and latent long thereafter, German realism remains undeveloped. The conservative realism of the Victorian
novel is prone to sentimentalization and narrow milieu studies. And,
finally, Russian realism offers an inimitable "immediacy of experience." In identifying coterminous differences, intra- and international, the Auerbachian theory of mimesis recognizes the operation of
a *synchronic differentiation,* one that complements that found on the
diachronic plane.

Both of the differentiations cited—diachronic and synchronic—
are methodological realizations of Auerbach's essential pluralism, a

pluralism from which the reception of postmodern fiction has not as
yet substantially benefited. Any postulation of mimetic function for
postmodern fiction must allow for differences *and* similarities on both
diachronic *and* synchronic planes.[3]

In the present context, diachronic investigation will highlight literature's (and humanity's) development within a period dominated by a
modern mimetic mode. Postmodern representation—a late variety of
modern mimesis within Auerbach's categories—both confirms and al-
ters previous modern modes, articulating an imaginative vision pecu-
liarly in harmony with its own time. On the synchronic plane, the critical reconstruction of the world represented in the text revolves
around the correct linking of intratextual phenomena, e.g., style,
themes, and generic strategies, to extratextual ones, e.g., history, epistemology, ethics—in short, the lived-world. *Mimesis* is sustained, both
in philosophical and practical hermeneutical terms, by a *cognitive* view
of the Western literary tradition. Literature says something meaningful about humanity that is *relatively* determinate. To posit for literature a mimetic function is to assert the presence of homologies, i.e.,
textual-existential correspondences, that patient, open study will be
capable of identifying. Yet, the identification of these homologies will
be tentative and contingent in that interpretation's historical nature
will leave it subject to constant revision and change. More needs to be
said about the contingent nature of interpretation and the consequences that the recognition of this contingency has for the classical
issues of authoriality and authorial intention.

Mimesis: A readerly problem

The act of meaning constitution that we call "reading" requires three
primary phenomena: an author, a text, and a reader. Throughout the
history of reading, theorists have typically emphasized one or another
of these components at the expense of the others. While the critical
theoretical trend today is toward reader-response criticism and reception history, toward the sharply individuated, even idiosyncratic,
reading, there exists more than a residual interest in both author-
centered and text-centered criticism, as my review of the critical reception of postmodern fiction documents. Certainly, Auerbach's dual
interest in both textuality and the reader's historicity was atypical for
the forties and remains instructive today. Many of the critics discussed

in chapter 1, particularly the formalists, are too quick to privilege what the author himself claims for his or her fiction in interviews, essays, and metafictional commentary. The preoccupation with authoriality and authorial intention delays or even preempts the examination of those second order references in the text, i.e., homologies, that link its world to the world of the reader. Before considering how a reader discerns in a text a mimetic function, it will be helpful to consider why mimesis is construed here not as an authorial problem but as a *readerly* one.

The most coherent, most developed theory of author-centered criticism in the English-speaking world is that of E. D. Hirsch. Over the last two decades, Hirsch has presented his position with consistency and vigor.[4] His intentionality thesis is well known: "respecting an author's intention" remains "the basic moral imperative of speech" (*The Aims of Interpretation*, 91). Hirsch proposes a "deliberate reconstruction of the author's subjective stance to the extent that such a stance is relevant to the text at hand" (*Validity in Interpretation*, 238). He ascribes validity only to those interpretations that *recognize* and *reconstruct* (Schleiermacher's *nachkonstruieren*) authorially intended meaning (*Validity in Interpretation*, 126). In citing *original* meaning as "best meaning," Hirsch calls for a hermeneutics of origins, of presence. Hirsch sees no difference between written and oral discourse; "the ethics of language holds good," he writes, "in all uses of language, oral and written, in poetry as well as in philosophy" (*The Aims of Interpretation*, 91).

However, many theorists insist, as I do, that a distinction between oral and inscribed discourse needs to be made. For Paul Ricoeur, for example, reading does not establish a dialogical relationship between author and reader (through a mediating text) in the manner that speech does between speaker and auditor (*Hermeneutics and the Human Sciences*, 146–47). In the latter instance, the auditor can attend, more or less, to the speaker's intended meaning. Through the exchange of questions and answers, the identification of intended meaning offers a goal that is both desirable and possible to achieve. Further, as Gadamer points out in *Truth and Method*, "The spoken word interprets itself to an astonishing degree, by the way of speaking, the tone of voice, the tempo, etc., but also by the circumstances in which it is spoken" (355). The auditor, though ever reliant on his or her own understanding of significatory codes, on personal *worldly* experience, respects nonetheless the freedom of the speaker to speak a meaning and to have that meaning given priority over other meanings. Through gesture, question-and-answer, and an analysis of the circumstance enframing the dialogue, author and auditor may enjoy a genuine "meeting of minds."

A reader's relationship to a text is quite other, however, for Ricoeur. Dialogue with the author does not occur. The text produces what he calls a "double eclipse"—of the writer and of the reader: "the reader is absent from the act of writing"; "the writer is absent from the act of reading" (*Hermeneutics and the Human Sciences,* 146–47). Ricoeur's hermeneutics—in sharp contrast to Hirsch's intentionalism—posits the author as "dead," the text as "posthumous." The "emancipation of writing" (Ricoeur's formulation) from the conditions of speech production and reception also emancipates the reader, permitting one to acknowledge one's own historicity in the act of textual interpretation. Derrida makes a similar point, though in more strident, polemical fashion. His deconstruction of traditional theories of reading is also critical of the conflation of oral and inscribed modes of discourse, of what he calls "logocentrism." Of the logocentric impulse he writes, "the humbling of writing beneath a speech dreaming its plenitude . . . [is] another name for death, historical metonymy where God's name holds death in check" (*Of Grammatology,* 71).

A simple scenario will illustrate the difference between the interpreting of spoken and written language. Suppose we receive in the mail—in the absence of any earlier correspondence—a note from a friend that directs us to "ignore the first letter." Our ensuing confusion is understandable, for there are a great many ways to interpret this communication, the more obvious of which are perhaps the following. Assuming a first letter has indeed been written, we might direct our wrath at the postal service—its very name often an oxymoron—for an unconscionable, if unsurprising, delay and concern ourselves no further with the matter. Or, if we assume no first letter has been penned, we may interpret the letter in one of two obvious ways: either as a somewhat worn practical joke perpetrated by the author of the letter or as an indication of an unrealized intention of the author to write a "first letter." Our interpretation notwithstanding, it is clear that we must privilege one of several distinct (or not so distinct) interpretive possibilities.

Consider alternatively, however, the very different situation that prevails if we receive the intelligence "ignore the first letter" directly and orally from the author. While on first audition the import of the imperative is unclear, we can, upon questioning our interlocutor, establish an authorially intended meaning for the statement. Assuming a simple, candid response to a simple direct question—"What do you mean by 'ignore the first letter'?"—the auditor becomes privy to the true, incontrovertible meaning of the author/interlocutor. Manifestly, our experience in reading literature is analogous to receiving a letter that bears no obvious, univocal meaning. A work of literature harbors the possibility of an illimitable number of significations. We, as readers, act out (consciously and unconsciously) a strategy of inclusions and exclusions. We, as readers, delimit a field of signification that is coherent and pregnant according to our sensibilities and historical context.

In its respect for plurality and its rejection of absolute knowledge, reader-centered hermeneutics enfranchises the reader. Interpretive virtuosity is not commensurate with methodological sophistication. Interpretive mastery is no longer the aim of reading. Establishing personal rather than antiquarian relevance for texts becomes the goal of hermeneutics. In the author-centered hermeneutics of Hirsch, for example, we see the operation of a religiosity that one would normally associate more with *hermeneutica sacra* than with *hermeneutica profana*. Herein the moral fervor that inspires religious hermeneutics crowds out the time-conditioned interests of secular hermeneutics. Indeed, Hirsch's rhetoric of authorial domination and readerly subservience—his own terms—draws its prescriptive, legislative biases from the politics of biblical exegesis. Traditionally, of course, the latter has been concerned with the reconstruction of original, that is, divine meaning. To propose that this divinely conferred meaning is either unsharable or, worse, chimerical would be an act of impiety, if not outright heresy. An omnipotent god is capable of expressing itself with clarity and decision. The exegete merely serves as a conduit.

Both Barthes and Foucault discuss the valorization of the author and the implications of the gesture. Barthes, in his suggestively titled essay, "The Death of the Author," assails two tenets of traditional criticism: the "biographical fallacy" and, its corollary, the subjugation of the reader and history: "The *explanation* of a work is always sought in the man or woman who produced it, as if it were always in the end, through the more or less transparent allegory of the fiction, the voice of a single person, the *author* 'confiding' in us" (*Image-Music-Text,* 143). Barthes rejects, of course, the notion of a "single 'theological' meaning (the 'message' of the Author-God)" (146). Rather, the text is polysemic, "a multi-dimensional space" in which the writer reiterates, not so much himself or herself, but a panoply of anterior, preexistent conventions and modes of discourse. The writer can only translate personal thoughts through recourse to a "ready-formed dictionary" (146). For Barthes, a hermeneutics of origins—whether through a preoccupation with "original" meaning or authorial "originality" or "original" intentions—privileges presence, method, and stasis at the expense of the reader and reception, in short, at the expense of history, itself. In Barthes' view, the rejection of a "secret," "ultimate" meaning is a liberating, revolutionary act that at once rejects "God and his hypostases—reason, science, law" (147). Nietzsche, using a radically transvalued lexicon, echoes this sentiment at the beginning of *The Dawn of Day*—"Does not almost every exact statement of an origin strike us as paradoxical and sacrilegious?" (11).

In his essay "What Is an Author?" Foucault engages many of these same issues. He explores how Western attitudes toward authoriality have affected our ways of reading texts. Discourse has become, for Foucault, "a possession caught in a circuit of property values" (*Language, Counter-Memory, Practice,* 124). In my view, those who promote interpretive objectivity and intentionalism see meaning as a kind of authorial wealth. As self-professed custodians of this wealth, the intentionalists ensure that authorial meaning is not "devalued" through errant, delinquent interpretations. We are invited to "borrow" what we will from the text but must always return what we have borrowed undamaged, intact—without, as it were, having accumulated our personal "interest." Here, text is integrated into a system of ownership that jealously protects "property rights" (the author's) at the expense of experience, being, and history (the reader's). In all of this the professional critic retains his or her status as the high priest of literary truth, an intermediary between the benighted masses and the authorial demiurge. "(Hence) there is no surprise," writes Barthes, "in the fact that, historically, the reign of the Author has also been that of the Critic, nor again in the fact that criticism (be it new) is today undermined along with the Author" (*Image-Music-Text,* 147).

Foucault brings up another interesting point in his essay on authoriality. The "author" has come to constitute a "principle of unity" that allows the reader easier access to texts (128–29). The principle of unity allows the reader to dissolve (or ignore) contradictions and incompatibilities that exist within and between texts by a given individual, within what the author says of his or her work and what the reader may read into it. (And, of course, the assemblage of unified, linearized biographies and histories has long been a venerable tradition in the human sciences [*Geisteswissenschaften*].) Having defined the author as a particular closed field of characteristics—style, tone, philosophy, etc.—one can certify a reading through a purportedly objective process of cross-checks and referencing. In fact, here, one merely certifies conventional reading practices. The principle of authorial unity provides a spurious validation for objectivist hermeneutics. Hirsch implies that authoriality can be objectively defined by consulting the appropriate documents and by making correct inferences on the basis of these. In such a project, theory and method precede and dominate the activity of reading. Theory and method homogenize literature to a very great extent. Consensus—what Hirsch calls the "practical goal of every genuine discipline"—becomes a realizable, indeed inevitable, achievement (*Validity in Interpretation,* ix). The purported recuperation of original authorial meaning becomes, rather, a recuperation of theory. "Difference and conflict are," as John Brenkman writes, "subordinated to bourgeois universality" (25). A routinization of reading follows, one that obscures the individuality of the reader and the formative role this individuality has in determining for the literary work what will presently be defined as a "significant mimesis."

Significant and private modes of mimesis

All literature is mimetic to a greater or lesser degree. That which is humanly inspired and which takes form through human mediation is necessarily a representation. Mimetic conventions have changed along with humanity's shifting conceptions of itself. What has not changed, however, has been the referent of artistic forms. Art has always been and remains an act of narcissism, a reiteration of a notion of self. This holds equally for those who embrace established generic conventions and for those who, as in the case of postmodernists, redefine such conventions. A statement by Robbe-Grillet merits quotation:

> All writers believe they are realists. None ever calls himself ab-
> stract, illusionistic, chimerical, fantastic, falsitical. . . . Realism is
> not a theory, defined without ambiguity, which would allow us to
> counter certain writers by certain others; it is, on the contrary, a
> flag under which the enormous majority—if not all—of today's
> novelists enlist. And no doubt we must believe them all, on this
> point. It is the real world which interests them; each one at-
> tempts as best he can to create "the real." (157)

In his statement, Robbe-Grillet begs the question of what constitutes
"reality." Let us look into the synonymous concepts of "reality" and
"real world" in an effort to understand the cornerstone of any mimetic theory of literature—a notion of *real world referentiality*.

Quite obviously we can no longer endorse the empiricist model that
holds reality to be the sum total of one's sense perceptions. This view
coincides with what we have called earlier a crude and naive theory of
mimesis. Humanity invests a great deal of itself and its culture in analyses and creative depictions of sensual impressions. One remains a
"faithful recorder" of one's experiences but "faithful" in a transvalued
way. It is not the faithfulness with which the light-sensitive paper of a
camera film records the relative presence of light at a given shutter
speed. One does not merely record the brutely physical. One records
rather a domain that, while tenuous (even "invisible") to the insensitive individual, is in every sense "real." We may term the domain that
engenders one's creative vision the *Lebenswelt* of the author—his or
her "life-world" or "lived-world." The lived-world is, as Alfred Schütz
tells us, "the intersubjective world which existed long before our birth,
experienced and interpreted by others, our predecessors, as an organized world" (72). The lived-world takes on an organized aspect because we cannot operate without "typification," i.e., the reduction of
experiences to certain common denominators. Through the application of a culturally determined frame of reference, the individual is
able to type or typify his or her experience. This frame of reference—
really our cultural heritage—is, however, open to alteration. Change
occurs through the formative roles of personal experience and personal genius. In Schütz's words, "we work and operate not only within
but upon the world" (73).

From the point of view of literary production, innovation occurs
when the author's experiences are no longer explicable within the

range of tried and true conventions. The dynamism of human history leaves the lived-world highly protean. The author of genius, once called the "conscience of his or her people," is really their eyes, more adept than they (we) at discerning change. The author of genius aesthetically "concretizes" or "objectifies" relationships—personal, social, political—that have as yet passed unnoticed. Whether or not we accept the thesis of Althusser and others regarding the artist's purported objective, supra-ideological perspective, it is hard to deny the revelatory or epiphanic quality of great art—whether an etching by Rembrandt, a great symphony by Beethoven, or, indeed, a postmodern literary work. Formal innovations earmark shifting perceptions of the *Lebenswelt*. These formal innovations, while responsive to a changing lived-world, help condition the quality and quantity of this change by adding to the cultural artifacts that constitute, to a very large extent, our "reality," our *Lebenswelt*. To represent through literature one's contemporary *Lebenswelt* is a mimetic act but, as we shall presently see, one that may be for some readers mimetically insignificant.

Except for the brief mention of Aristotelian *catharsis,* and the discussion of Auerbach's recognition of the historicity of interpretation, we have, following tradition, implicitly posited mimesis largely in terms of authorial production. Herein, mimesis has taken on the aspect of a solo performance by the author—one that the text *captures* and that the reader *absorbs*. This, in fact, has long been a model of textual understanding, one sanctioned by Romantic hermeneutics and more recently by E. D. Hirsch. Influential over the last two hundred or more years, classical Romantic hermeneutics has sanctioned an objectivistic, prescriptive bias in theories of mimesis. As shown in the first chapter, some critics have criticized as unmimetic works that frustrate the reader's ability to outline an unambiguous authorial meaning or an authorial meaning that does not subscribe to traditional values; and, curiously, others have praised these same works for having realized the expressly formalistic interests "intended" by authors as they have indicated (however equivocally) in their fiction and, in many instances, in interviews and discursive writing. The readings offered by Graff and others are cases of intentionalist criticism wherein the intentions of postmodern writers—often self-professedly pessimistic and formalistic—are deemed unworthy and suspect, and consequently the reception of their work produces frustration, disappointment, and, ultimately, disparagement. Similarly, the readings put forward by Kostelanetz, Gass, and other kindred minds have an intentionalist bias, but in these instances the authorially intended formalism of the fiction is deemed praiseworthy.

In each of these cases, in emphasizing authorial vision, the respective critics deny the performative nature of interpretation itself. Certainly, in rehearsing the ancients-versus-moderns debate, in their hypostasis of content and form, each group falls into a routinized reception with neither able to posit or pursue new interpretive alternatives for postmodern fiction. In each case, critics see mimesis in a nonrelational way as either a process that should objectively *reconstruct* an author's "social reality" and propose courses of amelioration for social problems, or one that is essentially confined to the depiction of fiction's very birth and the author's maieutic function therein. Contrariwise, the view of mimesis being developed here will show that mimesis is in fact a relational process that implicates, in the first place, the author and his or her lived-world in the production of the literary text and, more importantly in the present context, the reader and his or her lived-world in the reception of the text. Mimesis is, then, an interpretive project, a *pas de deux* involving text and reader, not an authorial *pas seul.*[5]

Nietzsche asserted long ago the chimerical nature of "disinterested" knowledge. In *The Will to Power* he calls scientific knowledge the "greatest fable of all" (301). One can never step out of one's *Lebenswelt* in order to reconstruct the *Lebenswelt* of another in terms faithful to the latter's self-understanding. As I pointed out, the author is responsive to his or her own cultural milieu in the creative act. Similarly, the reader is responsive to his or her own culture in the interpretive act. Literature is only significantly mimetic where reception and text take on a mutually implicated aspect. Otherwise expressed, literature becomes significant representation when it allows a relationality to take root. Mimesis becomes significant when the reader replicates the author's textual *performance* in an interpretive performance of his or her own. Actually, because of the substantialist Aristotelian connotations that traditionally adhere to "mimesis," when it is taken out of the domain of production and placed in that of reception, it might seem appropriate to coin a new term for my transvalued, reader-centered view of mimesis. I steadfastly reject such a move, however, because it would covertly give credence to the Hirschian view that there is a difference between textual "meaning" and that "significance" a given reader may attribute to the text. Because interpretation is always an instance of historical understanding, I regard as spurious the separation of meaning and significance.[6]

As this discussion implies, I am concerned here with a taxonomy of mimetic effectiveness. Literature that is *significantly* mimetic is relational; it is mutually implicating of text and reader; it allows the reader to realize a *performative* (rather than *reconstructive*) mode of interpretation. One might ask how we can characterize literature that does not permit this kind of reader response. What accounts for its failure (or is it the reader's?) to achieve significance? What follows is a taxonomy of mimetic effectiveness.

Significant mimesis issues from the mutual implication of text and reader. Literature that is significantly mimetic permits the reader to see his or her own world better through the apprehension of the world of the text. This process is founded on what Joseph Bronowski calls "recognition"—the recognition of one's self and one's world in the world of the text (127). *Recognition* is the prerequisite of all communication (with communication being the obvious purpose of all art). When recognition fails to occur, a text necessarily remains mysterious and closed, its communicative intentions stymied. As a point of departure, I have asserted that all that springs from humanity is a representation of humanity. Literature that fails to be mimetically significant is nonetheless mimetic. It "mimes" or "reflects" an authorial/ textual vision that is, for one reason or another, largely inaccessible, a vision that cannot be contextualized within the experiences and aspirations of the reader. We will term mimesis of this variety "private."

To describe a text as *privately* or *significantly* mimetic is an interpretive act. In the absence of a readerly self-recognition, a text will appear purely "formal," "literary," and "self-referential." To the reader such a text will seem to inform issues that pertain not to the lived-world in general but rather to a rather negligible portion of it—the world of textuality. The reader, if mature, will usually recognize the manipulation of rhetorical tropes and generic conventions, but this manipulation will appear to be largely gratuitous, if not onanistic. One's interpretation of mimetically private literature will predictably remain stuck on a summary of the latter's tropologico-rhetorical strategies. Unavoidably, such interpretation will imply a separation of life and art, as we saw in Kostelanetz, and, as in the case of Gass, a form–content dichotomy.

A given work of literature can embody a private mimesis for one reader and a significant mimesis for another. The point of the present study is to show how postmodern fiction, particularly those works considered here, is significantly mimetic, claims to the contrary notwithstanding. As stated, the assignation of a *private* or *significant* mimetic status is in every instance an interpretation. Each kind of interpretation responds to the issue of readerly recognition—the latter positively, the former negatively. Literature embodying a significant mimesis affords the reader the possibility of identification and recognition. The original self-realizing act of production finds a parallel or, better, its complement (in the communicative process) in the self-realizing response of the reader. Such literature enables the reader to make the text his or her own, to relate the text to the lived-world that he or she shares with peers. This making-one's-own of the text on the part of the reader, what Ricoeur (borrowing from Heidegger) calls *Aneignung,* establishes the relationality of interpretation. *Aneignung* or "appropriation" is, as Ricoeur asserts, the "aim" of interpretation. This appropriation does not mean that the reader merely imposes his or her own subjectivity upon the text. Appropriation is, rather, the process by which the reader apprehends, through the text, "new capacities for knowing himself" and his or her historical world (*Hermeneutics and the Human Sciences,* 192). Appropriation occurs, as Ricoeur informs us, only when the reader overcomes the "cultural distance" and "historical alienation" that separate him or her from the text (185).[7] This describes anew what I have identified as the basis of valid interpretation—the mutual implication of text and reader wherein understanding emerges osmotically and not through reconstruction or "divination" (Schleiermacher/Hirsch).

A given reader will deem as "privately mimetic" literature that denies him or her any substantial recognition. In such an instance, the reader can only juxtapose his or her own lived-world and that of the text. The text will have a foreign aspect. It will resist an integrative reading. It will embody the above-mentioned dichotomies of form–content and life–art. Such an interpretation can only emphasize reader–text alienation. The text seems preoccupied with a private or hermetic concern—its own textuality, for example. It fails to generate the relationality that is the essence of significant mimesis. The reader dwells on the formal performance of the text without enlivening his or her interpretation with any substantive performance of his or her own. Rather than appearing to put forward a world into which the reader can step, the text seems to present itself as a mere artifact that the reader can explore and describe but not make meaningfully his or her own.

Why would a reader regard certain works as significantly mimetic and others merely privately so? What differences exist among various works, among different readers? Conceding the relationality of all interpretation, we will need to investigate not only textuality but also the interpretive frames that readers bring to their reception of this textuality. On the one hand, it is a question of verbal usage, rhetorical devices, and generic conventions and, on the other, a matter of the kind of readerly expectations through which a reader filters his or her reception of the text. In assuming the capacity of the text to communicate, I now focus on the issue of readerly competence.

The problem of competence

Competence is a word of broad currency. It suggests a capability or aptitude to perform some kind of task in a more or less effective manner. We might see competence as a faculty that a given phenomenon has and which an observer merely recognizes. Thus, we might say someone is a competent tennis player. At first glance, it seems that *competence* here is a kind of absolute condition that exists whether or not one recognizes it. However, upon reflection, we see that the assignation of competence is in fact a judgment, one that presupposes the importance of certain criteria and the insignificance of others. As a predicate, competence becomes, then, not only relative to the event under judgment but relative to the one making the judgment. What Arthur Danto says of art in general certainly holds for literature—it is only through interpretation that an object's aesthetic status is established (37). In both the production and reception of the literary text, competence arises from the mastering of cultural codes. Within a literary text, strategies of symbolization and typification *encode* a meaning. A reader can perceive a meaning in every text he or she encounters. An impatient or unskilled reader or one conditioned by different cultural codes can still make some sense of most texts. As with the contemporary reception of postmodern fiction, however, the "sense"

that such a reader makes of the text frequently extends not much further than claiming that the text makes little sense or, in the language
of the current discussion, that the text embodies a mimesis that is in-
sular and private and only narrowly significant (if at all). In such an
instance, it may in fact be the case that the text is, in its own way, incompetent. Incompetence here would involve the setting up and subsequent frustration of readerly expectations in an apparently pur-
poseless, erratic manner. These expectations might concern a text's
thematic resolution of some internal problematic or they might concern certain stylistic particularities. In rigidly conventional literature,
a category that subsumes most literary works, texts usually appear
consistent in their (internal) intentions. The absence of inconsistency
and ambiguity will allow a "coherent" reading to emerge. The conventions that structure a reader's point of view are echoed in the conventions that the author manipulates in the text. Neither the competence
of the text to "speak" a meaning nor the competence of the reader to
"hear" a meaning is at issue. The presence of the minimal requirements of all communications—similarities in the codes of the text
(broadly defined) and those of the reader—allows the reader to find
the text to be an exemplar of significant mimesis.

Private mimesis "occurs" when the "strategies of symbolization and
typification" seem, to the reader, to be ends in themselves. In such a
case, the surface luster of these strategies blinds the reader to the cognitive import of the text. The reader sees the text as "incompetent."
He or she cannot escape a preoccupation with form and textuality.
The world of the text seems self-enclosed and autotelic. Interpretation cannot move beyond the outlining of the private mimesis of the
textual monad. The reader is like a phonologist who can record the
sounds of a language without knowing anything of their significance.
The lived-world of the text is only obliquely similar to that of the
reader.

Whose task is it to guarantee the kind of substantive competence
required to leave a work perceivable as mimetically significant? Those
critics propounding prescriptive theories of mimesis would doubtless
reply that it is the author's responsibility. Implicit in this is an intentionalist bias. This bias minimizes or denies the historicity of the
reader by claiming that true meaning is apodictic and constant. If the
author *does his or her job,* the reader will have no difficulty in bringing

to light the author's intended meaning. When the author departs from the "correct" representational mode, e.g., modernist-liberal or formalistic, he or she ceases to communicate and indulges, rather, in "solipsism." I have already rejected this approach to the question of competence.

The innovative text compels the reader to struggle to achieve competence. This struggle is the price the reader must pay in order to use the conceptual horizons of the innovative text to extend his or her own self-understanding. If literature is to remain unprogrammatic, the reader cannot demand that the author rely on a stable body of conventions. The reader cannot insist that the author be the first and final guarantor of the reader's own competence. Literature ceases to be revelatory when it reenacts dated conventions in the name of communicative efficacy. For a spirit of freedom to prevail in literary communication, the reader must grant the text the right to say what it wills to say. A passive reception, while never desirable, may not be all that inappropriate when the text at issue is highly conventional. Postmodern fiction, however, requires something quite other of the reader.

The question of competence becomes problematic to the degree that a text departs from established conventions. The onus is on the reader to come up with a competent reading. Our "competent" reader will understand and accept this responsibility. Admittedly, however, postmodern fiction frequently "turns off" even the "competent" reader. The thematic minimalism of *Watt* (not to mention that of later works by Beckett), the verbal sport of *Ada*, the inventive typographies of Federman's *Take It Or Leave It* all require a patient absorption in the act of reading that not every reader is willing to devote to the task. As Ricoeur says, citing Joyce's *Ulysses*, the experimental text almost "abandons" the reader, forcing the latter to bear the "burden of emplotment" (*Time and Narrative* 1:77). Experimental works challenge, of course, the sacrosanctity of conventional narrative interest. They can engender in the reader what Jauss calls "aesthetic indifference," a posture that leads the reader to abandon the text rather than muddle through it:

> The dismantling of the narrative function can go too far and become a contentless language experiment; dematerialization can turn into a monotonous ascesis of perception, and ambiguity

can be exaggerated and decline into the directionlessness of arbitrary solutions. (*Aesthetic Experience and Literary Hermeneutics,*
187)

In *Aesthetic Experience and Literary Hermeneutics,* Jauss emphasizes the
need for aesthetic pleasure. He criticizes Marxist thinkers, particularly Adorno, for negating aesthetic pleasure in their whole-hearted
promotion of *aesthetic reflection.* The latter, an analytic faculty, allows
the reader to perceive, through the artwork, the essential negativity
of his or her contemporary world. For Adorno, aesthetic pleasure is
the product of the bourgeoisie's co-option of art, its reduction of art's
status from an instrument of learning to an "article of consumption"
(27). Only through the aesthetics of negativity, in itself only recogniz-
able through *aesthetic reflection,* can art perform its legitimate pedagogical function. In their discouraging of a "pleasurable" aesthetic experience, Jackson Pollock and Beckett, would, for example, in Adorno's
view, make difficult the kind of culinary reception (*kulinarische Rezep-
tion*) that more conventional works allow of their receivers (28).

It may very well be that in his critique of Adorno Jauss has merely
differentiated between the role that he has assigned himself in human
studies, i.e., literary historian-methodologist, and that which Adorno
assumed in his studies, i.e., moral philosopher and political scientist.
In any case, its validity notwithstanding, Jauss's critique does have implications for the present study. We have paid scant regard to the part
played by pleasure in the reading of avant-garde literature. Can the
development of reading competence be a pleasurable activity for the
reader? Does the competent reception of innovative literature issue
primarily from "aesthetic reflection"? Is it only through the rigors of
formal analysis that the reader apprehends the mimetic significance
of a work (be it supportive or critical of the social status quo)? What of
Jauss's assertion that aesthetic pleasure is quite as significant as cogni-
tion and the socio-ideological critique it may avail?

We have stressed the difficulty of interpreting postmodern fiction.
In this context, however, pleasure and intellectual demands are not
mutually exclusive, though Jauss, for his part, does not see a concilia-
tory relationship between the two. In the quotation above, alluding
apparently to certain *nouveau roman* fiction, he speaks of the de-structuring of narrative technique going too far. In such a situation, it becomes

. . . wholly incumbent on the reader or observer to generate the
equivalent of the aesthetic pleasure being denied him, where, in
other words, there is no aesthetic inducement that would make
him prefer the reflection or activity demanded of him to some
other way of spending his time. (187)

However, a work that leaves it "wholly incumbent" upon the reader to
achieve *aesthetic pleasure* will not yield significance through aesthetic
reflection (in Jauss's sense) either. Such a work would not satisfy the
minimal conditions of all communication—similarity in the representational codes of the text and reader. Rather, through the incommen-
surability of codes or sheer technical incompetence, such a text could
not sustain the relationality that we have asserted, again and again, to
be the frame in which a competent reception occurs. As noted earlier,
a reader rarely confronts such a text. In studying twentieth-century
fiction, the reader will frequently come up against "difficult" works.
These may, at a first casual reading, appear to withhold pleasure and
meaning. It is only later, upon subsequent readings, that fun and intellectual profit, the traditional benefits of serious literature, can
emerge.[8]

Jauss appears to be legislating, covertly, a standard of productive
competence that conforms to the reading conventions of a given public. Nothing could be more incongruous than for a historian of literary reception to lend tacit sanction to a prescriptive theory of mimesis.
The realization of such a view would quite obviously stunt creativity.
In fact, it would usher in the kind of aesthetic stasis that remains the
goal of all politically affirmative aesthetics. "Aesthetic indifference" is
usually more symptomatic of a readerly failing than of a textual one.
It would seem unreasonable to chastise the author for a reader's shortcomings. Whatever their temporal priority, aesthetic reflection and
aesthetic pleasure go hand in hand.

Elsewhere, in a short, insightful essay, Jauss emphasizes the need
for serious application, something like "aesthetic reflection," in literary reception. He acknowledges aesthetic reflection and aesthetic
pleasure to be inalienable adjuncts in reception. Referring to the
reading of detective novels, he notes:

The pleasure does not arise from the self-sufficient immersion
in a work qua work but rather from a generic expectation which

is at play between works. This expectation, together with each
new variation in the basic pattern, enhances the reader's enjoy-
ment. ("Theses," 144)

Competence arises only through familiarity with the art form in question. Competence arises only when the reader has appropriated the
"grammar" or "system of conventions" at work in the aesthetic medium. Or, expressed somewhat more dialectically, a competent reception occurs "as a way of reading which must negate the character of
the text as a unique work in order to renew the charms of a well-
known game with familiar rules but unknown surprises" (144). The
reader gains aesthetic pleasure through the successful operation of
aesthetic reflection. Ultimately—notwithstanding temporary, strategic separations of formal convention and "real world" referentiality—
aesthetic pleasure brings together form and content. The resolution
of the problem at hand—the intransigence of the text to be "meaningful"—provides the reader satisfaction and delight at his or her ability
to locate the mimetic significance of the text, that is, the point of intersection of his or her lived-world with that of the text. The bringing
together of lived-worlds, what Jauss (after Gadamer) refers to as a
"horizonal fusion," closes the circle of a competent reception. The
reader is left with what Gadamer calls "the joy of knowledge" (*Truth
and Method,* 100).

The very notion of *competence* has unavoidable *normative* overtones.
Competence is a prerequisite of understanding. It enables the reader
to give the reading a fullness that helps the text to be realized as mimetically significant. Only a competent reader can fully enliven a text.
Obviously, competence arises out of familiarity with texts. The more
one has read, the less likely one is to be puzzled by given texts. Competence is an achievement. It must be worked at. This is particularly
true for the competent reading of innovative texts. Jonathan Culler
stresses the need for an inventive faculty on the part of the reader:

> . . . the difficulty of interpreting some works provides evidence
> of the restricted nature of the conventions actually in force in a
> culture. Moreover, if a difficult work later becomes intelligible it
> is because *new ways of reading* have been developed in order to
> meet what is the fundamental demand of the system: the de-
> mand for sense. (*Structuralist Poetics,* 123; my emphasis)

We have already drawn attention to the need for a particular kind of performative hermeneutics. However, performance is not particularly meaningful as critical commentary—really no more than a personal or affective response—when it is largely self-motivated. We have spoken of private mimesis as a reception that records the formal qualities of a work without relating these to the lived-world of the reader. This kind of reading is *text-dominated*. There is yet another kind of private mimesis. A reading that is essentially *reader-dominated*—that sees the text as no more than a Rorschach blot encouraging self-exploration—is also a private mimetic reception. In each instance, the relationality of reader and text fails to take root. One or another of the elements of the communicative process dominates. Aesthetic experience ceases to be unifying; it either fragments the work into distinct formal and thematic elements or induces in the reader a self–other Cartesian fixation.

Readings based on a private mimetic reception can in themselves be of value. An understanding of stylistics and conventions is, as mentioned above, a condition of textual appropriation. Similarly, affective interpretations may be helpful to an individual in a variety of ways, for example, as mental therapy, as recuperation, as simple entertainment. Affective interpretation can help one to understand oneself in certain limited ways. Though both self-understanding and sensitivity to textuality are necessary components of a competent reception, in isolation they tend to distort, denying interpretation its legitimate relationality that binds together text and reader.

The primary innovation of avant-garde literature is conceptual in the broadest sense. Contemporary avant-garde literature puts forth new models of thinking. Finding it impossible to represent novel attitudes toward human existence through conventional means, the literary innovator radically displaces convention. A highly relativized world view will likely reject traditional formal standards. On the track of such a text's cognitive significance, the reader will have to identify the nature of this rejection, will have to place the text within the general vocabulary of other, more conventional texts. Without the interpretive benchmark of intertextual relations, the cognitive import of innovation would not be accessible to the reader. It is literature's status as text that provides the reader initial entry into a given work. (To deny a work's textuality is to reduce it to personal allegory.) Having identified the formal qualities of the work, the reader is in a position to assay their cognitive import.

It may appear that we are perpetuating the form–content dichotomy that we have already criticized in the theories of others. This
would certainly be the case if "form" and "content" were not seen as
mutual determinants. This would indeed be the case if the current
discussion stopped with formal considerations without establishing
form–content correspondences or if the text were reduced to personal allegory. However, as emphasized above, a reading that establishes the significant mimesis of a given text does so only through the
identification of internal form–content correspondences of a text and
the linkage of these to the lived-world of the reader. Competent interpretation issues from the denotation of an ever-expanding circle of
intertextual and reader-text relationships. The critical readings of
postmodern fiction offered in the second part of this study will enliven
through praxis these somewhat abstract claims.

The reception of postmodern mimesis

In light of the preceding sections of this chapter I am now in a position to summarize the conditions necessary for a competent reception
of postmodern mimesis. Through the insight afforded by Auerbach's
differentiations, we may adduce that normative theories of representation can only frustrate the reception of innovative literature. Alternatively, *diachronic differentiation* sees shifting strategies of verisimilitude as an inevitable and healthy development. Similarly, *synchronic
differentiation* emphasizes mimetic diversity within a given time frame
to be inevitable and positive. I am not putting forward a catalogue of
correctly "postmodern" mimetic strategies. Drawing primarily from
phenomenological hermeneutics, I offer not a theory of postmodern
mimesis (in itself an impossibility), but rather a theoretical outline for
its competent reception. A "theory" of postmodern mimesis, per se,
can be no more (and no less) than the critical explication of given
works. The descriptive claims arising from particular readings will
constitute our theory.

Hans Magnus Enzensberger denies that innovative literature can
have a positive social praxis:

> Even the most extreme esthetic contraventions no longer meet
> with serious resistance. . . . by way of detours via advertising, de-
> sign, and styling the inventions become part and parcel of the

consumer sphere. This means the end of an equivocation which
has ruled progressive literature for fifty years: the parallelism or
even equation of formal and social innovation. (91)

Enzensberger's argument overreaches itself here. In aligning the reception of innovative literature with our exposure to the, yes, often
clever, always self-serving ploys of advertisers and salespeople, he ma-
ligns our intelligence as readers and betrays, inadvertently or otherwise, his patriarchal attitudes. Innovation, as shown in chapter 1, is
not quite so "co-optable" as Enzensberger would have us believe. (The
critical readings that follow will augment this same demonstration.)
Certainly, professional readers like Graff and Newman, for instance,
have resisted the "esthetic contraventions" of postmodernism, have
found it difficult to shrug off innovation. Clearly, the general thesis
that intellectual rigor and moral responsibility are preempted by economic prosperity—call it materialism or consumerism—is reductive
in the extreme. Preoccupied with formal innovation, and the assault
on expectations such innovation advances, many readers overlook the
strongly satirical elements in much of postmodern fiction, elements
that, while not necessarily proposing practical, ameliorative options,
are socially responsive. John Aldridge remarks that contemporary
American writers have not been able to achieve "a critical or satirical
perspective on their society" (153), a view I contest. Aldridge regrets
that the satiric themes of contemporary black humorists, e.g., Vonnegut and Pynchon, have been too "obliquely suggested" or "altogether
absent" (139). At the same time Barthelme can be too negative, rep-
resenting a generally defiled human condition without delimiting the
sociohistorical circumstances that have given rise to such a condition
(141). Aldridge's paradigm of effective, responsible satire suffers from
an arbitrary exclusionary bias. I agree with John Tilton that "the major obstacle to a true perception and sound evaluation is a rigid pre-
conception of what satire is or ought to be. . . . Satire is and ought to
be what the creative satirist makes it become" (*Cosmic Satire in the Contemporary Novel*, 14). Like those of Graff and Newman, Aldridge's interpretation remains stuck in a private mimetic reception. His reading
oscillates between the text- and reader-dominated modes, sometimes
concentrating on the senselessness of formal play, sometimes on the
divergence of postmodern attitudes from his own.

The critical receptions we have reviewed reflect a narrow, normative view of mimetic efficacy. Many of these receptions judge postmodernism by modernist standards. They laud those whom James Mellard calls "critical modernists," essentially unexperimental writers like Bellow, Heller, and Updike, who have consolidated the achievement of Fitzgerald, Hemingway, and Faulkner (85–124). They criticize avant-garde writers for failing, as Aldridge says of Kosinski, to give shape and significance to their visions (64). Aldridge even goes so far as to assert that no contemporary novelists provide the "intellectual and imaginative leadership" that important writers of the twenties and thirties purportedly did (2).[9] Such critics quite clearly burden the text with a series of static expectations, often hearing in their readings merely their own voice and not that of the text's as well.

In *The Act of Reading* Wolfgang Iser makes a clear distinction between the voice of the text, i.e., its "implied reader," and the voice of any given "real" reader. The implied reader is a "textual structure"; it "prestructures the role to be assumed by each recipient" (34). Along with the reader's own expectations, the implied reader determines meaning. The implied reader is the textual perspective to which the real reader responds. The implied reader is a system of four main perspectives—narrator, characters, plot, and the fictitious reader. It transmits the "individuality of the author's vision" (35). In our language, the implied reader is the textual embodiment of the lived-world of the author. Those critical of postmodern fiction, who see it as narcissistic and nonmimetic, claim, implicitly, to be guided by the implied reader of the text in question. I have argued, on the other hand, that they are in fact guided by the implied readers of those texts that shape their own personal canons.

In postmodernism, the reader confronts a number of radically eccentric visions—what have been called "idiolects." While not "private language" in absolute terms, the idiolect is not widely accessible. Julia Kristeva points out the grave danger of "idiolectic" works. They stand the "enormous risk of becoming solitary monuments, gigantic but invisible, within a society whose general tendency, on the contrary, is toward conformity" ("Postmodernism?" 141). Postmodern fiction represents the implied reader in an idiolectic or quasi-idiolectic manner. However, the empirical reader will be capable of relating the textual lived-world to his or her own if he or she has come to terms with the text's form–content correspondences and its intertextual relations.

As Western humanity progresses deeper and deeper into a nonverbal age, the sensuous titillation of sound and sight media is increasingly supplanting the more cerebral excitements of reading. Jauss defines three levels of reception: a high, paradigm-forming level of dialogue between "great authors," such as Pascal reading Montaigne, Rousseau reading Saint Augustine (and, to update his examples, Barthes on Balzac, Derrida on Rousseau); a middle level of "professional," "professorial" reception that tends to "traditionalize and authorize meaning"; and, finally, a lower or "prereflective" level that "represents a subversive process of canon formation" ("Theses," 139). Both the higher and lower levels can produce substantive canonical revision. When viewed theoretically, Jauss's analysis seems reasonable. Both the upper and lower levels have a greater capacity to be original—one by token of its superior intellectuality, the other by its lack of the kind of methodological "superego" one takes on through scholarly training. The journeymen scholars of the middle level lack the generativity of the former and the untamed imagination of the latter. When, however, we locate Jauss's taxonomy within a particular frame of empirical reception, when we historicize it, its validity is less demonstrable. In the reception of innovative literature, the ability of low level receptions to influence canon formation is greatly compromised.

The radically innovative character of postmodernism makes the serendipitous insight Jauss attributes to the lower level of reception highly improbable.[10] In picking up the postmodern novel, the unschooled reader (as well as, quite often, the nonspecialist reader) will often find himself or herself denied easy textual access. Such is less likely with the reading of premodernist masterworks and indeed with many modernist works. The meaning of these latter works is *relatively* determinate and unambiguous. They will appear to be "overdetermined," replete with a great many meanings from which to "choose" (*The Act of Reading*, 48). But the overdetermined quality of contemporary innovative works will seem less obvious to the "casual" reader. Without sufficient awareness of postmodern conventions, i.e., of the relationships existing among various postmodern fictions, the latter may very well appear "underdetermined," exhibiting only a vague preoccupation with "form" or what I have called private mimesis. Consequently, given the highly allusive, complex literary texts that many postmodern fictions represent, it is an important obligation of the period specialist to engage in critical readings of works which, as I believe is the case with the texts I consider here, deserve inclusion in the canon but are not yet sufficiently known to permit this. A primary aim of this study, then, baldly stated, is *canon revision,* however modest or tentative.

While, as chapter 1 seeks to show, a certain amount of haggling with critics of contrary mind is necessary—not to mention conventional—canon revision's most powerful tool is not debate over periodization or the identification of critical trends. Similarly, though general philosophical constructs need to be examined and certain abstract premises established—I have attempted as much in the present chapter—the pursuit of these tasks does not in itself produce canon revision. No, canon revision is most ably advanced through the individual reader's engagement with literary texts. (New Criticism had that much right.) To recapitulate, my study aims to enhance the aesthetic qualities of postmodern fiction by illustrating the latter's world referentiality. Interpretation bound largely to formal issues or to a work's *purely* aesthetic status continues what one critic calls the "ideology of the aesthetic" which serves as "the social analogue of religion in our secular age, exuding a pervasive and tenacious idealist notion of 'culture' as the *soul* of society" (Kavanagh, 120). As I will show, the "ideological practice" of specific postmodern fictions is frequently obscured by the novelty of their mimetic strategies. Calvino poses a very poignant question in *If on a winter's night a traveler* (and elsewhere):

> How is it possible to defeat not the authors but the functions of the author, the idea that behind each book there is someone who guarantees a truth in that world of ghosts and inventions by the mere fact of having invested in it his own truth, of having identified himself with that construction of words? (159)

I would reply that, ultimately, only actual critical readings—not summaries of receptions or theories—can "defeat" traditional notions of authoriality and the methods of reading the latter inspire and compel. The ball is in the reader's hands. Mimesis is not an authorial problem but *ours,* mine and yours.

3

Postmodern Fiction and the Possibility
of Mimetic Significance

THE FORMALISTS' REPUDIATION OF MIMETIC FUNCTION has been dealt with considerably over the last century and a half. Many of the arguments advanced against the aestheticism of the Romantics, the *l'art pour l'art* school, against Pater and Wilde, against the New Criticism, can be applied to the formalists' reception of postmodern fiction. This contemporary strain of aestheticism/formalism is no more philosophically compelling than its antecedents and nothing more needs to be said of it here (though in the interpretive essays to follow I take up, where appropriate, formalistic readings of given fictions). On the other hand, the denial of mimetic significance put forward by a diverse body of cultural critics—including, notably, Graff et al., as well as Marxists like Fredric Jameson and Terry Eagleton—represents a more serious challenge to my thesis. To be sure, the claim of mimetic significance gains its full resonance only through illustration, only through exegesis of postmodern works. Yet, these critics' arguments necessitate a temporary postponement of actual interpretation and further elaboration on what I have called *mimetic significance*.

The preceding chapters have emphasized in a general way that postmodern fiction is mimetically significant, or more accurately, that this literature allows and indeed encourages readings that postulate mimetic significance. The latter term requires further specification. None of the cultural critics discussed deny postmodern fiction a mimetic function. Postmodern fiction represents contemporary atti-

tudes toward contemporary society; it has what Jameson calls "a moment of truth," a verisimilitude (Stephanson, 14). The real problem
with this literature, in their view, is that this mimesis has for its subject
human despair, human misery, and general anomie, all of which are
unattenuated *in* the fiction *by* the author. For them, this fiction lacks
moral exemplarity, whether defined by character, narrator, or plot,
and consequently it lacks for them a salutary moral significance. For
them, postmodern fiction is representational but not moral; or, to
adapt my language, it is mimetic but not significantly mimetic, not
importantly mimetic.

For these critics, postmodern fiction depicts problems but not solutions; its pessimism is illimitable and paralyzing. Thus, John Aldridge can characterize Coover's *The Public Burning* as "shrill sopho-
moric bombast" because it fails to depict morally redeeming elements
in America in the fifties (145). And, similarly, in *The Rhetoric of Fiction*,
Wayne Booth criticizes Robbe-Grillet's *Le Voyeur* for its depiction of an
unrelieved moral pathology (384). Gerald Graff's and John Gardner's
essays also express a similar concern for the "positive hero." In *Truth
and Method*, Gadamer maintains that correct interpretation involves
the discernment of the particular "questions" that every work asks. In
the case of Aldridge, Booth, et al., the critic has read postmodern fiction with the "questions" in mind that realism and modernism pose.
There is, I think, something distastefully patriarchal in suggesting
that a moral elite, i.e., writers, can (and must) present to the morally
deficient, i.e., readers, unassailable moral truths. While such a tack
might be suitable in an age dominated by a single world view, or for
children in any epoch—we recall Plato's views on education in *Laws*—
there is every possibility such a strategy will seem unappealingly naive
to contemporary readers, or that it will encourage in them passivity
and dependence, often synonyms for moral cowardice. Neither postmodern fiction nor life in the late twentieth century, for that matter,
presents scenarios with unambiguous moral significance. Each demands that we as readers and citizens *choose* (and, given the influence
of the existentialist ethos on much of postmodern fiction, *choice* seems
an appropriate term). In compelling in the reader self-choice, postmodern fiction is, it seems to me, both a logical and desirable response
to mass pluralistic democracy in the West in the late twentieth century.

Clearly what is at issue here is the capacity of postmodern literature
to inspire in readers a morally productive response to their lived-

world, what Marxists would call a positive praxis. Graff et al. do not dispute that postmodern fiction can affect readers but claim that the effect is not likely to be a healthy one. This latter reading is founded on a traditional humanistic liberalism, a position earmarked by seriousness, optimism, confidence, and what has historically often been a pseudo-pluralism, one that has in fact enacted unspoken valorizations based on class, race, gender, political ideology, and, as we have seen in the context of this study, literary representational modes. In asserting for postmodern fiction a mimetic significance, I do not divorce myself from traditional liberalism but suggest the need to redefine it now in the late twentieth century in an age when moral verities are no longer timeless but time-bound. Traditional liberalism has of course emphasized the capacity of free men and women to effect positive, progressive change, the capacity of the enlightened, committed individual to conquer all. However, as a host of germinal thinkers have forcefully established in recent intellectual history—the familiar list includes Darwin, Marx, Nietzsche, Freud, Heidegger, Wittgenstein, Foucault—the individual's power to respond unilaterally is seriously challenged by powerful and often "invisible" forces, what are called "supra-individual" determinisms. A redefined *postmodern* liberalism seeks to renegotiate human subjectivity in the context of the personal and historico-structural determinisms that, through their interaction, determine human destiny. This enterprise is not founded on an antihumanism but rather on a revised notion of human possibility.

In contrast to traditional liberals who apotheosize subjectivity, writers of postmodern fiction consider the limits placed on individual agency by such supra-individual determinisms as language, class affiliation, race, gender, and history, all of which go together to shape one's lived-world. Were this the entire story of postmodern fiction, the latter would indeed be as bleak and morally irrelevant, even invidious, as its harsher critics maintain. But postmodern fiction is not about a docile capitulation to historical circumstance. Postmodern fiction is about tension, a tension already evident in both realism and modernism, as Lukács's *The Theory of the Novel* points out, a tension that exists between the present and the past, the individual and the collectivity.[1] In exploring this tension, postmodern fiction is *traditional*. Its manner of exploration is, however, decidedly untraditional as is its reluctance to dissolve the tension through some kind of closure.

Postmodern fiction is about paradox. Indeed, generally, as Lyotard suggests in *The Postmodern Condition*, the study of paradox, i.e., "para-doxology," is a preeminently postmodern exercise. As noted above, the central theme of postmodern fiction is the tension that exists between the individual subject and, generally stated, society. Perhaps the most common theme in all of fiction, this tension has historically yielded two different kinds of stories. Where the overcoming of the tension has not destroyed the individual, we find the traditional bildungsroman. Where the protagonist perishes in the overcoming of the tension or simply opts out of society, we have a tale of alienation. Realist and modernist fictions have of course explored both of these emplotment options with the former emphasizing more social integration and the latter alienation. In each instance, the treatment of this tension has normally involved the ultimate dissolution of the self–other tension. In the "novel of development," the protagonist conforms to, and is co-opted by, social expectations. In the alienation novel—the more dominant mode in the twentieth century—the oppressed subject does one of a number of things to dissolve the self–other tension, all of which involve either self-destruction or a retreat from society. Some protagonists go (or stay) mad like Dostoevsky's Underground Man, the protagonist of Hamsun's *Hunger*, and Rilke's Malte; others indulge in the grand gesture as do Turgenev's Rudin and Faulkner's Bayard Sartoris; some commit suicide like the many tragic heroines of nineteenth-century realist fiction, or like Quentin Compson; others turn to a romanticized aestheticism as in Joyce, Proust, and Mann; and, still others simply relocate themselves like Huck Finn, Ford's Tietjens, and Dos Passos's Jimmy Herf.

In each of the above instances, the tension between society and the individual is eased, whether through conformity/co-option or defiant withdrawal/self-destruction. Closure is imposed upon the protagonist's dilemma. In every instance, the fundamental paradox of human existence—we choose ourselves but we are also chosen—is dissolved and hence denied. In the end, the protagonist acknowledges either supra-individual social determinisms or idiosyncratic private ones—but not both concurrently. The basic paradox of existence yields to the orthodoxy of liberal teleology. This paradox is captured most economically in a statement by the protagonist in Handke's *Across:* "I am determined and self-determined" (101). It is illustrated by Oedipa Maas's inconclusive (and unconcluded) quest for social justice and truth. It is of course this same paradox that is summoned up in John

Barth's two celebrated discussions of postmodern fiction, the "Exhaustion" and the "Replenishment" essays, the former emphasizing the limits of narrative freedom, the latter the imaginative capacities of individual writers and readers.

The absence of closure in postmodern fiction inspires its critics to pronounce it as nihilistic, as frivolous, as bereft of mimetic significance. Espousing the central tenets of traditional liberalism—the integrity and potence of the subject—such critics demand that the alienated condition of humankind be either overcome or that the subject perish in the process of seeking to overcome it. This is the necessary *telos* of a moral life, and it must be represented in literature. Here, the self–other tension is a very serious topic and must be treated as a grand dramatic theme. There is no place here for (postmodern) playfulness, for the recognition that this tension, given its inevitability, is equally open to the kind of parodically melodramatic handling we find, for example, in Vonnegut, Pynchon, and Barth. Richard Rorty offers an interesting distinction between what he calls "philosophical liberalism" and "postmodern bourgeois liberalism."[2] The former posture bears much in common with what I have been calling traditional liberalism. Calling the former position Kantian in its metaphysical preoccupation with "intrinsic human dignity" and "intrinsic human rights," Rorty goes on to criticize "philosophical liberalism" for its reliance on a "metanarrative" (after Lyotard) that fails to consider fully human historicity ("Postmodernist Bourgeois Liberalism," 214–16). It seems to me that the cultural critics most suspicious of postmodern fiction are burdened in this way by a number of a priori assumptions about human possibility and how it is best depicted in fictional narrative. These assumptions, explored in detail in chapter 1, define these critics' particular metanarrative, one that juxtaposes their humanism and postmodern "nihilism" (Graff, *LAI,* 51–52), their solvency and postmodern inflation/bankruptcy (Newman), their hopefulness and postmodern "frustration and disappointment" (Aldridge, 9–11).

Rorty's "postmodern bourgeois liberalism" accepts contexts. It rejects "first principles," the delineation of which has traditionally been the primary task of the philosopher. Postmodern fictions endorse this revisionist liberal position, I think. In them we find a rejection of a number of ideal constructs, values that undergird the arguments of the critics of postmodern fiction: *faith* in reason; traditional liberal teleology (which manifests itself in narrative closure or claims of closure); the absolutization of subjectivity; the "High Art" versus "Low Art" distinction; suspicion of unresolvable dialectical thought, i.e., paradox; suspicion of formal innovation; and the primacy of absolutist, nonsituational ethics. In postmodern bourgeois liberalism, Rorty informs us, "the moral justification of the institutions and practices of one's group—e.g., of the contemporary bourgeoisie—is mostly a matter of historical narratives . . . rather than of philosophical meta-narratives" (218). And it is the arts, in Rorty's view, and not philosophy, that provide "the principal backup for historiography"; it is the arts which "serve to develop and modify a group's self-image by, for example, apotheosizing its heroes, diabolizing its enemies, mounting dialogues among its members, and refocusing its attention" (218).

Are postmodern fictions capable of some or even any of these things that Rorty claims as central functions of the contemporary arts? I obviously believe they are, yet what accounts for the failure of so many readers to agree? There are several reasons, some philosophical in nature, others more a case of rhetorical strategy. Those cultural historians critical of postmodern fiction have brought unhelpful metaphysical biases to their readings, biases that compel what I have called earlier a private mimetic reading of this literature, biases that foreclose all possibility of the mutual implication of text and reader needed for an interactive reception. Other considerations have made a significantly mimetic reception unlikely. As discussed already in chapter 1, formal experimentation, by definition, calls attention to aesthetic properties and can distract us from the work's referentiality. Further, many critics define the field of postmodern fiction too narrowly and base their discussions on too few authors and too few works. Additionally, many cultural historians, intent on defining the central premise(s) of postmodernism generally, have neglected the fiction of the period and have made general, often abstruse claims that are refuted (with greater or less ease) when actual literary works are considered. Though a fine essay—the best on the subject by a Marxist—Fredric Jameson's "Postmodernism, or The Cultural Logic of Late Capitalism" focuses very little on literature, attending more to architecture. Whatever its interpretive validity, debatable in my view, Jameson's brief look at Doctorow hardly defines the postmodern novel.[3] Taking this principle of the "representative" sample one long step further, Eagleton's "Capitalism, Modernism and Postmodernism" fails to mention a single postmodern writer and opts to caricature postmodernism by defining it simplistically in terms of Andy Warhol and a single, unnamed (apocryphal?) sculptor. In his "Modernity versus Postmodernity" essay Habermas offers abstract taxonomies that are generally unsupported by examples (though passing references are made to the autonomist aesthetics of the Dadaists and Surrealists). While it can be argued that these Marxist critiques of postmodernity are after bigger game than narrative experimentation, the premises of these essays would be more fully tested were a broader sample of literature explored, and explored in detail.

But to return to the central issue, how can postmodern fiction "refocus" our attention in a positive way? What is the relationship between a positive praxis and postmodern fiction? Certainly *praxis* is an unsettling term. It is burdened with neoplatonic, utilitarian associations; it seems to emphasize pedagogical function at the expense of aesthetic accomplishment, and not a productive interaction of form–content. Further, it is exceedingly difficult to *prove* that a single work of literature or some constellation of literary works has actually influenced human behavior. One can usually only make an interpretive case for "influence," whether positive or negative. Indeed, the critical readings that I will presently offer do not go beyond the *postulation* of positive influence; they have no basis in statistical fact, the kind that empirical studies seek to provide. (Few novels have the direct, certifiable effect of, for example, Goethe's suicide-inducing *Werther.*) Certainly, the praxis that postmodern fiction encourages is not fundamentally political, though there may be political implications. Jameson is obviously correct when he says that one's view of postmodernism involves either affirmation of the political status quo or a repudiation of it ("Postmodernism," 55; "The Politics of Theory," 53). I believe American and European postmodern fiction is quite clearly a politically *conserving* gesture but not necessarily a *conservative* one, as political labels go. (The case of Latin American postmodern literature would have to be considered separately.) Consequently, it is not surprising that this literature is devoid of what Habermas calls "utopian content," a (Marxist) prescription for radical social reformation or indeed outright revolution (14).

Yet, as is well known, there is no consensus among Marxists on the need of literature to offer problem resolution, i.e., "utopian content." In contrast to Lukács, Jameson, Eagleton, and Habermas, who all emphasize the need for positivity, there are those who stress the importance of delineating problems, of negativity, for example, Engels (in the already mentioned 1888 Harkness letter) as well as first-generation Frankfurt philosophers like Adorno and Horkheimer. What Horkheimer, for example, says of philosophy can be applied to postmodern fiction: "Philosophy is inconvenient, obstinate, and with all of that, of no immediate use" (694). The key qualification here, I think, is the word "immediate," for philosophy, like postmodern fiction, can in time influence the way we act in the world. Interestingly, another important critic-theorist much preoccupied with social reform also denies the need for explicit positivity. Rabelais, writes Bakhtin,

> taunts the deceptive human word by a parodic destruction of syntactic structures. . . . But the truth that might oppose such falsity receives almost no direct intentional and verbal expression in Rabelais, it does not receive its *own* word. . . . Truth is restored by reducing the lie to an absurdity, but truth itself does not seek words; she is afraid to entangle herself in the word, to soil herself in verbal pathos. (*Dialogic Imagination*, 309)

Problem resolution should not be an a priori requirement in literature.

Eagleton's criticism of a "certain wing of the Western liberal intelligentsia"—generally, what Rorty calls postmodernist bourgeois liberalism—for failing to attend to the problems of the Third World strikes me as a non sequitur ("Last Post," 111). The oppression of Third World peoples is an important issue but it is not the *only* significant topic for debate. It is certainly not the only topic for Western intellectuals to consider even as one acknowledges the complicity of many corporations and Western governments in this process of subjugation and the timeliness of the divestment debate in the United States and elsewhere. It does not follow that the discussion of intellectual and moral problems peculiar to the democracies of the North Atlantic suggests moral failing or outright decadence. Many Third World countries would indeed benefit from radical political change, even revolutionary change. The same cannot be said for Canada or the United States or the nations of Western Europe. Eagleton's Marxist metanarrative obscures the historico-cultural specificity of very diverse traditions.[4] I would maintain that the content of postmodern fiction is morally ameliorative, rather than politically "utopian," and that this is satisfactory. The fictions that I consider here document the moral failings of fictional and historical characters in specific contexts. No attempt is made in these fictions to revolutionize society; there is indeed a loss of Lukács's desired "epic significance" (*Writer and Critic*, 127). The stories offered here are presented on relatively small canvases. There is no sense of a "great collective project," the sort of which Jameson longs for, as any consistent, totalizing Marxist must ("Postmodernism," 65). Unlike the great milieu studies of realist and modernist fiction, these fictions provide little scope for the paradigmatic exercises of Marxist literary criticism. Postmodern fictions are "little narratives" (*petits récits*) in the Lyotardian sense of small "local" stories with small "local" truths (60). Postmodern fictions are focused tactical assaults on certain injustices in our society; they are not total war on the social totality.

Clearly, if postmodern fiction promotes a positive praxis, it is not "political" in the strict sense of the word. Yet, I would argue, it is "political" in the term's etymological sense of having to do with people and how they behave toward one another. Walter Abish addresses this issue in an interview:

> My work is indeed political, but I very much doubt that any American political entity, left or right, would recognize this. I am interested in describing how people function and adjust to the hierarchical in everyday life. . . . in my writing I like to call attention to as well as seek to undermine the so-called political stability of our society. (McCaffery/Gregory, 21–22)

What Abish says of his own work also applies to the other fictions I discuss here. These have a variety of themes, but they all make significant social critical statements, or better, to avoid essentialistic overtones, they allow readers to postulate, to construct and reconstruct, something like morally significant claims. Though rejecting traditional humanism, one clearly allied with "philosophical liberalism," a humanism that in his view is excessively metaphysical, Walter Abish takes an obvious "ethical position" on a number of social issues—consumerism, the fetishization of culture, anti-Semitism, bourgeois conformity, historiographical amnesia. Abish engages contemporary moral problems by illustrating how *values*—in this context *suspect* values—are invested in linguistic conventions and, more particularly, the

material objects of the lived-world. Robert Coover is similarly concerned with language but in his *Spanking the Maid* he looks at how
language, indeed how the "linguisticality of being," in the current
buzz phase, shapes our attitudes on issues related to epistemology and
especially gender relations. Peter Handke, for his part, investigates
how expectations—literary-generic, emotional, social—shape the
narratives we "write" for ourselves in order to understand our lives.
Finally, Gilbert Sorrentino, in *Mulligan Stew,* analyzes how human subjectivity—in this instance the special case of the creative writer—is
assaulted by the "culture industry" and its commodification of the aesthetic object.

As I have argued throughout, reading is a contingent process in
which an individual "historical reader" interacts with a literary work.
The various issues that these fictions take up will obviously not be
judged by readers to be of equal importance, nor are they by me. This
is understandable and suggests the contingent nature of literary reception. Certain issues are more central to certain readers than are
other issues. In selecting the fictions to be interpreted in this study, I
had two basic choices—to consider works that deal roughly with the
same theme or to consider thematically disparate texts. Clearly, as my
brief catalogue of themes reveals above, I have pursued the latter
tack. Rather than select fictions devoted to a single, primary interest,
e.g., gender relations, history, ecology, materialism, the artist, race,
ethnicity, etc., I have elected to consider a group of works concerned
with a variety of topics. While I have done so in part for flagrantly
idiosyncratic reasons, it is also my view that my thesis can be more
fully explored and, if my readings are persuasive, more fully justified
by consulting a diverse body of texts. Another factor has influenced
my selection of texts. The formal inventions of these works pose an
attractive hermeneutic challenge, though inventiveness should not be
construed in romantic terms of "genius" and (absolute) "originality."
Indeed, and this is of course a postmodern truism, innovation here
occurs in the context of established rhetorico-narrative conventions:
the ("experimental") realism of Abish; the chronological fragmentation evident in Coover and Handke; the parody and pastiche of
Coover and Sorrentino; the essayistic digressions of Abish and
Handke.

Another consideration has determined in part my selection of
texts. These particular ones have not received the attention I think

they deserve. This last point may raise a question in the reader's mind. In acknowledging that these fictions have not been considered much, I also admit implicitly that the two reception constituencies I criticize—the formalists and the cultural historians/philosophical liberals—have not offered readings of these specific works. A conventional and sound rhetorical strategy when offering a new, uncanonized reading of a literary work or corpus of work is to consider the *same* texts that canonized receptions have taken up. This strategy, while logical, is difficult to implement here because much of the reception of postmodern fiction has been summary, has been dedicated to general principles and a review of prominent, "representative" authors, with little close attention paid to particular works.[5] Would Gerald Graff perhaps reject *Spanking the Maid* for some purported glamorization of sadism? I don't know. Most of Graff's positions that I consider here date from the seventies but, I must admit, I have seen no retraction of those positions. Would John Aldridge find Handke's deliberations on the conventions of biography petty and onanistic? I don't know. And what of Charles Newman? Would one or another of the fictions I consider here merit praise were he to consider it in detail? The vituperative rhetoric of *The Post-Modern Aura* suggests not, but who is to say? Yet, it seems to me, in each instance, with minor qualification in the case of Graff, postmodern fiction and postmodernism are synonymous with general moral and intellectual entropy, and are subjected to a blanket condemnation. Obviously, in my mind, this embracing condemnation—endorsed by the Marxists I have cited—also threatens the works I consider here and needs to be rebutted both generally and exegetically. The critical readings that follow seek to demonstrate that these works deserve a careful, sympathetic look, that they can both teach and entertain, the two classic functions of "good" literature.

As I have continually implied here, canon revision is one prominent aim of this study. I seek to garner for postmodern fiction, or at least for some of it, the prestige enjoyed by fiction endorsing other (and earlier) representational modes. In her pursuit of a similar project in the field of women writers, Lillian Robinson notes correctly that the "gentleman's agreement" that founds the accepted central canon can be effectively challenged and ultimately altered by offering new, noncanonical readings of literary works (573–74). Obviously, Robinson is concerned here not merely with the "correction" of literary history (as it is written by a mostly male constituency), but with the far more significant enterprise of improving the status of women generally, a move with clear moral implications for our culture generally. Robinson has assumed what I regard to be the proper role of the literary scholar in that her scholarship encourages a positive praxis for herself, her students, and her peers. Like Robinson, I also seek to reduce the emargination of a particular body of literature but not merely as a response to an internecine quarrel among academics. My objective is to investigate what postmodern works tell us about ourselves, about our culture, and therein to postulate for it a positive praxis.

Jauss, like me heavily indebted to Gadamerian phenomenology, outlines in his "Provokation" essay the conditions necessary for literature to have a social function:

> The social function of literature manifests itself in its genuine possibility only where the literary experience of the reader enters into the horizon of expectations of his lived praxis, preforms his understanding of the world, and thereby also has an effect on social behavior. (*Toward an Aesthetic of Reception,* 39)

It is quite obvious that my readings, like all readings, attempt to influence the literary expectations of the reader, particularly the academic reader. But, in contrast to the formalists' project, my readings are based on what Gadamer calls, somewhat ponderously, "aesthetic nondifferentiation," a process emphasizing the indivisibility of (aesthetic) form and (existential) content (*Truth and Method,* 104–8; *Relevance,* 29, 51). It is only through aesthetic nondifferentiation that literature has the possibility of a social function. It is only through aesthetic nondifferentiation that we as academic readers can avoid the specialization of function promoted for us by formalists, a specialization encouraged by the technocratic society in which we live.[6] Even though I reject the reception of postmodern fiction tendered by the cultural critics, I am in obvious sympathy with the basic premise of their readings, that literature and life should not be separated by the "expert" who chooses arbitrarily to thematize formal elements. No, it is precisely the expert who has a professional obligation to assist the layperson in fashioning links between self and text and the lived-world in all of its plenitude. I hope that the readings offered here provide other academics examples of how a significant mimesis can be construed for contemporary noncanonical fiction. Having rejected the aesthetic differentiation of formalism, my readings seek to occupy a place somewhere between the nostalgic yearnings of the less radical liberals and the millennialist prospections of the Marxists, a place I would quite simply call the postmodern present. And, if my readings do indeed act as an incitement to others to consider both postmodern mimesis and the reception problem—both largely neglected, in my view, to date—they modestly succeed, though admittedly not as the last words on these subjects but as some of the first ones.

4

Walter Abish and the
Topographies of Desire

VIENNESE JEWS, WALTER ABISH AND HIS FAMILY fled Hitler's Austria
for China. Unbeknown to him, there lurked below Vienna's surface
decorum, concealed by the refinement and prosperity of a former im-
perial center, a most virulent ethno-racial hate. And how did such a
world appear to a boy of seven or eight? Life, Abish tells us, was very
much an affair of surfaces for him, a mistaking of the *apparent* for the
real. Reassured by the props of his childhood—favorite toys, a com-
fortable home, a supportive family—Abish viewed life as a harmonious arrangement of people and objects. Writing recently in a lengthy
essay on his Viennese roots, Abish, referring to himself in the third
person, retrospects:

> . . . from the very beginning he sensed a smoothly functioning
> world in which his needs were taken care of with a scrupulous
> attention to detail, a world in which pleasure had to be negoti-
> ated, in which the gramophone, the radio, the telephone as
> much as the tiny bell on the underside of the dining table, the
> bell with which his mother summoned the maid, highlighted the
> perfection of a designed world. Everything was always planned,
> all contingencies *appeared* to be covered. Nothing was left to ac-
> cident . . . ("The Fall of Summer," 121–22)

In its various allusions to perfection, familiarity, orderly surfaces, and
naive confidence, this brief passage highlights key thematic interests

of Abish's innovative short stories, collected in *Minds Meet* (1975) and *In The Future Perfect* (1977), and his novels, *Alphabetical Africa* (1974) and, most notably, *How German Is It,* winner of the Faulkner/Pen award for the best fictional work of 1980.[1]

Pleasing surfaces

Abish's fiction depicts the surfaces of things, of people, of events, compelling the reader to ponder the moral and psychological interests that shape life's visible contours and condition our response to them. He attributes his reluctance to intrude with "clarifying" narratorial commentary to his own perception of the world, while growing up, as "bewildering in its profusion of stylized drama . . . a drama that remained forever highly elusive" (Klinkowitz, "Walter Abish," 97). In Abish's view, we, in the twentieth century, present images of order and perfection to ourselves in order to assuage the demands of psyche and conscience for emotional and moral solvency. The world of Abish's fiction is preeminently urban, a not surprising preoccupation given Abish's professional training as an urban planner. The characters that populate this world strive for urbanity, a presentation of self suggesting confident mastery of the codes of bourgeois taste and personal comportment. "Taste," in this narrow context, involves the recuperation of familiar standards of social grace, the repetition of an unreflective "perfection."

Abish's characters strive to achieve "familiarity" and "perfection." They dexterously arrange objects in space, from domestic bric-a-brac and furniture to major institutional architecture, in an effort to present iconically the values and achievements most revered in the late twentieth century: self-confidence, material success, taste, stability, and power. Whether involving the markers of bourgeois affluence— designer clothes, a "good education" for our children, fashionable holidays—or the signs of sociopolitical prowess—sleek technologies, polished executive performances, well-publicized philanthropies— we live in an image-conscious era in which style, artfully and strategically, subverts substance, in which the ephemeral often supplants the ethically responsible. Whether considering our collective preoccupation with appearances in the context of personal crises, as he does in many of the short stories, or in light of a major historical issue such as contemporary attitudes toward the Nazi pogroms, as in *How German*

Is It, Abish, a subtle social critic, always returns to a single question: "Is there any other way to live?" (Klinkowitz, "Walter Abish," 96).

Abish's work, like the fictions of Pynchon, Handke, Vonnegut, and many Latin American writers, effectively rebuts the argument that contemporary, innovative writers neglect history in their preoccupation with formalistic vanguardism and (what Jameson cites as) postmodern stylization of "past-ness" ("Postmodernism," 66–71). As in the best postmodern fiction, technique and content are interactive in Abish's work. The discernment of the "familiar" is a central imperative in Abish's fiction, for it is only through discernment that the "familiar" can be displaced by something more morally profound, more profoundly insightful. Abish would risk unintended, unfortunate self-parody were he to discuss the "familiar" in familiar literary-generic terms. The "familiar" can only be effectively depicted through a representational mode that denudes it of its familiarity, making of it something foreign, something unsettling, something perhaps even hateful to the reader.

Abish's most succinct statements on his narrative aesthetic come in interviews, one in 1974, the other in the early 1980s, each appearing after the publication of a novel. In the earlier interview, he analyzes the uninflected description that figures so prominently in *Alphabetical Africa* and *Minds Meet* (and that we also see in later work):

> In my writing I try to strip language of its power to create verisimilitude that in turns shields the reader from the printed words on the page that are employed as markers. Writing as close as possible to a neutral content, everything, the terrain, the interiors, the furniture, the motions of the characters are aspects of a topography that defines the limits of the situation being explored. (Klinkowitz, "Walter Abish," 96)

Though indicating a concern for the empirical, this statement quite obviously defines no standard mimetic realism, nor indeed a neo-naturalism. Abish's realism, really an "experimental realism" as Jerome Klinkowitz has observed, presents a highly nuanced vision of a world only superficially stable (*The Self-Apparent Word,* 128–31). Unlike conventional realists who supplement description with much straightforward narratorial analysis and commentary, Abish manipulates language and images in a more self-conscious, subtle manner in order to show the capacity of communicational codes to constrict thought and to preempt moral introspection.[2]

Structurally, both in the stories and the novels, we find an emphasis on spatiality. Not a great deal happens in Abish's fiction, typically. He juxtaposes a series of short, narrowly enframed scenes involving, for example, a character considering the contents of a shop window, or a sparse narratorial description of an interior, or a bland conversational exchange. His realism offers no expansive, slice-of-life tableaux. His is the art of the photographer, not the mural painter (and we find frequent references to photographs and photographers in his fictions). Abish's verbal vignettes flaunt the surfaces of life. Abish is not after a deep, hidden truth. For him, "everything is on the surface" (Lotringer, 165). Characters are presented to the reader very much as people present themselves to us in our daily interactions with them, replete with apparent goodwill and not always scrutable motivations and desires. Yet, though he offers neither conventional psychological analysis nor exemplary characters, Abish, in a resolutely Bakhtinian spirit, consistently manipulates an understated irony to deride the superficiality of our age. Unlike Robbe-Grillet, for example, Abish pursues "neutral content" in order to achieve a value-charged end. His fictions relate the epistemological to the moral.

As has been suggested above, in order to isolate phenomena, and therein render them less "familiar," Abish uses a kind of scenic enframement in his fictions roughly analogous to the spatial limits placed upon a photographic image by the aperture of a camera lens. Abish, like many twentieth-century writers and philosophers, is acutely aware of another "enframing" device—language. As we find with other modern, native-born Austrian writers like Musil, Thomas Bernhard, and Handke (all of whom are mentioned by Abish from time to time), Abish interrogates the constrictive function of language. Through the isolation and repetition of clichés—the verbal bedrock of human interaction—Abish considers language's seductive capacity to domesticate objects and events in the world by reducing them to the rhetorically familiar. Abish's characters take refuge in language, allowing the reassuring rhythms of trite conversation to lull them into intellectual and moral apathy.[3] In *How German Is It*, for example, the weather inspires an often repeated exchange that, incidentally, has embedded within it a reference to the war the characters are attempting to forget.

A glorious German summer.
Oh, absolutely.
A scent of flowers in the air.
Isn't it marvelous.
Easily the most glorious summer of the past thirty-four years
    [since 1944].
And how relaxing. (54)

The unreflective use of language represents, of course, an affirmation of the status quo and this affirmation has obvious and profound moral implications. At the conclusion of "Access," the narrator remarks both on the malaise of stereotyped speech patterns and the writer's capacity to effect partial remedy:

> I'm not really concerned with language. As a writer I'm prin-
> cipally concerned with meaning. What, for instance, does being
> a writer mean in the context of this society. . . . writers perform
> a vital task, they resuscitate words that are about to be obliter-
> ated by a kind of willful negligence and general boredom. Writ-
> ers frequently are able to inject a fresh meaning into a word and
> thereby revitalize the brain cells of the reader by feeding the
> brain information it does not really require. (*Future Perfect*,
> 72–73)

And, by helping overcome the intellectual entropy begot of formulaic language, the writer may also have a moral impact.

Though, as Wolfgang Holdheim has pointed out, "The boundary between ethical blindness and intellectual obtuseness has never been precisely defined," we may nonetheless consider Abish's fictions as preliminary cartographic efforts to draw this line of demarcation (147).[4] Before considering the novel *How German Is It,* his longest and most successful work, let us turn first to the short fiction and Abish's portrayal therein of contemporary urban society.

The short fiction

A materialistic society is controlled by the manipulation of, and its own absorption in, the apparent. It practices a crude, impatient phe-nomenology that "understands" through reduction and typification.

A priori notions of perfection render invisible the nuances of the moment. "This Is Not a Film This Is a Precise Act of Disbelief," the lengthiest of Abish's collected stories, starts off with some *apparently* reassuring observations:

> This is a familiar world. It is a world crowded with familiar
> faces and events. Thanks to language the brain can digest, piece
> by piece, what has occurred and what may yet occur. It is never
> at a loss for the word that signifies what is happening this instant.
> In Mrs. Ite's brain the interior of her large house with a view of
> the garden and the lake are surfaces of the familiar. . . . To some
> degree the objects in the familiar interior of her house channel
> the needs. (*Minds Meet,* 31)

The passage suggests, as Abish says of it, "the dubiousness of the familiar" (Klinkowitz, "Walter Abish," 96). Its naively confident tone excites in the reader the suspicion that all is not as it appears to be, that the verbal surface of the story must be attended to closely. As the story illustrates, Mrs. Ite's "understanding" of the world around her is based on myopia. She understands very little about the circumstances in which her life is enmeshed. This opening section concludes with Mrs. Ite remarking to her son Bud that something is missing, something normally present "among the familiar setting of her furniture" (*Minds Meet,* 31). Her son responds wanly that it couldn't be anything "terribly familiar," investing the scene with comic absurdity for, in fact, it is her husband who has disappeared.

Three years after his father's disappearance, son Bud discovers the keys to Mr. Ite's locked study. Upon casual investigation he and Mrs. Ite discover Mr. Ite's body, the seeming victim of foul play (though the cause of his fate is never identified). Mr. Ite, an architect by profession, was professionally engaged in the creation of new surfaces. At the time of his death he was involved in the design of the local mall, a fixture in the landscape of contemporary America. A mall, of course, bears testimony to our capacity (and desire) both to neutralize nature and to implant our own stylized vision on the world. (And, lest we doubt the compelling nature of this vision, there were, in 1985, more enclosed malls in the United States than cities, four-year colleges, or television stations, and almost as many as county courthouses [Kowinski, 20].)

In the story, a French Marxist film director who has come to "use" the mall as a set for a movie—actually to blow it up as a gesture of proletarian self-righteousness—refers to the new mall as a "Museum of Need," noting generally the "surfaceness of all American things" (*Minds Meet*, 34). Abish's story shows us that the mall must be read as a sociological marker. Apparently a "museum" that bequeaths to its clientele usable cultural artifacts, it represents, at the same time, equally apparently (if we defamiliarize "mall-ness" for a moment, as Abish does), the most recent stage in the commercialization of modern life. The architects of such structures are also, in concert with developers, retailers, etc., the would-be architects of our desires. Barthes, in the essay on the Eiffel Tower—another architectural paean to "progress"—notes that architecture has always been "dream and function, expression of a utopia and instrument of a convenience" (239). It remains of crucial importance that we consider self-consciously the dream, the utopia, the mall's authors are, quite literally, selling and that, if we accept this dream, we do so volitionally.[5]

Like many postmodern writers, Abish rarely puts forward exemplary ethical postures in his fiction. As noted earlier, his characters exhibit bad faith and bad moral judgment, typically. In "This Is Not a Film" the various characters represent different classes, varying intellectual interests, and conflicting political positions; therein, they serve as foils for one another. Yet, in the end, the cast behaves in a frighteningly undifferentiated way. The working class—represented by Hank notably—and the controlling bourgeoisie have essentially the same values, a situation that denies the Marxist claim—at once romantic and hopeful—that the workers are closer to historical truth than any other class. Hank, a worker in a local bottle plant, accepts unquestioningly both his wife's lavish wardrobe and the ease with which he himself receives well-remunerated employment. Hank, like his bourgeois masters, affirms a statement made by Cas Ite shortly before his death: "We're all trapped by our needs" (60). Hank's needs, emotional ones that are serviced by material well-being, compel him to overlook the source of his prosperity—his wife's efforts to copulate her way up the social ladder, a circumstance happily exploited (and paid for) by the town's oligarchy of professionals and businessmen.

In addition to class difference, there are two other noteworthy oppositions in the story though neither admits significant moral differentiation. Merce Ite, the brother of architect Cas, appears to be markedly dissimilar to his brother and the latter's cronies. A man of culture, a cosmopolitan, Merce seems admirable in his sensitivity to books and theater and his general aloofness from the maneuverings of the provincial business world. However, these aesthetic interests—call them "needs"—merely indulge a hedonism indistinguishable from those of his peers, a hedonism that is underwritten in part by brother Cas, who provides Merce funds for fine suits and trysts in Boston with male prostitutes. Finally, the seemingly disparate priorities of culture and corporation are subsumed by a common foundational priority—the satisfying of personal need. After seeing his sister-in-law and his brother's business associate Frank Ol together in a Boston hotel, Merce opts for the preservation of surface harmonies and does not inform his brother of the infidelity. Cas's death, though never definitely explained—was it murder or was it suicide?—seems most likely attributable to the treachery of Ol and Mrs. Ite, a treachery inadvertently abetted by Merce's moral passivity.

Completing this pattern of immorality in "This Is Not a Film" is the character Michel Bontemps, a leftist filmmaker after the fashion of Godard, who serves as a foil to businessman Frank Ol and his associates. As with the oppositions discussed above, Abish plays with stereotypes in this juxtaposition of the "Marxist revolutionary" and the captains of commerce. Written in the early seventies, "This Is Not a Film" rejects the fatuous assumption (more current then perhaps than in the opportunistic eighties) that antiestablishment rhetoric serves as the only necessary surety for ethico-political idealism. Though purportedly intent on producing an agitprop film depicting the general corruptness of American values—values that are embodied by Ol and Cas Ite—Bontemps' cinematic project is more an act of self-promotion than of social critique. The narrator makes clear in introducing Bontemps that the latter has developed a personality cult around himself by carefully fashioning a public image. Dark sunglasses, a myriad of affairs, temper tantrums, fifteen "innovative films," and the interior of his apartments are the markers that define "Michel Bontemps" (32). As his surname suggests, Bontemps is after a "good time"; he is a hedonistic media star, not a Marxist ideologue.

Bontemps and his aides—the unnamed narrator and his fiancée—have installed themselves in a local hotel:

> The hotel room is our center, our HQ. . . . our books, our pa-
> pers, our black-and-white photographs of Che and Mao have di-
> minished the bleak uniformity of the surfaces in our room. We
> have, for the duration of our presence, imposed on the neutral
> hotel surface the dynamics of our ideas and intentions. (37)

The narrator suggests that their alteration of the hotel's surface establishes a moral difference between themselves and small town America.
Their actual behavior, however, contradicts this implicit claim. In his
development of a glamorous public persona, Bontemps does not indulge in the revolutionary's characteristic self-denial. Significantly,
when Bontemps unexpectedly leaves the town, he takes along the narrator's Gillette razor, thirty-five of his Seconals, and the narrator's fiancée, Jill. In a farewell note, Bontemps admits having bedded Jill,
while denying that she holds any physical appeal for him. The note's
recurrent use of the pronoun "I" unambiguously denotes Bontemps'
central concern in life. The narrator remains in America to work out
filming details. Feeling that the film may improve mall business, Frank
Ol agrees to certain "eccentricities"—to allow Bontemps to blow up a
few houses, to burn a pile of consumer goods, and even to destroy a
portion of the mall. Paradoxically, the film, which intends to destroy
corporate America, may well accomplish the opposite end of finan-
cially buttressing it (a situation, incidentally, that often occurs when
"antiestablishment" books, recordings, and films are successfully mar-
keted through mainstream corporate entities).

Bontemps is a poseur, a conventional bourgeois artist for whom
self-expression and personal accomplishment are primary goals. In
his films the aesthetic overwhelms the ethical.[6] The narrator points
out this contradiction. Bontemps, he tells Frank Ol, "subverts the destruction of his enemies by his aesthetic concerns. In other words, the
placement, the color, the objects, the motions, the juxtaposition of
faces all combine to diminish the revolutionary content" (58). In
Bontemps' films, aesthetic novelty produces a strong visceral reaction, produces an aesthetic frisson, and undermines his ostensible
theme(s). This is a danger that every innovative artist courts. Unusual
formal designs can dominate semiosis rather than aid it, can produce
a formalistic reception. And we can legitimately ask how an innovative
story such as "This Is Not a Film" succeeds notwithstanding the risks
inherent in experimentation.

First of all, the "experimental realism" of the story obviously builds on the elements of conventional realism, the latter a mimetic form readily accessible to readers. Clearly defined characters occupy a clearly defined time and place. Characteral introspections are totally neglected. Settings such as domestic interiors and the mall serve as obvious symbols of a human desire for order at whatever moral price. The plot is progressive with few violations of natural chronology. Yet, notwithstanding these features, the fluidity of the conventional realist fiction is not apparent here. A number of elements block narrative flow and compel an active engagement on the part of the reader. "This Is Not a Film" has a complexity of plot unusual for a story or even a novella. There are a number of subplots that require contextualization within the main story. Relationships between people, for example, are only hinted at, requiring the reader to scrutinize the "surface" of the narrative carefully for clues indicating, variously, a love interest, corporate machinations, or a betrayal of trust. The three parts of the story are broken up into a total of thirty-one sections, a structure that further fragments the narrative, with the reader forced to relate each part and each section to the others, forced to fill in what Wolfgang Iser calls "blanks," those points in a story where focus shifts—sometimes subtly, sometimes radically (166–70; 190–203). In the absence of guiding narratorial commentary, the preoccupation with surface description results in an allusivity one associates more with the mystery tale than with a realist milieu study. And of course, as noted already, there is no moral center in the story, no exemplary character, no foil to define virtuous conduct. In "This Is Not a Film," as in other of his works, Abish skillfully marries fragmentation and allusivity to such conventions of realism as natural plot chronology, symbolism, and surface description. This marriage of the disparate yields a *relatively* original narrative that valorizes neither form nor content and thus avoids both aestheticism and an aesthetically barren tendentiousness. The story defamiliarizes both the reassuring surfaces of conventional realist fiction and the reassuring surfaces of the quotidian.

In "This Is Not a Film This Is a Precise Act of Disbelief," characters take considerable emotional and moral solace in the aura of order that emanates from the surfaces of their surroundings and the surfaces of their lives. They remain scarcely aware of the sexual predation, the avarice, the manipulation, the general misanthropy that motivate their behavior. The mall, Bontemps' films, and Hank's apartment all serve as calming, familiar surfaces to be recognized; they conspire to perpetuate moral and epistemological obtuseness. Similarly, in other stories, Abish uses such highly structured phenomena as contrastive symbols to highlight a desire, often distinctly neurotic, on the part of his characters to protect themselves from the contingencies of their existence. These contrastive symbols—photographic portraits, maps, mosques, formal gardens, and chic living quarters are notable—all present to the viewer a superficially ordered world. They offer a world enframed, one reduced to essence. Each symbol in its own way lies and conceals: the portrait, for example, seeking in a single glance to characterize; the map offering its custodian an illusory sense of mastery over space, its two-dimensionality emphasizing surface; the mosque and the formal garden objectifying metaphysics; the chic apartment exhibiting a tenuous self-assurance. These symbols bear closer scrutiny.

For the narrator-protagonist of "The Second Leg," mosques, actually photographs of them, provide endless fascination. Though he has never visited a Muslim country, mosques are part of his "turf" (*Minds Meet*, 105). On the other hand, the turf of Ludmilla, a former lover with whom he is staying while visiting New York, is "insidious sex." As the story unfolds, the protagonist and Ludmilla act out a sado-masochistic melodrama in which mosques, his images of completeness, and Ludmilla's misshappen leg, a living allusion to imperfection and death, provide symbolic polarity. Having failed in marriage and having been spurned by Ludmilla, the protagonist turns to his mosques. "Love," he observes, "does not have the resolute perfection of the courtyard of the Great Mosque of Kairouan" (117). The illustrations give him order, however vicarious and fragile. At the same time, they present a past that is neutral and hence not psychologically oppressive for him. He passes an ingenuous confidence: "Unlike most passionate involvements with the past, illustrations, it seems to me, are not necessarily regressive. I find this reassuring. I have no wish to be imprisoned in a Parthenon of rosy memories" (118). In fact, the protagonist's own past has enshrined in his mind oppressive memories of marital failure, of sexual confusion, of an enigmatic relationship with his mother.

The orderly volumes of the mosque, its pillars, its many naves, the striking chromatic contrast between the mosque's whiteness and the perfect blue of the Mediterranean sky, all these write a topography of his desires, a need for clear delineation and confident restraint and physical prowess:

> I now can clearly see the egg-white ribbed dome, the cobalt blue frames of the crosshatched windows and the gleaming white walls. . . . The eye is so tremendously selective. The exterior of the mosque is covered with many layers of whitewash, and when viewed below, the walls stand out in sharp contrast to the Mediterranean sky above. (118)

The protagonist's eye is indeed "selective," his mosque "fantastic" (118). He takes in surface detail without considering the mosque as a time-conditioned artifact. Just as his own dispiriting circumstances are forgotten in his contemplation of the mosque, so too is the mosque's cultural specificity overlooked when it is translated into a mere *objet d'art* existing beyond the contingent within the covers of the coffee-table book. In "The Second Leg," "culture," as it does in much of Abish's work, becomes a refuge for the emotionally (and morally) weak. In serving up time-honored analogues of perfection, that is, predefined "masterworks" stripped of cultural context, culture risks becoming an opiate that dulls the sensibilities. "The Second Leg" concludes, uncharacteristically enough for Abish's fiction, with the protagonist achieving some degree of self-understanding. The protagonist and Ludmilla sit contemplating her legs, first the healthy one, then the misshapen one. "Poor Ludmilla, no amount of loving will replace your deformed leg," he confides to himself, acknowledging, symbolically, the imperfections of his own life (124). The story ends with the protagonist and Ludmilla in emotional union, the former having accepted "the second leg," an emblem of the contingency and death that his mosques had striven to negate.

A numbing concern for perfection also surfaces in stories of the second collection, *In the Future Perfect*. The same quote from Whitehead occurs in two of them, "Parting Shot" (25) and "In So Many Words" (79, 87): "Even perfection will not bear the tedium of infinite repetition."[7] Both stories are set in chic Manhattan. The characters in both have not come to terms with Whitehead's remark. In each instance they use money to achieve "perfection" repetitively, unconsciously calling into question of course, at the same time, the very notion of perfection. Television, shop displays, glossy magazines, the small private galleries, all these mold notions of value, identity, and world:

> Did Whitehead know that wealth enables people to acquire the perfect apartment, the perfect country house, the perfect haircut, the perfect English suits, the perfect leather and chrome armchair, the perfect shower curtain, the perfect tiles for the kitchen floor, and a perfect quiche available only from a small French bakery near Madison Avenue, and the perfect Italian boots that look like English boots but are more elegant, and the perfect mate, and the perfect stereo, and the perfect books that have received or undoubtedly are just about to receive a glowing review in the *Saturday Review.* Wealth makes it easier to have the perfect encounter with a stranger, enjoy the perfect afternoon, make perfect love, a sexual encounter that is enhanced by the objects that are in the room, objects that may at one time have attracted a good deal of attention while on display in a Madison Avenue shopwindow. (*Future Perfect*, 25)

The narrator's mock rebuttal of Whitehead's statement illustrates well Abish's technique of defamiliarization, in this case of a crassly materialistic view of perfection. In response to Whitehead's succinct, seemingly credible assertion, the narrator offers a droning anatomy of "perfection" as construed by an upper-middle-class urban milieu. The appending of "perfect" to a great number of mundane objects ultimately derides the values that define "perfection" in this context. The litany of "perfect" objects is interlarded with references to human relationships, indicating of course that some equate the two or, more accurately, emotional satisfaction is, for some, a mere derivative of bourgeois faddishness. Objects combine in their settings to serve as a panoply to protect their proprietors from the vagaries of open, forthright relationships. Perfection is accomplished only through reification of self and others. People wear brand names, rather than clothes. People become "generic," mere mannequins posturing within "sets" appropriated from shop windows and department store displays.

In the tastefully appointed prison houses of the urban chic, stylish perfection is an end in itself. In "Parting Shot," Maud acknowledges, from her midtown Manhattan apartment, that she and her husband have become "two collectors of the perfect experience, assessing the degree to which we have arrived at the state of perfection" (26). Maud herself is an object on display. At her parties she serves as another prop within the fashionable ensemble of her apartment. Certainly, the "perfection" of her surroundings in no way protects her from sexual frustration and a general sense of displacement any more than it does the heroine of "In So Many Words." She too seeks, and fails to find, ecstasy in the perfection of surfaces:

> Standing at one of the elongated windows, munching a Sara Lee croissant (quite delicious) she is taking in the American perfection, the American splendor—absolutely no irony intended. It is true. From a certain height and perspective, the eighth floor of her building, America is convulsed with perfection. (*Future Perfect*, 75)

Again, name brand consumer goods are the primary patrons of this perfection, e.g., Abercrombie and Fitch binoculars, Gillette and Schick razors, Sara Lee pastries, and Draino. Yet, these fail to neutralize the existential malaise that envelops her. (Or do they enhance it?) At story's end, in a desperate attempt to escape the "familiar perfection" of her social set, she invites three leather-jacketed men from small town Arizona into her bed for "in bed something else besides perfection was wanted, needed, desired" (97). Finally, the familiar, perfected topography of her milieu yields to long repressed desire.

How German Is It: *Perfecting notions of German-ness*

The Nazi reign of terror remains, decades after its defeat, an enduring nightmare. It crops up regularly as a primary theme in various artistic media as well as in contemporary current events.[8] There is, as Elie Wiesel tells us, a double moral imperative to remember—to honor the innocent victim (living and dead), and to ensure that history never again takes such a vile turn. And indeed, in the face of a fundamental human inclination to gloss over the savage, there can never be too many reminders. *How German Is It* is Walter Abish's reminder. Abish first considers the Holocaust in "The English Garden," a story which provides the setting and general tone of the novel. The "garden" of the story's title has a symbolic rather than ontic presence in the story, appearing as it does only in an epigraph that Abish takes from John Ashberry's *Three Poems:*

> Remnants of the old atrocity subsist, but they are converted into ingenious shifts in scenery, a sort of "English Garden" effect, to give the required air of naturalness, pathos and hope. (*Future Perfect,* 1)

Both the short story and *How German Is It* explore how the "English Garden effect" strives today in contemporary West Germany to subdue an unseemly past.[9] Since the novel's techniques and themes subsume, for the most part, those of the story, I will focus on it.[10]

"The presentation of the 'familiar world' is not," notes Abish, "an innocent one."

> To me, the familiar details are also *signs* of a familiar world. In projecting these *signs* I am aware of my own preoccupation with the "familiar" and the presentation of it. Essentially, I am questioning how we see and write about something. . . . I feel that the text I write lies between me and the experience. (Lotringer, 162)

How German Is It studies how the familiar signs of the world—linguistic, kinetic, iconic, etc.—are perceived and processed. For Abish's characters, just as for Abish himself and the reader, the variegated "textual" signs that the world offers us help configure our general attitudes. The world looms as a dynamic semiotic field, one that is open to manipulation, one that demands of us an interpretive gesture. Both the manipulation of the semiotic field and the interpretation of it have obvious ethical ramifications. *How German Is It* considers the production, maintenance, and reception of the field of signs in the context of a small West German town in the seventies, paying particular mind to the ideological bias that responses to signs betray.

Abish uses a number of techniques to defamiliarize the milieu of the novel: the detailed listing of "typical" features; unaccentuated references to the past and the past in the present; the posing of blunt, leading questions; and the double entendre. In part 1 of the novel, entitled "The edge of forgetfulness," the protagonist, Ulrich Hargenau, Jr., a writer, returns home to Würtenburg after an extended

French sojourn. "The edge of forgetfulness" offers a subtly ironic catalogue of what, for the native German or the returning expatriate or the tourist, constitutes "German-ness." Like a tour book or a Chamber of Commerce pamphlet, the images presented strive earnestly for typicality. Great emphasis is placed on the visible splendors of Germany's past but, as the narrator observes in "This Is Not a Film This Is a Precise Act of Disbelief," the brain is "highly selective" (*Minds Meet*, 36). The typical portrait of German typicality is indeed laudatory. Germany *is* culture: Gothic and Baroque architecture; Wagner and Beethoven festivals; Dürer and Cranach and Holbein and Grünewald; and Goethe, *natürlich*. Germany *is* punctiliousness: clean streets, obedient trains, civic order, well-stocked shops, and precision-engineered automobiles coursing along precision-engineered *Autobahnen*. Germany *is* economic progress (if not "economic miracle"): industrial plants, well-designed dams and bridges, modern farms, and new urban centers. These are the familiar signs of German typicality that greet one pondering "this smooth and agreeable surface" (3). These are the familiar signs that present German history as an unbroken series of achievements and civilized national gestures.

Yet, punctuating this familiar, univocal semiotic system, we find brief, hushed allusions to the "atypical," to past events and current attitudes that lie beyond the conventionally familiar. In these passages, Abish strictly controls the flow of information, presenting only a superficial description and, consequently, leaving the reader to his or her own resources. Ulrich von Hargenau, Sr., Ulrich's *apparent* father, a Nazi officer executed in 1944 for treason—he is not "familiar," remaining for many ever a traitor to national ambitions. Passing mention is made of a local Jewish furrier who converted to Catholicism earlier in the century (6). Why? Perhaps to escape the wrath of anti-Semitism, and perhaps not. Abish compels the reader to consider the bare facts of the anecdote, i.e., its "surface," and to postulate their implications. The narrator does not guide the reader through commentary. Pointing out the many "tall blond men and women" wearing leather coats and jackets, the narrator asks, "But why this curious predilection for leather?" (3). The linking of fabled Aryan racial traits to leather overwear stirs images of Hitler Youth donning martial leather. Or does it? Again, Abish neither confirms nor denies such readerly associations. It is only through a slow accretion of such allusive references and images that the reader becomes suspicious that

traditional notions of German typicality are compromised by a strategic blindness to certain "obvious"—at least in Abish's defamiliarized
context—moral failings. Indeed, these unsettling references to an immoral recent history, and its residual influence, are largely beyond the
ken of the protagonist who, until the novel's conclusion, disregards
visible suggestions of a dark past—collective or private—preferring
to write self-indulgent autobiographical novels about male-female relationships.

At the end of part 1, Ulrich plays the *boulevardier,* drinking beer,
observing others, and taking in the sights. But Abish allows the reader
no such anesthetized point of view. He heightens the reader's sensitivity to his thematic concerns through questions and the double entendre. The narrator probes: "The question remains, do the Germans
still expect to be asked embarrassing questions about their past and
about their present and what, if any, ideas they may have about their
future?" (7). And, as Ulrich considers the reconstructed version of a
bridge destroyed in the war, the narrator ironically acknowledges that
"replicas of this kind testify to a German reverence for the past and
for the truth, a reverence for the forms and structures upon which so
many of their ideals have been emblazoned" (7). We will later learn
that this interest in replicas is "highly selective" and that it does not
extend to replicas of Durst, the local Nazi death camp that now lies in
ruins (7). At the conclusion of "The edge of forgetfulness," a series of
questions focuses unequivocally on the novel's key interests. The last
two questions are central: "What is seen? And what is said" (9). Most
of the novel focuses on the major disjunction between, precisely, what
the eye recognizes, and what the mouth reports.

In parts 2 ("The idea of Switzerland") and 3 ("Sweet truth"), the
setting shifts from the "Old World" splendor of Würtenburg to a new
town, Brumholdstein, with Ulrich spending a brief interlude in Geneva. Brumholdstein is a civic embodiment of Ashberry's "English
Garden" effect in very many ways. Constructed as it is on the site of
Durst, it literally covers the "surface" of an unsavory remnant of Germany's Nazi past. Brumholdstein offers a clean, new topography. The
town emblematizes the "New Germany," presenting a revision of "typical" qualities, ones apparently at odds with those honored in the thirties and forties. The novel of course will demonstrate that now, as in
the period of the most heinous persecution of innocent people, there
exists a conspiracy of silence that, effectively, puts the best face on the

past and the present. In the only concentrated description of Brumholdstein (77–82), the narrator shifts registers continually, modulat-
ing with these shifts the degree of irony within the respective sections.
These registers range from a bald promotional tone to objective description to a subtle criticism of the townspeople's "forgetfulness."
The town has become a modest center of culture offering concerts
and operas, international films, and lectures on such compelling topics as excavations in Outer Mongolia (79). Brumholdstein also happens to be home to author Bernard Feig, whose novels Burghermeis-
ter Kahnsitz-Lese praises for not being "immersed in the past," and
for offering characters "happily free of that all too familiar obsession
with the 1940–45 period of our life" (82). Feig is, as his name indicates, "cowardly" and "fainthearted" in his forgetfulness of history.
Ulrich's views on authorship suggest his own aversion to plumbing the
unhappy depths of his nation's past. In comments given in an interview in Geneva, Ulrich denies for his own novels any political import,
or at least any politically revisionist function. The novel is not, Ulrich
tells us, "a process of rebellion," but rather "it validates and makes
acceptable forms of human conduct, it also validates and makes acceptable societal institutions" (53). In viewing writing as an apology
for the status quo, Ulrich's views are obviously at odds with Abish's.[11]
Like Feig and the good citizens of Brumholdstein, Ulrich neglects the
archeological study both of local historical "treasures" and of the soul,
preferring to concentrate on the surface of a temporally disembodied
present.

Brumholdstein is named after "Germany's greatest contemporary
thinker," a world-renowned philosopher who happens to be a native
of its environs (80). Over his long career, Brumhold has concentrated
mostly on ontology except during the thirties when social ethics and
political philosophy attracted his attention. Notwithstanding the tribute paid him by his fellow citizens, this august figure, now in venerable old age, refuses to mix with the good burghers of Brumholdstein,
eschewing the highways and byways of urban society in order to pursue his contemplative life amid the fields and forest paths (*Holzwege*)
of a rural setting, in order to advance his study of *Dasein* and "thinking." "The forest continues to beckons us," writes Brumhold.

For in the forest are located our innermost dreams and desires.
In order to reestablish our roots and our purpose and return to

a simplicity of life that can no longer be found in the German
community, we turn to the forest. We wander off by ourselves,
packs on our backs . . . confident that in what we are doing, we
are coming closer to our past, to our history, to our German
spirit. (167)

And, like Martin Heidegger whose words these echo, and on whom
the character Brumhold is based, the latter returns to university
teaching after an enforced absence, "the result of too many reckless
speeches in the '30s and '40s, speeches that dealt with the citizen's responsibility to the New Order" (19).[12]

Abish harbors ambivalent feelings toward Heidegger.[13] Though
admitting the astuteness of Heidegger's observations on the linguisticality of being—"Language is the house of Being. In its home man
dwells" ("Letter on Humanism," 193)—Abish is openly scornful of
Heidegger's philosophy of history:

His [Heidegger's] history, as I see it, was always a universal history that he somehow managed to locate in his own beloved forest. But was his history not shaped by specific historical events?
When Heidegger, a most remarkable thinker, touches on German history he verges on the banal. That is perplexing. (Lotringer, 169)

Though *How German Is It* offers no rigorous critique of Heidegger's
rapprochement/cooperation with Nazism—Heidegger's famous 1933
rectorial address calls Hitler the "greatness and glory of this new [na-
tional] dawn"—it makes a number of suggestive observations through
its characterization of Brumhold (quoted in 'Only A God Can Save
Us,'" 269).[14]

Heidegger and Brumhold both appeal to German "rootedness,"
what in his *Discourse on Thinking* Heidegger calls *Bodenständigkeit,* to
support their views of German history and national destiny (48–49).
Brumhold's withdrawal from society emulates Heidegger's; both re-
tire to the *Schwarzwald* to seek philosophical clarity in its foggy
reaches.[15] Isolation in the German countryside allows each to recuper-
ate that special relationship between spirituality and the land that
makes Germans special. Of the German spirit Heidegger writes:

For "spirit" is neither empty cleverness, nor the noncommittal play of wit, nor the endless drift of rational distinctions, and especially not world reason; spirit is primordially attuned, knowing resoluteness toward the essence of Being. And the *spiritual world* of a people is not the superstructure of a culture . . . it is the power that most deeply preserves the people's strengths, which are tied to earth and blood, and as such it is the power that most deeply moves and most profoundly shakes its being (*Dasein*). ("Self-Assertion," 474–75)

Like much of the *Rektoratsrede*, this passage represents a strange amalgam. Here, to the philosopher's sincere affirmation of the importance of truth, Heidegger weds an appeal to an obscure romantic nationalism, one that is not much elevated above the tabloid editor's, the soapbox sage's, or indeed the populist politician's. National-racial pride is not far removed here, if it is at all, from a banal chauvinism.

In his characteristically deflated way, Abish satirizes the preoccupation with "rootedness" and what is for Brumhold an overweening concern for the etymological purity of the German language, the latter issue also important to Heidegger as both his Germanophilia and his often ingenious, often interminable "word studies" would seemingly suggest.[16] Indeed, for Brumhold, the special relationship between "earth and blood," between land and race, is enhanced by the unique character of the German language itself.

Their language, *die deutsche Sprache,* as once before is again absorbing words from other languages. Still, notwithstanding the doubtful foreign elements in the language today, the German language remains the means and the key to Brumhold's metaphysical quest; it is a language that has enabled him, the foremost German philosopher, to formulate the questions that have continued to elude the French- and English-speaking metaphysicians. How German is it? Brumhold might well ask of his metaphysical quest, which is rooted in the rich dark soil of *der Schwarzwald,* rooted in the somber, deliberately solitary existence that derives its passion, its energy, its striving for exactitude from the undulating hills, the pine forests, and the erect motionless figure of the gamekeeper in the green uniform. For that matter, Brumhold might well ask of the language, How German is it still? Has it not once again, by brushing against so many foreign substances, so many foreign languages and experiences, acquired foreign impurities, such as *okay* and *jetlag* and *topless* and *supermarkt* and *weekend* and *sexshop*, and consequently absorbed the signifiers of an overwhelmingly decadent concern with materialism? (5)[17]

In this seemingly neutral, innocent engagement with key ideas of Brumhold the narrator identifies a number of questionable elements in his world view: his intellectual chauvinism, his obscure religious attachment to German topography, his linguistic xenophobia, and an undergirding nostalgia for a simpler, premodern time. Interestingly, we find guarding over Brumhold's Baden idyll the gamekeeper, whose uniform is a subtle reminder of the Germanic need for order, and often order at any price, as history documents.[18]

The reception of Brumhold by his fellow Germans is marked by strategic oversight and self-congratulation. Brumhold's writings are read by few and understood by fewer yet. His major public political addresses, unable to take refuge in abstraction and terminology, are "platitudinous": "We have completely broken with a landless and powerless thinking" (19).[19] Yet, upon death, he becomes another national treasure. Helmuth Hargenau, Ulrich Jr.'s brother, a celebrated architect, delivers a memorial address at a service for Brumhold, who dies midway through the novel. His speech can be read on two levels—as a straightforward eulogy or as a clear instance of "indirect authorial word," to borrow from Bakhtin. Viewed from the latter perspective, Brumhold's views exemplify neither virtue nor insight, particularly, but rather ethnic arrogance, irrationalism, and romantic obfuscation.

Helmuth links Brumhold's "metaphysical quest for *Dasein*" to a concern for "universal history" (170–71), tying Brumhold to a metaphysical-idealistic tradition that phenomenology, Heidegger's certainly, seeks to undermine, though not always with success as Adorno points out in *The Jargon of Authenticity*. Helmuth's speech contributes to Brumhold's canonization as an important cultural artifact, comparable to other German cultural "goods" such as Bach, Grünewald, and Hölderlin. For Helmuth, as for his auditors, Brumhold becomes another signifier within the semiotic field of "German-ness." Adorno offers some trenchant comments on this sort of commodification of one's national cultural legacy (and obviously it is not an exclusively German tendency, by any means):

> Those who most loudly proclaim Kant, Goethe or Beethoven as German property as a rule have the least concern for the content of these authors' works. They register them as possessions despite the fact that what these writers taught and produced precludes transformation into something that can be possessed. The German tradition is violated by those who neutralize it into a cultural property which is both venerated and yet has no consequence. Meanwhile those who know nothing about the implications of these ideas are quickly seized with indignation when even the slightest critical word is dropped about a famous name which they want to confiscate and exploit as a brandname product 'made in Germany.' ("On the Question," 122)

"Brumhold," rendered less than human at this point by idealization, contributes to the *familiar* and favorable stereotype of the intelligent, civilized Teuton and in so doing serves as yet another instrument of official culture. Yet, as Abish maintains throughout *How German Is It*, official culture is forgetful or, as Heidegger would have it, "lethetic." Neglecting many of the colors of the historiographer's palette, Helmuth—an exponent of universal history—presents a portrait of Germany that is too reliant on pastels, that neglects the delicate chiaroscuro that best captures the variegated story of any nation.

In his address, Helmuth actually identifies, inadvertently, a typical German "dualism," as Thomas Mann calls it—the coexistence, historically, of the "boldest [philosophical] speculation" and "political immaturity" (188–89). While the magnificence of German achievements in the arts and letters is undeniable, the German record in social and governmental reform is far from exemplary. Even the briefest survey documents the regressive, reactionary tenor of German political history, a tradition that long resisted substantive democratic reforms and general social reorganization. Certainly, the leader cult is not an isolated post-Versailles phenomenon that culminates in the Hitlerian *Führerkultus*, a point Heinrich Mann makes in his sardonic novel *Der Untertan*, which ridicules the Kaiser cult and therein the average German's blind commitment to "order and duty" (*Ordnung und Pflicht*). Helmuth's historiography fails to write these chapters in German history, ones that would compromise the superficial harmonies of his own definition of German-ness. Certainly, such a revisionist project would have to contend with four hundred years of political autocracy, a trend already highlighted, as Thomas Mann notes, by Martin Luther's betrayal of the peasants (186–89). Such a project would acknowledge the slow development of what Mann calls "social maturity":

> The Germans are always too late. They are late, like music which is always the last of the arts to express a world condition—when that world tradition is already in its final stages. They are abstract and mystical, too, like this, their dearest art—both to the point of criminality. (193)

Though Helmuth does not acknowledge it, Brumhold's immersion in philosophy after his political phase in the thirties and forties is an escape from social responsibility and a flight to the security of the "ivory tower." Brumhold effects a kind of faustian pact wherein he acquires philosophical knowledge but fails to exercise the moral and social leadership one might expect of a great mind, the kind of leadership exercised, for example, by Sartre. Helmuth concludes his speech by praising Brumhold for enabling Germans to see themselves as they really are, indicating that the philosopher's meditations are both exemplary and illuminating (171). Yet, in the context of *How German Is It*, this is at best ambivalent praise. Read as double entendre, Helmuth's claim becomes an indictment of the German nation.

As noted, we can transvalue many of Brumhold's seemingly positive attributes, seeing his writings, and life-style generally, as reproachable—his spiritual unworldliness can be viewed as a flight from social problems, his preoccupation with German culture as simple chauvinism, his ontological meditations in the Black Forest as dreamy, self-indulgent romanticism. Similarly, though most of the key figures in the novel are cultivated, intelligent, and professionally accomplished, they remain nonetheless morally myopic, both in their relations with others and in their neglect of their national past. Quite simply, they separate intellection and ethics. The examples are many. Ironically, Anna Heller, a schoolteacher, attempts to sensitize her students to the world around them through a phenomenological study— she does an ontology of chalk—yet she opts to marry Jonke, bookstore owner and collector of Nazi memorabilia, not out of love but because she does not wish to become an old maid.

Intelligence and cultivation are alienated from moral vision in the cases of Egon and Gisela as well. Egon, a book publisher and therein a patron of the arts, is a paradigm of the "New Germany," a prosperous, civilized democracy that has apparently conquered its past. Indeed, a popular magazine—suggestively entitled *Treue,* which can mean either "honesty" or "loyalty"—runs a photographic essay on Egon and Gisela that extends to its subscribers an "invitation . . . to reinterpret Germany":

> A new Germany. Certainly not the Germany that was once firmly ensconced (the saddle, after all, is an appropriate metaphor) in the Prussian tradition of honor and obedience, old money and authority, the saber, the crumbling castle overlooking the Rhine. (129)

However, concealed beneath the topography of civility that the photos write lies an unmistakable recidivism. In comments given to a photojournalist from the magazine, Egon, seemingly an exponent of a politically reformed Germany, offers a crypto-fascist political philosophy. For him, democracy has become depleted of "its meaning, its energy, its power" (131). "If anything can be said to represent the new Germany," he explains, "it is the wish, the desire, no, the craving to attain a *total harmony*" (131; my emphasis). (And the very term "New Germany" carries with it an unfortunate but, in the context of the novel, symptomatic echo of another slogan, Hitler's "New Order.") Curiously, neither phenomenologist Anna nor Egon nor their peers reach beyond the surface of the familiar to grapple with difficult moral issues; they use the artifacts of culture and material prosperity to fashion for themselves a "New Germany," a topography that leaves them reassured and unthreatened.[20]

Though offering an unflattering view of right-wing politics, *How German Is It* does not see in leftist extremism a tenable alternative. Throughout the novel, the Einzieh group, a leftist terrorist cell, conducts various violent acts, many of which involve, or appear to involve, Ulrich's former wife, Paula. Yet, the blowing up of public property has no clearly delineated purpose other than to disrupt public life. The Einzieh group issues no manifesto and seems to find its incendiarism

an end in itself. Events at the end of the novel suggest that the group
has little genuine sympathy for the working class, the constituency
whose causes it apparently wishes to champion. With the aid of the
very ambiguous Daphne (who is in turn Ulrich's lover and apparently
Paula's, who may be a terrorist or a counterterrorist agent or even a
double agent), Paula recruits a simple drawbridge attendant, Gottfried Mühler, to blow up the bridge where he works.

> When Daphne and Paula visited his [Mühler's] control room on
> the tower, it was Paula who asked him: Is this what you will be
> doing for the rest of your life? Raising the bridge for yachts, the
> pleasure boats, and nothing to show for it except a small pension
> at the end of thirty-five years? He pointed out that most of the
> boats during the off season were fishing trawlers, not yachts.
> (222–23)

Clearly, the destruction of the bridge will cause more harm to working
men and women than to vacationers and the monied leisure class.
Though it is by no means obvious exactly how, Paula is able to trigger
some latent rage in Mühler. She is able to "draw him in," to "recruit"
him, to "draft" him—all meanings of the German verb "einziehen,"
from which of course the Einzieh group takes its name. Ultimately, in
what seems more Gidean-Camusian *acte gratuit* than political statement, Mühler does indeed destroy the bridge and gun down two po-
licemen. And, as he and Paula laughingly acknowledge earlier while
discussing the destruction of the bridge, the result of his act is simply
public inconvenience (and needless carnage), and not the overthrow
of the government (217).

Ulrich, along with the reader, considers the politico-moral alternatives outlined in the action of the novel. On one side, we have leftists
who seek to overthrow the status quo while failing to offer a compelling vision of social progress; on the other, we find right-wing tradi-
tionalists who blindly ape the (in)glories of the past. The implication
in the novel, certainly in its conclusion, is that the individual must
carefully attend to the issues of the day and not be swept along by
either a corrupt tradition or by corrupt visions of progress and futurity. There is obviously an existentialist overtone here and, we might
say, Ulrich's tribulations throughout the novel clear the way for what

is depicted at the end of the novel as an inchoate process of moral self-determination.

Protagonist Ulrich, not coincidentally a former student of Brumhold, is, until the end of the book, a study in bad faith/inauthenticity, one study among many in *How German Is It*. A writer, ideally one gifted in seeing and describing what others cannot, Ulrich consistently defines his world in terms of culture, fleeing the contingency of the moment for the assurance of the aesthetically pure. The primary preoccupation of his writing as well as his life is private relationships. Yet, paradoxically, he avoids a crucial personal issue until the penultimate chapter of the book. Having long suspected that the man from whom he takes his name was not his actual biological father, having long suppressed his curiosity about the matter, Ulrich finally contends with his doubts by consulting a psychoanalyst. He admits that he has been afraid to learn who his father was and what role he played in the war. To seek out his father's identity would have violated "convention" and "good taste," and Ulrich, like his fellow citizens, has obsequiously guarded the harmonious topography of the "New Germany" through his reticence (250). The book concludes with his analyst using hypnosis to unearth Ulrich's suppressed past. Ulrich's right hand slowly rises and he nods as it does so, the entire scene marking an incipient process of historical recollection, the recollection of Hitler's "dream to end all dreams" (252).

"Living in the material world"

Though devoid of Madonna's panache and hysteria, Walter Abish's fictions too explore what it means to live in the "material world." Abish investigates how our desire for an untroubled self-consistency and social harmony manifests itself in the perceptible surfaces of our lives. In documenting the visible markers of our conformity—as apparent in our speech patterns, for example, the shape we give our physical environment, and the use we make of cultural goods—he divests these familiar surfaces of their familiarity and therein encourages us to interrogate our own values. In *For a Critique of the Political Economy of the Sign*, Baudrillard identifies consumption as a universal value of contemporary Western society and illustrates its operation as a morality and instrument of power. Though Abish does not share Baudrillard's sympathy for leftist politics, he does consider, like the latter, our material world and the ethical implications of consumption.[21] In his essay, "Self-Portrait," Abish addresses the issue of moral reformation in a typically postmodern way: "If we were to receive a message from outer space that read: Is there any other way to live? Our reply might be: No, there is not, but we try" (13). The pessimism revealed here is obviously qualified, and is not sustained in the bulk of his fiction, which has a clear moral tendency without being merely tendentious. Though Abish depicts humankind as the product of many powerful determinisms—objects, language, history, instinct—his fiction does not depict these determinisms as incorrigible or purely self-perpetuating. They are open to revision, to the influence of human agency. His fictions are not simply exercises in formalistic legerdemain.

In the 1982 interview, Lotringer characterizes *How German Is It* as a "machine made of broken pieces of mirror that flash elements of meaning to attract the birds" (177). Abish's response indicates his clear disagreement with this characterization (which seems to imply the absence of a clear moral center to the novel): "I wouldn't write in order to trap or fool the reader. To elicit a false response deliberately or intentionally mislead would be to reduce the meaning this book has for me as a literary accomplishment" (177). In this remark Abish effectively ties the aesthetic to the moral and implies that a "good" novel always does so.[22] Though Abish rejects traditional humanism because he feels, as does Heidegger of course, that it imposes a scheme of arbitrary, absolute values upon the historically conditioned circumstances of life, he does not advance the skepticism that is much in fashion in contemporary criticism and contemporary philosophy.[23] (Clearly, as Butler points out, the subject matter of *How German Is It* does not permit playful distortions of historical fact [64–65].) Abish realizes that life is full of moral quandaries, of inexplicable situations, yet, at the same time, he acknowledges that these aporias elicit from us interpretive responses. Abish's fictions are his response to these aporias. Though his works offer the reader few positive moral paradigms, they do suggest various moral courses that we should eschew.

5

Gender Relations and the Ways of
Paradox in Coover's *Spanking the Maid*

ROBERT COOVER'S FICTION preoccupies itself with the philosophical problems connected with the construction of a world view, with self-mythification, with ethical, ontological, and epistemological patterns. He acknowledges that we must schematize our perception of the world. "Men live by fictions," notes Coover.

> They have to. Life's too complicated, we just can't handle all the input, we have to isolate little bits and make reasonable stories out of them. . . . There are always other plots, other settings, other interpretations. So if some stories start throwing their weight around, I like to undermine their authority a bit, work variations, call attention to their fictional natures. (McCaffery, "Robert Coover," 50)

Coover's early major fictions, *The Origin of the Brunists, The Universal Baseball Association,* and *The Public Burning,* illustrate how pattern and idea, when pursued religiously, can conquer life, reducing the specificity of phenomena to unproductive allegorical generality. In each of the novels, metaphysics undermines a dynamic relationship to the world. In *The Origin of the Brunists,* intrigue, treachery, and alienation arise out of a cult's lunatic absorption in its creed. Henry Waugh, author of the elaborate parlor game that gives its name to Coover's second novel, *The Universal Baseball Association,* becomes the slave of his own invention, alienated and aloof from his immediate world. *The Public Burning,* a fictional documentary of McCarthyism and the ritualistic bloodletting it fostered (notably the persecution/prosecution of the Rosenbergs), reveals how the metaphysics of hate and xenophobia comes to dominate a nation that prides itself on its Enlightenment origins and egalitarian ideals.

Spanking the Maid is a difficult, convoluted novella. Given its concerted manipulation of ambiguity and paradox (built on the shifting sands of short, quick-cut sections), the novella may well strike one, at first glance, as little more than yet another formal exercise in the displacement of the conventions of writing and reading of the kind more ably (and humorously) taken up, for example, by Coover himself in *Pricksongs and Descants,* Barth in "Lost in the Funhouse," and more recently by Calvino in *If on a winter's night a traveler. Spanking the Maid* is indeed a parody of literary forms, but its parody is ultimately rooted in human behavior and human attitudes and not merely in literature or "literariness." Like Coover's earlier novels, which discuss, variously, the ethical implications of cultist religion, solipsism, and politics/nationalism, *Spanking the Maid* also focuses generally on the constrictive power of metaphysics but with particular attention paid to specific epistemological concerns and their implications for gender relations. In considering, variously, the significance of empirical evidence, the capacity of language to be "truthful," the efficacy of reason, the limits of traditional theories of knowledge, and the definability of space-time, the novella establishes epistemological critique as a starting point for the revision of dehumanizing notions of gender and gender-defined behavior. In the following, I will consider how meta-fictional conventions are worked subtly and productively to parody traditional modes of reasoning. "Of all the ways of paradoxes," writes Quine, "perhaps the quaintest is their capacity on occasion to turn out to be so very much less frivolous than they look" (18). The paradoxical and ambiguous ways of *Spanking the Maid* reveal the foibles of classical strategies of pattern making, both in narrative fiction and epistemological thought. The novella shows that world views—notably as they relate to gender relations—are dependent on social customs, that, as Rorty has pointed out, knowledge is a social practice and not a "mirror of nature" (*Philosophy,* 171).

Spanking the Maid: *Just a metafiction?*

Very little has been written on *Spanking the Maid*. One can speculate
on the reasons for this. Certainly it is a recent publication, having appeared only in 1981.[1] Few will find in its subject matter, loudly heralded by its title, any obvious moral appeal. Further, neither the frag-
mented form of the work nor its ambiguity is particularly new within
the corpus of Coover's fiction. Other of his shorter works raise ambiguity to a major structural device. His early short story collection,
Pricksongs and Descants, demonstrates a comparable use of ambiguity,
the interweaving of a great number of fictive possibilities within single
short narratives. Martin, the protagonist of "The Elevator," moves
through a myriad of fates, most mutually exclusive, a puppet of authorial mastery. Similarly, in "The Babysitter," Coover intersperses
plots of melodramatic, comic, and tragic import, enacting what Ronald Sukenick has called "The Mosaic Law" of postmodernism: "the
law of mosaics or how to deal with parts in the absence of wholes"
(*98.6,* 167). Ambiguity arises here through a kind of temporal fragmentation where the present becomes multiple and where a number
of mutually exclusive events seem equally plausible. A rivalry persists
among contending plots. The reader is incapable of harmonizing
these various plots into a unified, unambiguous reading of the text.
The reader confronts something seemingly similar to this in *Spanking
the Maid* wherein Coover extends and refines his technique of "multiple" or "cubistic" fiction.[2]

Yet, there is a significant difference in the novella's orchestration of
ambiguity and that which is evident in the early short fiction. This
difference in itself makes *Spanking the Maid* worthy of detailed study.
Ambiguity in the earlier works arises from the above-noted mutual
exclusivity; this exclusivity has nothing to do with organic character
development within the fictions themselves but is rather the product
of a bold, even at times bumptious, intervention of the author. (And,
significantly, in Coover's early metafictions—as in others like Vonnegut's *Slaughterhouse-Five* and *Jailbird,* Sukenick's "The Death of the
Novel," and Canadian George Bowering's *Burning Water*—this intervention involves the historical author, and not some fictional persona
in the guise of narrator.) Such direct authorial intervention illustrates
simply and clearly the ludic, performative nature of writing, the latter

admittedly a thematic commonplace by the eighties. In contrast, as I will discuss, ambiguity in *Spanking the Maid* has an altogether different basis, occurring as it does on the level of character (and not on that of narration), and an altogether different thematic significance.

Spanking the Maid leads us away, slowly but inevitably, from the confusions of its two characters to certain moral quandaries of life in the late twentieth century. This moral (or moralizing) function of the novella has been largely overlooked in readings offered by Evelyne Pieiller in a 1984 review and, more recently, by Jackson Cope in his Coover monograph (and quite frankly by me, to some extent, when I first considered the work).[3] Both Pieiller and Cope identify important aspects of the novella. Pieiller's reading highlights the "limits of language" theme, that is, language's incapacity to encode for us in a reliable, unmediated way our worldly perceptions and experiences. Accordingly, *Spanking the Maid* represents all that which gives form to the unformed as simultaneously necessary *and* ridiculous. Pieiller's remarks are valid but limited. In placing *Spanking the Maid* within an intellectual continuum that includes Saussure, Beckett, and poststructuralist skepticism, she overlooks the specificity of the novella's scenario, a male-female relationship, and its relevance to what has become a major social project over the last decade or two, the evaluation of gender ideologies. While Coover's works clearly postulate that all value systems are, in an absolute sense, provisional and arbitrary, they do not go to Beckettian extremes of nihilism (and Coover's rather catholic list of favorite writers admittedly includes Beckett). Rather, Coover attempts to debase inferior moral and philosophical "fictions" while rarely, perhaps never, drafting for the reader the contours of exemplary alternative "fictions." Coover states this unambiguously enough in the 1973 Gado interview:

> I've always been contentious with my writing; I've never turned away from unpleasantness in order to provide escapism. The world itself being a construct of fictions, I believe the fiction maker's function is to furnish better fictions with which we can re-form our notions of things. (149–50)

In Coover's work, and postmodern fiction generally, moral exemplarity is posed implicitly as a readerly problem; and, to be sure, moral

issues are embedded in even the most opaque self-reflexive work. Unlike John Gardner, Coover sees no obvious antagonism between the
aesthetic and the moral in fiction. Calling the art/life dichotomy a
"phoney issue," Coover asks, "Who's to say, for example, that self-
reflexive fiction, dealing as it assumes it does with a basic human activity, is not, by examining that activity as it celebrates it, engaged in a
very moral act?" (McCaffery, "Robert Coover," 51). It is necessary, of
course, for the reader to construe the nature of this moral act.

In its general emphasis on language, Jackson Cope's reading of
Spanking the Maid does not differ from Pieiller's. However, Cope considers the language question in more literary and formalistic terms.
He construes the novella as a "pastiche of nineteenth-century styles
from the literature of pornography" (55).[4] One can hardly quarrel
with this assertion. Indeed Coover has identified anonymous Victorian "Guides for Domestics"—with their suppressed eroticism and re-
petitive style—as the novella's central metaphor (Salgas, 20). I agree
with Cope that Coover's handling of the metaphor clearly reveals the
shortcomings of formulaic genres such as pornographic fiction. In
this, the novella's metafictional interests are manifest. The master in
Spanking the Maid can be viewed, as Cope asserts, as a writer. Con-
fronting the "blank page" of the maid's psyche (and buttocks), the
master opts not for creative self-expression but retreats into repetition
and formula, and marks his creative spirit as inferior and derivative.
Implicit in all of this is an oblique moral judgment on the pusillani-
mous writer who seeks emotional comfort, not to mention the critical
acceptability that disciplined mastery of (and conformity to) the conventional often brings. (As Sorrentino establishes in *Mulligan Stew,*
and I will later discuss, writers are always susceptible to co-option by
the standards of the official "critical community.") However, curiously
and paradoxically, the master/writer (no "masterwriter" he) writes an
incoherent tale because he has plotted words that bear only mute testimony, because he has adopted and combined conventions that no
longer speak. The novella is then for Cope an "allegory about writing
within genres, styles, and limits" that illustrates how "one can, with the
manual of generic prescription, proscription, with 'method and habit,'
write oneself out of 'communication' with an audience, with one's own
text, with one's own self" (57–58).

I do not agree with Cope that one's interpretation of *Spanking the*

Maid should end with the novella's reduction to either simple formal parody or a mere version of the classical *Kunstlerroman*—with the master the failed writer and the maid the uncomprehending audience—though I readily admit these perspectives to be a good place to begin. Cope's reading, as does Pieiller's, withholds from the novella its legitimate world-referentiality and moral relevance. In order to establish for the novella a "significant mimesis," the reader—and, as I have noted, this is precisely a *readerly* problem—must establish a relationship between the inanities of the parodied form, i.e., pornography, and the inanities of human behavior. Obviously, this project is founded on axiology, which itself is founded on the notion that certain outlooks (or what Coover would call "fictions" and Ricoeur "narratives" and Bakhtin "discourses") are superior to others. In his Coover monograph, Cope uses certain Bakhtinian notions—dialogicality and carnivalization—to effect a fine detailed reading of *The Public Burning*. However, in limiting his discussion of *Spanking the Maid* to its formal parodic elements, Cope seems to overlook a fundamental enabling premise of Bakhtin's theory of language, that, as Bakhtin tells us, "verbal discourse is a social phenomenon—social throughout its entire range and in each and every of its factors, from the sound image to the furthest reaches of abstract meaning" (*Dialogic Imagination*, 259).

The events of his day, and his own moral response to them, left Bakhtin ever on guard against the seemingly natural inclination of critics and scholars to become bogged down in narrow stylistic analysis, the latter endeavor reducing a literary work to a "closed authorial monologue" confined to "its own single hermetic context" (*Dialogic Imagination,* 274). But our own age exerts pressures on scholars and critics too, however different these pressures may be. There remains a need to make assertions related to fundamental human dignity and human worth, for, although such claims are commonplace, their objectives are not yet common practice. Yet, given the muddled perspectives of the master and maid, the absence of any exemplary authorial persona, and the novella's inconclusive conclusion, it is not immediately clear to the reader how this protean work can yield any kind of uncontingent moral claim. Certainly, moral assertion can only be credible if it comes from the reader's full engagement with the novella's most striking characteristic, its ambiguity.

Ambiguities that master

The ontic status of the events depicted in *Spanking the Maid,* whether centering on the maid, her employer, or their relationship, cannot be initially defined with any degree of certainty by the reader. Or, put somewhat differently, the reader struggles to determine which events refer to "objective reality" and which events are in fact the product of dream or conscious fantasy. This situation, in itself, need not render the work ambiguous. The patient reader is usually able to discern the difference between "objective" and "subjective" reality in fiction. The work of Joyce, Woolf, and Proust, among many others, has left the contemporary reader rather adept at discerning shifts in point of view. As Stuart Gilbert pointed out over fifty years ago in his landmark monograph on *Ulysses* and as Mitchell Leaska brought home in his meticulous study of Woolf's fiction, rash narratorial shifts can be plotted out. They are unambiguously determinate to a careful reader sensitive to delicate changes of tone, of vocabulary, of psychology. One finds something quite different in *Spanking the Maid.* The novella is not lacking in signposts, but these signposts point in a great many directions. It remains to be seen how the narrator's careful orchestration of conflicting signals leads the reader through a series of false starts, blind alleys, and dead ends on the way to a realization that the novella's internal contradictions can only be reconciled ultimately by going outside the fiction itself, by establishing a relationship between the literary work and the readerly world.

Spanking the Maid comprises thirty-nine short, paragraph-length sections, some minority of which contain dialogue. Eighteen sections focus exclusively or primarily on the master, fourteen on the maid, and in seven sections both characters figure prominently. The novella repeats a single, spare scenario several times. The maid enters her master's bedchamber early in the morning to attend to her domestic duties and discovers her master in various postures, e.g., in bed, at bedside, urinating in an adjoining bathroom, contemplating an early morning erection, muttering confusedly in a sleepy stupor about a recurring dream, walking dazedly about the room. Her master chastises her for her tardiness and general professional incompetence. His admonitions are sometimes expressed directly to the maid, sometimes maintained as prespeech ruminations. Emotionally and profession-

ally committed to servitude, the maid acknowledges her master's nig-
gling criticisms; she identifies him not as a petty tyrant, not as a morbid solipsist, but as one capable of bringing about her moral
improvement, perhaps even moral perfection—because it is perfection she strives for even as she understands the futility of her efforts.
In the narrator's words, "She is driven by a sense of duty and a profound appetite for hope never quite stifled by even the harshest punishments" (21). As for her punishments, the title of the novella speci-
fies their type—a bare-bottomed spanking at the hands of her
employer. As for the instruments of her abuse—whatever the master
finds handy or has time to devise, e.g., a hairbrush, his hand, a cat-o'-
nine-tails, a bull's pizzle, a ruler, and so on (45). The master sees his
self-styled "disciplinary interventions" as the honest efforts of one intent on the edification of an inferior (25).

The precise nature of the master-maid relationship is the major of
a number of conundra in the novella, all of which are occasioned by
the epistemological confusions of the two characters. It remains unclear throughout the novella, both to the reader and the protagonists,
which events actually take place and which are dreamed (and recol-
lected) or merely fantasized. The efforts of the characters to assemble
this conceptual puzzle, to dissolve ambiguity, to neutralize paradox,
all fail. Immersed in the fictional scenario, the reader's attempts are
no more successful.

The master-maid relationship has several *possible* colorations. The
master expresses repeatedly (to himself? to the maid?) dissatisfaction
with her domestic performance. To remedy the situation he lectures
her (actually?) on discipline and diligence and, frequently, accentuates
his lessons (actually? in his mind?) with bare-bottomed paddlings. The
maid absorbs his (actual?) chastisements—catechistic and corporal—
without complaint and, in one instance at least, encourages (actually?
imaginatively?) her otherwise distracted master to spank her. Again,
the essence of their relationship is unclear. Perhaps each fantasizes a
similar relationship in which the master serves as father-confessor
and moralist, wherein paddling has no sexual implications; perhaps
each fantasizes a similar sadomasochistic relationship and shrouds it
with religious implications; perhaps the former situation is actual; or
perhaps the latter is; or, perhaps, some amalgam of the above characterizes their interactions. In their analysis of their relationship, maid

and master (and reader, ever peeking over shoulders) investigate etiology, language (especially homonymity), logic, instinctual drives, and social role-playing, all in an effort to understand their experiences.

The novella's opening frame appears to locate the action in the empirical realm. The maid is described as entering her master's bedroom "deliberately," "gravely" (9). After a brief portrayal of this entrance, however, the narrator unaccountably chooses to redescribe the event: "No. Again. She enters" (9). The second description repeats certain of his original verbal formulations but then builds upon them. After this apparent false start, the scene takes shape. The maid daydreams as she busies herself with her work. Given the false start, given the maid's strange obsession with her wash "bucket" (both the object and the word's metaphorical possibilities), the opening frame puts the reader on alert even as it promotes the events it describes as empirical fact.

Frame two portrays the master awaking from a dream, struggling over its reconstruction: "something about utility, or futility, and a teacher he once had who, when he whipped his students, called it his 'civil service'" (11). (In the course of the novella, such semantic ambiguities will come to reinforce the factual ambiguities already mentioned.) The master's sleepy stupor (or perhaps the dream itself) denies him clarification. He wonders what mistakes the maid will make this day. At the end of the short frame, he remains sitting, apparently ready to leave his bed. At this point, it is evident to the reader that frames one and two do not refer to the same day. In the first, the maid has arrived; in the second, her master awaits her arrival. Frame three seems to continue the description begun in the opening frame with the master yet unaware of her presence. This temporal disjunction may seem insignificant to the reader intent on reading these introductory frames as straight empirical description. The narrator is merely setting up the thematic counterpoint of the novella—the contrast between the servant's submission and the moral pretensions of the employer—in the clearest possible manner. It is not until the fourth frame that the reader meets clear signs that lead him or her to question the reliability of the points of view thus far encountered and the objective status of the events being depicted.

Frame four opens, like frame two, with the master awaking after a night's sleep and puzzling over a dream:

Something about a teacher who had once lectured him on humility. Severely. Only now, in the dream, he was himself the
teacher and the student was a woman he knew, or thought he
knew, and in his lecture "humility" kept getting mixed up somehow with "humor," such that, in effect, he was trying, in all sever-
ity, to teach her how to laugh. . . . the curious strained expression on the woman's face as she tried—desperately, it seemed—
to laugh, and wondering why this provoked (in the dream) such
a fury in him, when the maid comes in. (16–17)

The dream has him in a teacher's role, attempting to instruct a
woman. This is analogous to his relationship to the maid as outlined
in the earlier frame (and as will be outlined in later frames). While his
chastisement of her involves no more than appending a forgotten
"Sir" to her discreetly expressed statement, "I'll start in the bathroom," the tenor of their relationship takes firm shape for the reader
(17). There is a covert suggestion that the master's dream and his response to his maid may have some, as yet undefinable, interdepen-
dence or, otherwise stated, that the fantastic and the empirical do not
so much stand in contrast to one another as perhaps overlap.

In frames five and seven, as in one and three, the maid enters her
master's chambers. In frame five she finds the room deserted. She
takes up her domestic tasks. The point of view oscillates between her
own and the narrator's. In frame seven, the reader finds the maid
wondering when this macabre scenario began. Here, as usual, she surprises her master beset by his matudinal erection: "some kind of lux-
uriant but dangerous dew-bejeweled blossom: a monster in the garden. 'I was having a dream,' he announces sleepily, yet gravely.
'Something about tumidity. But it kept getting mixed up somehow
with—' " (22). Once more the mysterious dream; again the verbal ambiguity. With master caught between the realms of dream and the empirical, with maid bound to a somnambulant state where fantasy and
fact freely interact, the reader is unable to locate the old benchmarks
of time and place.

The befuddlement of the protagonists very soon conditions the
reader's own outlook. There are the displacements of time where
maid and master sometimes appear to operate in different dimensions; the peculiar interaction of dream, fantasy, and empirical world
that leaves point of view unreliable, adrift; the master's semantic con-

fusions that seem to offer a potential source of resolution and yet yield no substantive insight; the bizarre objects the maid unearths in her master's bed, e.g., old razor blades, broken bottles, crumbs, mirrors, even her own underpants. All of these circumstances tempt the ingenuity of the armchair psychologist. Two further sources of readerly disorientation materialize in subsequent frames, namely the maid's obsessive submission to her employer's sadism, to what he calls his "divine drudgery," and, second, the cause of his violent urges. In most instances, the maid submits to her punishments with trepidation but, in at least one instance, she clearly courts her master's wrath and is disappointed when he fails to respond in his typical, violent manner (97). Through indirect interior monologue (*erlebte Rede*), both characters recurrently suggest that neither takes joy in the maid's corporal abuse, yet the contrary seems often the case. The title, for example, yields the letters "S" and "M." The reader struggles to determine whether sadomasochism, a morbid religious zealotry, or indeed some other issue—political autocracy perhaps, or the literary creative act— is in fact the central theme of the novella.

Frames ten, twelve, fourteen, and seventeen involve awakening scenes. The master's reconstruction of his dream remains a failure; semantic incongruities build up: "lecture" or "lecher" (29), "civil service" or "sibyl service" (32). He makes reference to strange manuals, moral tracts of sorts, from which he draws his "lectures." The master's seigneurial rights extend to the invention of the maid's very soul (34). The maid, for her part, accepts unquestioningly her master's spiritual superiority and the attendant spankings, for "she knows he is just" (46). Her utter subjugation is a condition of her salvation. But she is not the only victim of the manuals. They tyrannize her master as well, his existence solipsized by his morbid application of their pious cant. These manuals litter his dreams along with the unidentified woman. Or have the manuals and the woman merely an oneiric presence all along? In his dreams, his role as a molder of souls has become "a sort of fever of the mind" (48). Perhaps, the reader surmises, this "fever of the mind" is a fit characterization of the master in his waking hours as well. In fact, maybe the entire preposterous scenario is but the waking fantasy of one controlled by inscrutable fascinations with pain, the domination of women, and the female posterior. Perhaps the narrator is reliable to the extent he faithfully depicts the master's confused integration of dream, fantasy, and empirical fact. Perhaps the only incontrovertible "facts" of this tale are the existence of the man, the maid, and narrator. Or, then again, maybe only the man and the narrator. Or maid and narrator. Or, finally, a narrator, one intent on manipulating the innocent reader through a series of semantic confusions, violations of verisimilitude, and logical incongruities. But to what avail? Before discussing the ramifications of employing ambiguity as an organizing principle, we turn to the final frame of the novella in which Coover's ambiguity has its most unambiguous realization.

The ultimate frame begins with the master walking in the garden with an old teacher of his. The discussion falls to the condition of *humanity*, the latter word getting continually confused with *homonymity* (99). A morning glory metamorphoses into a woman that the teacher (or is it the master?) once knew on the "civil surface," a verbal play that may indicate sexual intimacy or merely verbal confusion (99). There is an interruption—" 'What? What?!' " exclaims the master. The narrative continues: "But she only wants him to change his position, or perhaps his condition" (100). The pronominal "she" seems to refer to the maid, in which case we have another awakening scene with the maid disturbing the man *in medias somnium*. In that case, the reader is directly privy to the master's dream for the first time, not merely to his inadequate reconstruction of it. The many semantic confusions seem, for the moment, explicable. The juxtaposition of *humanity* and *homonymity* brings to mind the many not quite homonymous pairs of words and phrases that have perplexed the male protagonist and the reader alike throughout the book. The master appears to fall back into the dream, but the maid's continued presence proves a distraction, and the scene dissolves into a dizzying conflation of dream, fantasy, and empirical event. The teacher of the dream mentions "callipygomancy." Apparently derived from the model of "necromancy" (Greek, literally "black divination"), this nonce word suggests supernatural powers through, literally, "beautiful buttocks." An explanation for the master's morbid preoccupation with his maid's posterior suggests itself.[5] Yet, why is callipygomancy mentioned only at the book's conclusion, *post facto* as it were? Is it part of a recurring dream? An aspect of a daytime fantasy? Or is it constitutive of the master's actual relationship to his maid?

In *Spanking the Maid*, the author offers the reader a single promising tool to dissolve or conflate this myriad of juxtapositions, antitheses, contradictions, dichotomies, and paradoxes—the ordering

symbol. Traditionally hermeneutic and/or heuristic keys used to un-
lock the most resisting of thematic doors, the ordering symbols in
Spanking the Maid are two—flowers and the blank sheet, the latter
more adequate than the former (and to be discussed later), but neither capable of establishing hermeneutical linearity. At the conclusion
of the novella, the master's former teacher, the interlocutor of his
dream, turns lilacs into roses. Traditional endings crystallize themes,
recapitulating in a symbol or summary statement what has been thematically developed in the course of the work. Traditionally, endings
and beginnings are informationally "denser" than the middles that
connect them. Aware of these conventions, the reader ponders the
final frame expectantly. Roses are, for the Freudian, symbolic of the
female sex organs. A bibliographical search unearths Barbara Seward's study of the rose as a symbol in literature—the rose in Dante, in
Romantic literature, in Yeats and Joyce, in Eliot. Eliot, the reader recalls, in his most famous poem, mentions lilacs.

> April is the cruellest month, breeding
> Lilacs out of the dead land, mixing
> Memory and desire, stirring
> Dull roots with spring rain. (lines 1–4)

If roses are femininely sexual, can lilacs not be the masculine equivalent? The shape is right. And . . . However, finally, flowers hold no
particular symbolic significance. The reader is soon stymied by this
line of inquiry. His or her efforts unearth no new mysterious hidden
meanings. When confined, like the maid and her master, to the fictional scenario, the reader too is unable to make sense of things.

The final frame, while first appearing to offer grounds to surmise
that the action of the novella is primarily confined to the conscious
fantasizing of its male protagonist, offers no real legitimate grounds
for any univocal reading of *Spanking the Maid*. The conventional function of a concluding chapter is not realized. Questions are not an-
swered; doubts are not dispelled. In fact, the final frame only serves
to multiply doubts. Closure of plot is but one more readerly expectation that the novella frustrates. The reader wends blindly, unpredict-
ably, through the undefined mental states of the protagonists. The
reader is trapped in a labyrinth, made sport of by a wealth of interpretive possibilities that are, when considered selectively, viable but, when

taken up *in toto,* utterly inadequate. But what can such a fiction mean or has the very notion of meaning as a set of unambiguous truths lost its relevance in Cooverian postmodernism?

Mastering ambiguities

While concentrating *solely* on the fictional scenario, the reader is quite as lost as the master and the maid. Like the latter, the reader remains paralyzed; ambiguity and paradox seem unconquerable. Yet, unlike the protagonists, the reader is not confined to this confusing realm. The reader can "leave" the fictional scenario or, at least, place it in the background while foregrounding his or her own experiences and opinions. If the reader is to make of the novella something more than a mere metafiction, more than a ludic project, more than an ingenious display of authorial imagination, he or she must establish a homological relationship between the events of the novella and events in the lived-world. Of the feminist critic, Alice Jardine has written that she (and he) is "at her best when drawing the painful analogies between those written plots [that circumscribe female characters] and their mimetic counterparts in 'real life' " (56). Indeed, the need to outline such analogies holds for any reader wishing to establish a moral dimension for a literary work, irrespective of topic or theme.

The central ambiguity of the novella involves of course the master-maid relationship. As I have noted, it is not immediately clear if its basis is sadomasochism or moral proselytization or some measure of each. Readers find themselves within what Coover calls the "vibrant space between the poles of a paradox" where "all the exciting art happens" (McCaffery, "Robert Coover," 50). For the protagonists, this "vibrancy" takes place within the closed system of their own psyches, their thoughts condemned to oscillate aimlessly between two poles. Master and maid cannot discover the denominators common to abusive sexuality and assumed moral superiority, such elements as moral hypocrisy, chauvinism, gender stereotyping, and self-deceit. All of the latter are common aspects of traditional Western gender ideology. (And, although Coover may have had specific nineteenth-century attitudes on sex in mind while writing *Spanking the Maid,* the Victorian era—the least original of major cultural epochs—merely nuanced traditional views on sexuality.) The relationship depicted in *Spanking the Maid* presents a logical, if parodic, extension of what I would call a "metaphysical" conception of gender identity and gender role. Metaphysics entails an abstract, unworldly ("anti-worldly"?) reduction of human possibility. The plenitude of existence is replaced by a limited set of possibilities fashioned by arbitrary design. Metaphysical reduction in the area of gender simplifies our choices; it responds to the inherent human desire for power and mastery, and the security these bring. And, to be sure, metaphysical reduction can make of human consciousness and behavior something crabbed and schematic and uncontingent. Like people in Chaplin's *Modern Times* and Fritz Lang's *Metropolis,* the master and maid are two-dimensional and stick-like, driven by codes and forces that are a cultural inheritance.

In her discussion of Sade's female characters, Angela Carter also characterizes as "metaphysical" many of our views on sexuality and gender roles. Justifiably, she derides pornography for its role in sustaining stereotypes. "Pornography," she writes, "involves an abstraction of human intercourse in which the self is reduced to its formal elements" (4). However, interestingly, even paradoxically, the thesis of her monograph maintains that pornography, at least some of it, can lead us to reevaluate sexual mores.

> When pornography abandons its quality of existential solitude and moves out of the kitsch area of timeless, placeless fantasy and into the real world, then it loses its function of safety valve. It begins to comment on real relations in the real world. Therefore, the more pornographic writing acquires the techniques of real literature, of real art, the more deeply subversive it is likely to be in that the more likely it is to affect the reader's perceptions of the world. The text that had heretofore opened up creamily to him, in a dream, will gather itself together and harshly expel him into the anguish of actuality. (19)

For Carter in *The Sadeian Woman,* and incidentally Simone de Beauvoir in her *Must We Burn Sade?,* Sade's fiction has a moral element in that it depicts, in an unrepressed, brutally honest way, fundamental male attitudes toward women, attitudes that are apparent not only in sexual relations but throughout the full range of male-female interaction.

Like Sade's pornography, Coover's essays in the pornographic form also inspire a reconsideration of gender relations. *Spanking the Maid* is

not Coover's first treatment of pornography as a genre. Two plays
from the early seventies, the short "Love Scene" and "A Theological
Position," parody pornography and the values that support it, values
that are held a priori, that are unresponsive to the complexity of human nature. In "Love Scene," a director of a pornographic play (or
film) exhorts an actor and actress from offstage. Coover's play is really
nothing more than a barrage of imperatives. The director wants a
"love scene" but his vision of love and sexual commerce is burdened
by cliché and iconic commonplace. The players stand paralyzed, depleted of all spontaneity by the harangue of the offstage "lovemaster."
"Come on," he cajoles, "this is a love scene, gang! This is the biggest
thing in your life! . . . It's the whole goddamn saga of the western
world!" (87). He grows increasingly incensed as the couple fails to respond. The director attempts to incite his "love scene" by cataloguing
the antinomic images that have helped historically to define Western
views of human love:

> . . . let's try the allegorical thing. Love embracing death, that
> kind of thing. The East and the West. Black and white. . . . The
> princess and the blackamoor. Hah! That thing he's got'll split
> you wide open, honey! She's old mother night herself, boy, full
> of sweet delirium. Smell that black horniness? Look at those
> chains! Look at those whips! . . . this is depravity and virtue! . . .
> This is night and day! sun and moon! yin and yang! Get ready
> now! Oh boy! This is beauty and the beast, order and chaos, ego
> and id, we're up to our ears in it, *feel* it! God and the Devil! youth
> and age! terrific! the intrinsic and the extrinsic! it's a seduction!
> fight it! grab it! resist! surrender! It's man and society! zero and
> infinity! oh yeah! time and space! will and necessity! hot shit! it's
> war and peace! master and slave! *the beginning and the end! SYN-*
> *THESIZE!* ("Love Scene," 91–92)

The director depicts human sexuality and human love as bellicose responses on the part of each gender to fundamental gender antagonisms. Sexuality courts then not so much genuine unity as a brief ces-
sation of hostilities. Synthesis is purely physical, of no longer duration
than orgasm itself. The various sets of oppositions reinforce conventional views of gender relations: physical prowess, typically a male attribute, governs relationships; submission, typically a female posture,

is central to sexuality; and, sexuality in itself is an act of personal de-
filement that calls attention to the perpetual clash between moral purity and moral depravity. What are missing here of course are spontaneity, individualism, and, to be sure, empathy, or, in a word, love. At
the end of "Love Scene," the director issues a stern chastisement:
"*IMAGINATION RULES THE WORLD*" (98). Yet, his inclination to
cast his "Love Scene" as an amalgam of pornographic cliché and soph-
omoric violation of taboo suggests that insufficient imagination rules
his own.

Many of the themes of "A Theological Position," the title piece of
Coover's collection of plays, prefigure those found in *Spanking the
Maid*. A priest-confessor ministers to a couple with a strange problem
that has heretical implications. The woman, though purportedly a virgin, is six months pregnant. Yet, to claim an immaculate conception is
heresy—Mary has cornered the market here—and burning at the
stake is the prescribed reward for the heretic. Clearly what is required
is penetration, an act that will render the conception "maculate," i.e.,
"spotted" and "stained" by human desire. Yet, the husband is unable
to couple with his wife in front of the priest whose "theological position" requires he witness the act. The priest agrees to an unusual so-
lution to this problem, one that will satisfy theological "statute" and,
incidentally (if unadmittedly), the priest's growing lust. He himself, in
a generous and compassionate act of self-abnegation, will enter the
woman and make her pregnancy "honest." Denying any personal
knowledge of sexual intercourse, he will rely on his marital counseling
"manuals" for direction.

For much of the play, the priest attempts to ejaculate into the
woman. Stage directions define the woman's conventionally passive
role throughout this "theological" exercise. She views her circumstance—the physical occupation of her body by an abusive cassocked
cleric—"demurely," "placidly," and "innocently," a metaphor for woman's (un)involvement in the phallocentric ritual of orthodox theology
(137, 139). For his part, the priest (like the master in *Spanking the
Maid*) shrouds his sexual desire in the theological cant that has historically authorized man as the agent of moral redemption and woman
as the agent of moral compromise. Certainly, the apple in the play
recalls Eve's role in Eden as a violator of a moral code. At the same
time, the concurrent indictment of the woman and the implied exon-
eration of the man recall various literary representations of double

standards in gender relations. Whatever the seduction scenario—
whether Mary Hamilton's in the eponymous medieval ballad or Hes-
ter Prynne's or Effi Briest's or Emma Bovary's—it has typically been
the woman who has borne the brunt of societal condemnation when
sexual mores have been violated.

The malignity of the priest's physical violation of the woman is
compounded by the steady stream of verbal abuse he trains upon her.
When she smiles "serenely" up at him, seemingly the very ideal of
accommodation, he reproaches her—apparently for her missing the
moral seriousness of his ministrations but actually to maintain the fiction that his purposes are not sensuous, but solely moral and altruis-
tic: "Now, stop that! There is nothing to smile about. . . . you can be
charged with witchcraft! Do you know what we do to witches, my pet?
We strip them naked and chase them naked through the public places
with whips!" (153). Here, as we see in *Spanking the Maid*, there is on
the surface an entirely disingenuous denial of the libido while the libido is simultaneously indulged covertly through appeals to moral order. Both the priest's threatened public punishment and his enact-
ment of *in camera* redemption offer him dual gratifications—that
offered by sexual pleasure and that offered by the exercise of moral
authority, an authority founded on a metaphysical disgust of orgasm,
and corporality generally. The woman becomes no more than a prop
in this delicately negotiated indulgence of seemingly antithetical desires, one physical, the other metaphysical. Indeed, historically, these
desires have often warred and often won, however bizarrely, mutual
accommodation. As Marina Warner writes,

> In Christian hagiography, the sadomasochistic content of the
> paeans to male and female martyrs is startling, from the early
> documents like the *Passions of Saints Perpetua and Felicity* into the
> high Middle Ages. But the particular focus on women's torn and
> broken flesh reveals the psychological obsession of the religion
> with sexual sin, and tortures that pile up one upon the other
> with pornographic repetitiousness underline the identification
> of the female with perils of sexual contact. (Warner, 71; quoted
> in Rigney, 43)

Paradoxically, clerics, theologians, and lay persons have historically
engaged in a kind of sexual experience, even as they aver the horrid-

ness of things sexual. Seen in this light, Foucault's claim that sexual indulgence, not sexual repression, characterizes Western culture seems insightful:

> Rather than the uniform concern to hide sex, rather than a general prudishness of language, what distinguishes these last three centuries is the variety, the wide dispersion of devices that were invented for speaking about it, for having it be spoken about, for inducing it to speak of itself, for listening, recording, transcribing, and redistributing what is said about it: around sex, a whole network of varying, specific, and coercive transpositions into discourse. Rather than a massive censorship, beginning with the verbal proprieties imposed by the Age of Reason, what was involved was a regulated and polymorphous incitement to discourse. (*The History of Sexuality* 1:34)

Certainly, both "A Theological Position" and *Spanking the Maid* illustrate how sexuality becomes a focal point within the discursive economy of theological cliché. Paradoxically, "sexual repression" in each work is a kind of unwitting, perverse celebration of sexuality in that "repression" produces a preoccupation with the very phenomenon it seeks to tame and mute.

There is a curious development at the end of "A Theological Position." Through the kind of radical conceit typical of Coover's fiction, the woman's vagina becomes a second mouth, capable of speech and mastication—a "talking cunt," in the characterization of the husband. This nether mouth bites the penis of the priest and launches into a philippic comparable to the priest's own. "I use your language," she says, "having failed with my own," and immediately acknowledges with this statement that women have not been allowed to develop their own gender identity in a unilateral way (161). The woman berates the priest because he, like other socially powerful males, has replaced the corporal with the abstract, the provisional with the absolute, the natural with the hypostatic. In the view of the talking vagina, "the soft letter of the soft law"—the imagery suggesting of course both contingency and female genitalia—has been denied by a masculine rigidity; as she says to the priest and her husband, "You work up a hard-on and like it so much you call it a system, but you are afraid of orgasm and call it death!" (162). The woman becomes an incarnation of a life-principle, the priest of a morbid, life-denying metaphysics. Given the distribution of power, the woman can hardly prevail in her struggle for personal sovereignty. She knows what her fate must inevitably be. "That's right," she acknowledges, "anything you don't understand, kill it, that's your road to salvation, your covenant with holy inertia! Kill and codify" (168). The priest restores moral order, simply and finally, by plunging a knife into the woman's pregnant belly.

The woman in "A Theological Position" is an unusual Cooverian character in that she seems to offer an unfiltered statement of the author's own views. Her exemplarity lies in her fierce denigration of hypocrisy, of self-censorship, of sexual inhibition, of chauvinism, all of which are mandated by the priest's "theological position." The pornographic implications of the play's scenario are quickly superseded by moral ones as is the case, for example, in works by Boccaccio and Rabelais that deal with similar "theological" proclivities. In Coover's play, the set figure of the lecherous cleric engaging in coercive sex (a practice at once licit and illicit) is depicted as a buffoon. The absurdity of the play's action neutralizes all possible sexual titillation. The use of sexually suggestive material is an important didactic stratagem in Coover's work. His views on the utility of erotica/pornography merit quotation:

> We are never more susceptible to our own doubts and fears and anxieties than when we are approaching the erotic, and so are most apt—and part of art is process—to discover something going that route and not being too programmatic and self-censoring. Understanding the self, approaching "the other" by way of its erotic impulses is a way of understanding everything— philosophy, religion, history. But this is what has led me over and over to the use of it. And I think it's led *all* artists to it, in a way that is ultimately not prurient but revelatory. (Smith, 45)

Although *Spanking the Maid* has no exemplary character, the reader can, with effort, draw out certain moral implications from the work.

The critique of conventional gender roles and metaphysics generally is continued in *Spanking the Maid,* though, as noted, there is no authorial spokesperson. In the novella, Coover illustrates two things: how metaphysical positions are enabled by epistemological reduction-

ism and how such reductionism aids the formation of gender stereotyping. In book 3 of *The Will to Power,* Nietzsche reviews humankind's
history of self-deception in epistemological inquiry. Metaphysical notions of truth have deformed, conformed reality to fit our emotional
need for univocity, consistency, pattern, plot, linearity. We, as inven-
tors of "formulas and signs," have been able to "reduce the confusing
multiplicity [of life] to a purposive and manageable scheme" (315).
Metaphysical truth, the product of programmatic reduction, allows
one "to become master of reality, in order to misunderstand it in a
shrewd manner" (315). In *Spanking the Maid,* maid and master see
their highly complex relationship in terms of redemption theology—
the master-lord, as priest, exacting high standards of performance
and accountability; the maid, the erring supplicant, bent on moral improvement, even moral perfection. Religious zealotry is indistinguishable here from gender bigotry. The former veils their ongoing (if
unexpressed) need for a conventional economy of power within their
relationship, for the emotional security conventionality brings. However, as becoming, change, contingency, slowly invade the cloistered
world of the master and the maid, the metaphysical sandcastles erode,
leaving them confused and circumspect.

Ritual attempts to bring time to a halt, to celebrate life not as a
series of discrete events but as a single unitary, unified phenomenon.
Ritual emphasizes *being,* stasis, the achieved condition. Nature, on the
other hand, is processual. It constantly becomes; it is dynamic and
changeful. The maid, as she observes her master's penis grow flaccid,
identifies the key distinction between being and becoming. *Being* has
no beginning and no end; only *becoming* and *change* respond to the
suppleness, the vitality of time. In contrast to the physiological change
she witnesses in the rise and fall of her master's penile humors, her
life plays itself out as ritual, an endless recuperation of a single, primal
scene of divine retribution that knows no change.

The master lives in a similar state of stasis, his sole function to play
his role as an agent of divine expediency. It is his task to mold the
maid's character. In an often repeated lecture, he informs her of the
importance of *method* and *habit,* "two fairies that will make the work
disappear before a ready pair of hands" (59). The master lives out a
curious paradox. Though apparently independent and sovereign—
free to propose and dispose—his existence is inextricably bound up

with that of the maid: he is "dependently independent."[6] Her improprieties are his sole reason for being and, as the following hints, his sole means of sexual gratification:

> To live in the full sense of the word, he [the master] knows, is not merely to exist but to give oneself to some mission, surrender to a higher purpose, but in truth he often wonders, watching that broad part destined by Mother Nature for such solemnities [the ritual beating of the maid] quiver and redden under his hand (he thinks of it as a blank on which to write), whether it is he who has given himself to a higher end or that end which has chosen and in effect captured him? (54).

In this passage, "higher end" points in two different directions. Figuratively, it suggests an ethical objective; literally, it conjures an image of the maid disencumbered of her underpants, in a posture of supplication. Religiosity or carnal need? Spiritual rite (however macabre) or sadomasochistic minuet?

Actually, these antitheses can be collapsed. Here, both religious zeal and sexual desire derive from the inclination of the master to dominate his gender complement, the maid, and her collateral inclination to submit to the male will. Though redemption and sexuality—the latter at once repressed and celebrated—are symbolically linked through his use of a bull's pizzle to "indoctrinate" the maid, it is power, and not morality or lust, that defines their relationship. Power—the imposition of one person's will upon another—expresses itself in verbal and physical abuse. "Spanking" is of course reserved for the young and the unformed. Through the spankings meted out to her, the maid is implicitly likened to a child who must be punitively informed of the patriarchal vision and who must be physically compelled to endorse the patriarchy's notion of redemption.

The maid and her master are hermetically locked within a paradigm wherein their "love" for one another manifests itself in two schematic ways (each of which is male dominated): as a beastly sadomasochism and as an ethereal spiritual love. Bound to convention, neither is capable of the critique necessary for their relationship to achieve a fairer, more humane distribution of power. Femininity has often been construed in rather Manichean terms. In *Spanking the Maid,* the maid is at once posited as an abject violator of the moral code and an important agent of the code's perpetuation. The master sees her capable of grossness as well as perfection. The maid embodies simultaneously both the whore and the virgin syndromes. Each syndrome is based on an idealized view of women; each extrapolates a single element and hypostasizes it, making of it an essence. Angela Carter calls such reductions of female possibility "consolatory nonsenses." As Carter correctly notes, "If a revival of the myths of these cults gives women emotional satisfaction, it does so at the price of obscuring the real conditions of life" (5). Clearly, Coover's novella must be seen as a satirical comment on a literary (and hence social) tradition of female stereotyping. For purposes of contrast, we might engage in a brief digression and consider two classic meditations on male-female relationships—Dante's *Vita Nuova* and Sade's *La Philosophie dans la boudoir.* In each instance, through reason and/or arbitrary valorization (the same thing, Nietzsche would claim) of one "kind" or aspect of love, the protagonist defines and justifies his relationship(s).

In his discussion of Renaissance Neoplatonism, the art historian Erwin Panofsky offers an insightful reading of the Neoplatonists' typology of love, notably as developed by Ficino and Pico and pictorially rendered, for example, by Titian in his "Sacred and Profane Love" (c. 1515; Borghese Gallery, Rome) (129–69). The Neoplatonists proposed three "kinds" of love—divine (*divinus*), human (*humanus*), and bestial (*ferinus*). Clearly, the divine and bestial modes reduce human being to a single proclivity. In the former instance, love is transcendental and spiritual; in the latter, love is vulgar and urethral/clitoral. Neither kind of love is contingent; each is in its way "pure," based more on metaphysical reduction rather than on imaginative play with human possibility. Both of these "loves" are parodied in *Spanking the Maid.* For their part, Dante and Sade, two important and seemingly very different writers, draft nonparodic treatments of particular kinds of love and, in so doing, emulate the reductive stance of the Neoplatonists. In *Vita Nuova,* Dante privileges *amor divinus* over *amor humanus.* Alternatively, the Marquis de Sade—the atheist and antiChrist—rejects *amor humanus* for *amor ferinus* throughout his writings. (*Bestial love* is not, apparently, an option Dante entertains, nor Sade *divine love.*) In each case, philosophical idealism rejects the vagaries of human love.[7]

In *Vita Nuova,* Dante uses reason to "triumph over" the impious thoughts occasioned by *amor humanus,* to define the "divine" or "holy" love he self-confessedly feels for Beatrice:

> Henceforward I say Love swayed my soul, which was so early espoused to him, and he assumed such complete mastery over me, through the power of the imagination, that perforce I was compelled to fulfill all his behest. . . . And although her image, which was constantly present with me, was a transport of Love to overmaster me, yet it was so noble and virtuous, that it never suffered Love to rule me beyond the counsel of reason. (5)

Dante dissolves the conflicting impulses he feels toward his beatific Beatrice by *claiming* the sovereignty of reason over carnal desire although throughout the book—both in its commentaries and poems—neither appears supreme. The ambiguity of Dante's response is evident to the reader though not, apparently, to the author:

> There awoke one day within me . . . a most vivid phantasy, wherein I fancied I beheld the verisimilitude of that most glorious Beatrice. . . . Then I fell a-thinking of her, recalling all the doings of my past life in their due order of time, and my heart repented bitterly the *desire* to which it had so basely yielded place for a short while, counter to the constancy of reason. (104–5; my emphasis)

Reason allows Dante to "emplot" the events of the past, or rather his memory of them, in such a way as to provide them consistency and sequence—in short, a linearity—and brings univocal meaning to his vision. Through the separation of mind (divine love) and body (human love), through the arbitrary promotion of the former, Dante is able to overlook the plurisignification of his relationship with Beatrice.[8] Paralyzed by epistemological and semantic breakdown, neither maid nor master achieves the comfort of this reductive position in *Spanking the Maid.*

The Marquis de Sade, a son of the Enlightenment, influenced by Rousseau's thesis of the "noble savage," similarly reduces the protean phenomenon of love to a single aspect of human behavior—raw sexual expression.[9] Reacting to the restriction on sexual mores promoted by society, Sade argues for libertinism, for unrestricted sexual activity—notably "sadism" but also masochism, sodomy, incest, and prostitution. Spiritual love is nothing more than an irrational prejudice *forced* upon the individual; in a radical transvaluation, spiritual love becomes for Sade a vice, and sadistic carnality a virtue:

> Cruelty, very far from being a vice, is the first sentiment Nature injects in us all. . . . Cruelty is simply the energy in a man civilization has not yet altogether corrupted: therefore it is a virtue, not a vice. Repeal your laws, do away with your constraints, your chastisements, your habits, and cruelty will have dangerous effects no more, since it will never manifest itself save when it meets with resistance, and then the collision will always be between competing cruelties. (*Philosophy in the Bedroom*, 253–54; *La Philosophie dans le boudoir*, 437–38)

Like Dante, Sade uses reason and personal caprice to valorize a particular love, in his case *bestial love*. Cruelty is naturalized. He fails to see the contradiction within his position. In a world where everything goes, where antinomianism is "natural," surely the state is as free to impose its will arbitrarily as indeed is the individual. The state's incarceration of Sade is not dissimilar in kind to his own abduction and assault of Rose Keller.[10] As with Dante, reason becomes an instrument of desire, put into service by an emotional need for consistency and self-justification.

Though they promote antipodal resolutions to the "two loves" debate, Dante and Sade employ reason to appease a very human need for a univocal truth. Reason gives phenomena determinacy; reason dissolves contradiction. As Nietzsche asserts, the will to truth has become, quite simply, "the desire for a world of the constant" (317). Unlike in the case of the protagonists of Dante and Sade, constancy eludes maid and master in *Spanking the Maid;* reason fails them. Paradoxes abound: the maid performs her domestic office *humbly* and *authoritatively* (9), grandly yet with circumspection (18); she knows *true service* is *perfect freedom* (47); her whippings are *divine drudgery* (76). Time no longer offers an epistemological mooring: "When, she [the maid] wants to know . . . did all this really begin? When she entered [the master's bedroom]? Before that? Long ago? Not yet? Or just now . . ." (22). Diachrony or synchrony? Change or condition? Ambiguity is sovereign. And he, her master, lives out a similar epistemological conundrum:

> Sometimes, as now . . . he wonders about his calling, how it came to be his, and when it all began: on his coming here? on *her* coming here? before that, in some ancient time beyond recall? And has he chosen it? or has he, like that woman in his dream, showing him something that for some reason enraged him, been "born with it, sir, for your very utility"? (30)

The fundamental riddle here relates to human free will. Has the master chosen his own role in his relationship with the maid, or has his role been mandated by tradition? Has the maid, like the woman in the dream caught striking an exhibitionistic pose, been born into socio-sexual servitude? Or is her servitude a freely elected one? Are the maid and the dream woman reducible to their callipygian charms? Is their personal worth to be measured in terms of mere "utility"? Is the worth of the master commensurate to his skill in perpetuating male dominance? Clearly, neither Dante nor Sade (nor pornography in general) problematizes gender relations in this explicit way. In Dante and Sade, reason remains a potent instrument in the justification of metaphysical notions of gender and love; in *Spanking the Maid* reason cannot negotiate the distance that separates moralistic assertion and immoral deed.

Like reason, language too breaks down throughout the novella, its failure revealing the rift between the apparent and the actual. For master and maid language loses its capacity to denominate and symbolize unambiguously. Words metamorphose in front of the characters' very eyes, separating, as if once and for all, signifier and signified. For them, language becomes opaque, ambiguous, plurisignificatory— pointing toward religion and lust, salvation and sex, saint and sinner. Wordplay illustrates how phonetic contiguity—proximate or precise—produces major semantic alterations: lectures / ledgers (66) / lechers (89); order / odor (39) / ordure (89); souls / holes (89); civil service / sibyl service (32) / civil surface (99); puzzle / pizzle (95); humility / utility / futility (16); hymnody / humidity (77) / tumidity (22).[11] It is immediately clear that these sets of homonyms and near homonyms are more than simple manifestations of the much heralded postmodern ludic sensibility. Looking at the sets closely, we see that in most instances the first term is in some way conventionally moralistic while the subsequent term(s) effects a revision or critique of the first. Consequently, moralizing "lectures," which aim to safeguard the moral economy, i.e., to keep its "ledgers" in balance, are made not by the morally superior but by the morally deficient, by "lechers." Protestations about moral "order" have about them a foul "odor," that of "ordure." Talk about "souls" is really talk about (sexual) "holes." The "civil service," emblem of reason and the societal superego, conceals the operation of the divinatory and superstitious—the "sibyl service"—not to mention the instinctual that leads us to the "(civil) surface" of carnality. "Hymnody," a religious observance, yields to (the) "humidity" (of carnal sweat) and penile "tumidity."

Homonymity involves the concurrence of phonetic similitude—actual or proximate—and semantic difference. Homonymity is, in a way, an ineradicable trick of language; it is sometimes innocent, sometimes not. Homonyms embrace simultaneously both identity and nonidentity. They are philology's paradoxes. In *Spanking the Maid*, homonymity—a simple philological fact—becomes a metaphor for human self-deceit, for the disjunction between the purported and the real. Master and maid claim to be actors in a morality play. Ministrant and supplicant respectively, they play out their prescribed parts. Their monologues and dialogues sound morally elevated; their discourse and actions *seem* to coincide, *seem* to confirm one another. Word and deed *seem*, in short, to be *synonymous* with one another, with synonymity in this context suggesting moral good faith. Yet, as noted above, the moralizing cant of master and maid obscures what is actually immoral and inhumane in their behavior: the endorsement of gender stereotyping, their flight from the truth of contingency into the embrace of metaphysical abstraction, and the explicit denial of their sexuality. Consequently, word and deed are really not so much synonyms as homonyms. That is, they are phenomena that look and sound the same but that actually signify different things. Their identity is only apparent; nonidentity is actual. Master and maid are not what they claim to be. Seen in this light, homonymity suggests moral bad faith.

Clearly, the actions of the master and maid have broad allegorical significance, a point implied throughout the present discussion. In the final section of the novella, there is allegorical closure of sorts when "homonymity" itself is aligned with "humanity," suggesting that humankind's inclination to misrepresent its actions is fundamental

and inalienable (99). Yet, we might legitimately ask, if deceit of self
and others is inevitable, given the nature of humankind, isn't Coover
wasting his time (and ours) bemoaning the fact? At this point, doesn't
tendentiousness become not only tedious, as it usually is, but point-
less? These questions lead us to a final consideration, to the metaphorical significance of the "blank sheet" that is referred to throughout the novella.

There are many references to the blank sheet. Literally, there is the
bed sheet with which the maid must daily contend. These are matters
in which the master takes keen interest:

> He lectures her patiently on the proper way to make a bed, the
> airing of the blankets, turning of the mattress, changing the
> sheets, the importance of a smooth surface. "Like a blank sheet
> of crisp new paper," he tells her. (36)

"Smooth surface" points both to bedclothes and the maid's bared bot-
tom, suggesting once again that appeals to order—domestic and
moral—actually mask sexual preoccupations. Elsewhere, the maid recalls one of her master's more importunate demands—that the buttocks she proffers him for flagellation be like "a clean sheet of paper"
(69). Later, we find the master despairing of the maid's capacity to
reach perfection, "staring gloomily at her soul's ingress which confronts him like blank paper, laundered tiffany, a perversely empty
ledger" (81). Toward the end of the novella, the master's mind becomes a "blank sheet" (92).

The inventor, in a manner of speaking, confronts a blank page at
the moment he or she commences his or her inventing (as does, of
course, the writer literally when he or she sets out). The reader is also
an inventor. The text, especially an innovative one, remains a blank
page until a reader has established for it a relevance, a meaning, a
mimesis, until the reader has established a relationship between the
text's world and his or her own. Barthes' notion of *écriture* makes this
point of course. The innovative text has no *obvious* mimetic import. (It
is this very quality that defines it as innovative.) It is, as Sontag points
out, using an aural metaphor, "silent" (3–34). Its blank page is a blank
cheque upon which the reader must inscribe value and specificity. If
the maid's soul is the invention of her master (as he himself claims
[54]), or at least the invention of the master's cultural traditions, then

the reader must be the inventor of any significance that inventor and invention hold. (And Coover, the author, is of course thoroughly and inventively implicated in all of this.)[12] Within this complicated skein of inventiveness, the blank page serves to inspire readerly activity, readerly involvement. As a controlling image, the blank page emphasizes contingency, potential, and self-accountability. Though the reader cannot step out of his or her culture any more than the master and the maid can, the reader can opt for a different cultural tradition, one that pays more than lip service to the ideals of tolerance and fairness, one that does not seek to cloak a desire for power in terms of a desire for moral transcendence.

In metaphorical terms, the blank page illustrates that value is the function of human volition and not something that is pre-inscribed once and for all. It suggests the bounteous presence of *absence*—absence of epistemological certainty, absence of apodictic truth. Yet, the absence of absolutes, whether in the domain of knowledge or morality, need not lead to nihilism or antinomianism. Quite as easily, these absences can provoke us to pursue the "better fictions" that Coover alludes to in the interview comment cited earlier. In *Spanking the Maid* Coover presents an unsubtle and unsettling deconstruction of those verities—epistemological, linguistic, and psychological—put forth by the first poet of the *blank page,* John Locke. Locke's truths were unconditional; Coover's are not. Coover has some interesting things to say in the Bigsby interview about the provisionality of moral truths:

> Is morality tied to some kind of stasis? . . . it seems to me that out there in the flux our moral values are being generated and regenerated all the time. Our politicians and sociologists, historians and literary critics are constantly up to that, creating value-generating metaphors or fictions by way of which we understand things, derive our sense of morality, as you [Christopher Bigsby] call it—and looking at fiction in a broad way, this is what always happens and must happen, it seems to me. I see self-conscious fiction as a willed passage beyond the functional definitions of the world, out where it can wrestle with the shapeshifting universe. That, for me, is a moral act. (87)[13]

Clearly, in the context of traditional Western philosophy, the postulation of a provisional, temporary truth involves something of a paradox, but paradoxes can just as well liberate as paralyze. Paralysis is the common fate of master and maid, but the reader need not share their destiny.

The productivity of paradox

Paradox and ambiguity have always troubled humankind. The paradoxes of Zeno, the debate on epistemological issues that Zeno inspired (notably the *Parmenides* of Plato, but also a good deal of isolated discussion elsewhere), the paradox of the Holy Trinity (each deity a part of an *indivisible* whole), all of these illustrate the early ubiquity of paradox. Of paradox, Gregory Vlastos writes:

> All-too-familiar beliefs may have implications which are fatal to the credibility of the implicands. In the whole history of philosophy no better device has ever been found for sensitizing us to the possibility that commonplaces may reveal absurdities and hence to the need for re-examining even the best entrenched and most plausible. (378)

Paradox and ambiguity have always stood in the way of *effective* action, a course deemed desirable by Westerners. Whatever the motive—financial profit, personal advancement, gender dominance—Westerners have found it necessary to dissolve and/or ignore ambiguities and paradoxes before setting out on praxis's road. The unfortunate thing has been, as Nietzsche notes, that "instead of seeing in logic and the categories of reason means toward the adjustment of the world for utilitarian ends (basically, toward an expedient *falsification*), one believed one possessed in them the criterion of truth and *reality*" (314–15).

Richard Nixon, the protagonist of Coover's *The Public Burning*, hates both dialectics and paradox, seeing in them an inducement to indecision and paralysis. To be effective, one must reduce, one must choose. In the view of the character, the genius of the American spirit allows the native son to be objective, to choose the *correct* course, the *true* course. A lengthy reflection of Nixon in *The Public Burning* merits quotation:

> What was fact, what intent, what was framework, what was essence? Strange, the impact of History, the grip it had on us, yet

it was nothing but words. Accidental accretions for the most part, leaving most of the story out. We have not yet begun to explore the true power of the Word, I thought. What if we broke all the rules, played games with evidence, manipulated language itself, made History, a partisan ally? . . . I love to debate both sides of any issue, but thinking about that strange space in between made me sweat. Paradox was the one thing I hated more than psychiatrists and lady journalists. Fortunately, I knew, I'd forget most of this—these errant insights always fled and something more solid, more solid, more *legal,* sooner or later took over. I'd find the right question, take a side, and feel on top of things. Gain perspective. Courage, Confidence, Perspective. . . . (136)

The problem with choice, of course, is that it excludes, often arbitrarily and unfairly. Choice inspires difference and dichotomy. In gender relations, choice can breed arrogance and disdain, the privileging, for example, of the interests of one gender over those of the other.

In *Spanking the Maid,* the deconstruction of epistemology and language illustrates how a world without univocal truths might appear to those with expectations of order and univocity. The maid and master (not to mention the reader) experience anxiety and insecurity. The use of paradox and ambiguity as ordering principles—narratorial, epistemological—remains novel, the accompanying experience of ontological uncertainty an as yet uncomfortable one. The novella shows, however, at least for the patient reader, that, once initial expectations of order and closure are revised, if not overthrown, paradox can be productive.

Men and women exhibit fundamental similarities and differences that must be respected. *Spanking the Maid* demonstrates that convictions of male superiority are based on tenuous epistemological grounds. *Spanking the Maid* affronts a distinctively Western sensibility that metaphysics yields *knowledge,* that bequest of hypotheses, inductions, deductions that orders and stabilizes the diffuse and disparate in human experience. Promoting a healthy skepticism (rather than outright Pyrrhonism), *Spanking the Maid* emphasizes (*unambiguously?*), like other postmodern fictions, the contrived nature of understanding, its "homemade," perspectival quality. The novella concludes with a riotous scene of epistemological displacement. The master's psyche floats freely among the realms of the ontic, the somnambulant, and the oneiric. Homonymity and paradox abound. Focus shifts vertiginously throughout, but no more so than in the highly contorted final sentence:

> "What? WHAT-?! An answering back to a reproof?" he inquires, taunting her with that civility and kindness due an inferior, as—hiss-WHAP!—flicking lint off one shoulder and smoothing the ends of his moustache with involuntary vertical and horizontal motions, he floats helplessly backward ("Thank you, sir!"), twitching amicably yet authoritatively like a damp towel, down a bottomless hole, relieving himself noisily: *Perhaps today then . . . at last!*" (101–2)

His orderly appearance—product of his fastidious preening—contrasts incongruously, ironically, with his disorderly state of mind. The master finds himself in a "bottomless hole," an epistemological *mise en abyme,* forever seeking a stable basis for knowing, for perfection—and forever stymied. Whatever possibilities the master-maid scenario had for pornographic titillation, these have long since dissipated. Master and maid wallow in a state of emotional and philosophical funk, victims of a metaphysics that bears no relation to the protean world in which they live, victims of an "inferior fiction."

Spanking the Maid offers us a blank page on which to write our own views on gender relations. There is no one in the novella to do it for us. For the postmodernist, the author is no Shelleyean man-god; literature is not tractarian. If *Spanking the Maid* teaches us anything, and obviously I think it can, it does so through parody and negative analogy. The relationship between master and maid fails because each defines self and other as an essence: man is essentially superior, woman inferior. But, as Nietzsche tells us in *The Will to Power,* "the essence of a thing is only an *opinion* about the 'thing',", and the experiences of master and maid do not confirm their essentialistic biases (302). The lesson for us here is an obvious one. Stereotypification is an expedient lie that wrongs both agent and subject. Two Adrienne Rich poems capture well the pressures that gender stereotyping places upon both women and men. "Aunt Jennifer's Tigers" describes a frustrated housewife with artistic talents who finds her marriage stultifying. Her only chance for self-expression lies in needlework; she is only able to experience freedom vicariously through the subjects of one of her projects, tigers. "Aunt Jennifer's Tigers" offers a rather conventional depiction of female subjugation. What is less typical is Rich's portrayal of the fate man suffers through the same stereotyping process. In "The Knight," the protagonist rides off into battle. The first stanza shows a proud, fearless warrior, invulnerable in his highly decorated mail. The second stanza deals not with regal appearances but with real panic and despair. Only the knight's "eye" is living, it "a lump of bitter jelly / set in a metal mask"; the knight's mail conceals nerves worn "to ribbons / under the radiant casque" (44). The third and final octave asks questions similar to those posed implicitly throughout *Spanking the Maid:* what will "unhorse" the knight? who will release him from the tyrannical rule of gender stereotyping? The knight, like Aunt Jennifer, and like the master and the maid, is compelled to perform in an unnatural way simply because of his gender. He cannot express his terror; he cannot seek refuge in his own humanity or in the human community at large. Fixed within a traditional gender ideology, he must act out his fate in a "manly" way, to all appearances inhumanly unconcerned and even unaware of his pending doom. Like many of Rich's poems, Coover's *Spanking the Maid* seeks to liberate the reader, to "unhorse" him or her from the morally and emotionally uncomfortable seat of gender discrimination. We number the latter among those fictions that have outlived "their usefulness," as Coover says, that "disturb life in some unnecessary way, and so it becomes necessary to break them up and perhaps change their force" (Gado, 152).

6

Auto-Bio-Graphy as Metafiction:
Peter Handke's *A Sorrow Beyond Dreams*

TYPICALLY, CONTEMPORARY METAFICTION has primarily dealt with a world of fictive events. The author—either directly or through a persona—reflects on the "made" or "constructed" quality of his or her fictional realm, dispelling notions of narrative omniscience and epistemological apodicticity as the fiction progresses. The reader infers that his or her own world resists definitive description in much the same way. Peter Handke, the contemporary Austrian poet-novelist-playwright-essayist, endorses such a view in *A Sorrow Beyond Dreams* (*Wunschloses Unglück*) and elsewhere.[1] His point of departure in this novella is not, however, a "fictional world" per se but rather personal history. Handke's subject matter would seem to distance him from metafictional considerations. After all, what have biography, autobiography, and history, in general, to do with imaginative literature? The response Handke fashions to these questions will be the subject of the present inquiry.

Though he has been long heralded in western Europe, critics in the United States—and not just Germanists—are now coming to regard Handke as one of the more gifted experimental authors writing today and one who largely concurs with American postmodern attitudes on history, epistemology, and fictional narrative. Prior to discussing *A Sorrow Beyond Dreams* as exemplary of the Handke opus, it will be helpful to place Handke's work within the context of contemporary narrativist historiography and "nonfiction fiction." In my view, Handke's work takes on new significance when located within a comparative frame of reference. *A Sorrow Beyond Dreams* is an important work, one that will prove instructive to readers interested in postmodern philosophy and narrative theory.

While sharing with other postmodernists a preoccupation with self-reference and generic redefinition, Handke's concern with the ethical implications of language usage is perhaps more serious and more urgent than that exhibited by many of his peers. Like many twentieth-century thinkers—his fellow Austrians Robert Musil and Wittgenstein, for example—Handke sees in language the operation of "invisible" social codes. In his fictions, plays, and poetry, Handke seeks to unmask the subtle, often insidious powers of language. *A Sorrow Beyond Dreams* is especially resonant today in two respects. Generally speaking, it investigates language as an (strong-) arm of coercive ideology. More specifically, it explores how language assists in society's subjection of women to sexist biases. In making himself and his reader more sensitive to the conceptual oppression language often effects, Handke opens up language usage to the possibility of a constructive revision. Revision, herein, entails a critique of "automatic language," that battery of axioms and idioms that is all too frequently our first refuge in moments of moral and intellectual lassitude.

Passivity and conformity have always been the enemy for Handke. His writing reveals nothing so much as a private appropriation of the contemporary literary tradition, as an *existentializing* of literary forms. An influence study would detail at length Handke's debt to Kafka and Camus in *Die linkshändige Frau* (1976) and *Die Stunde der wahren Empfindung* (1975); to Camus (*L'Étranger*) and Robbe-Grillet (*Le Voyeur*) in *Die Angst des Tormanns beim Elfmeter* (1970); to the theater of the absurd in *Kaspar* (1968) and *Der Ritt über den Bodensee* (1970); to the bildungsroman tradition in *Der kurze Brief zum langen Abschied* (1972).[2] Finally, however, the influence study could not fail to remark upon the originality of language, the subtle extension of conventions, and the fierce intellectual integrity that invest these works. These same qualities characterize *A Sorrow Beyond Dreams,* a work in which the author at once defines and exceeds the limits of traditional biography and autobiography.

Beyond fiction, beyond fact

A Sorrow Beyond Dreams is a meditation on the powers and limits of language to construct meaning. The novella-length study records the author's emotional and intellectual reactions to his mother's life and suicide, what he calls her *Freitod*—her freely willed death.[3] Typically, a biographer assumes a stance vis-à-vis his or her subject somewhere between enthusiastic engagement and dispassionate objectivity, the aim being to garner the reader's interest without sacrificing the illusion of critical inquiry. Handke's, contrary to this kind of unambiguous biographical project, embraces a multifurcated perspective. In *A Sorrow Beyond Dreams*, he acknowledges a complex of motivating factors that take him far beyond the generic confines of the biography form; he lists the following as "justifications" for the work: as an "insider," he is in the best position to tell the story of his mother's life (and death); the act of writing is, for himself, therapeutic; and he wishes to privilege his mother's story, to represent it as an "exemplary case."[4]

The first of these motivations would seem to put Handke in league with traditional biographers who, implicitly or otherwise, purport to capture something like the "essence" of their subject in the course of their research. Handke, however, defining auto-bio-graphy as a private reading of event, stands in an ironic relationship to the genres of autobiography and biography. He does not aim at a delineation of objective correspondences in *A Sorrow Beyond Dreams*. Text is neither a slice-of-life nor a crude reflection of onticity; text is merely a faint representation, partial and temporary. In *A Sorrow Beyond Dreams*, the objectivist's confidence in ratiocination and empiricism—typical of biography and, to a lesser extent, of autobiography as well—conflicts directly with an ironic mode that posits relative (or even absolute) uncertainty as the surety of *truth*. "Truth" has become insubstantial, existing only at the intersection of assertion and counterassertion, at a level of dialectical debate on the very impossibility of truth. Handke feels a filial and creative need to depict his mother verbally and yet declares openly his incapacity to achieve this goal. Through his self-reflexive mode of representation, his metafictional self-consciousness, Handke admits himself to be a "liar," a dissimulator, yet, paradoxically achieves something more than dissimulation through his admission.

There has emerged, of late, in the philosophy of history the view that historiography does, like imaginative literature, manipulate rhetorical tropes, that the historian imposes a narrative structure upon event as he or she writes history. The manipulation of tropes and the consequent narrativization of history determine a historian's understanding of his or her subject. In his *Metahistory*, Hayden White details at length the operation of certain tropes in nineteenth-century historiography, e.g., metonymy in Marx, metaphor in Nietzsche, irony in Croce. Like the novelist, the historian must establish, White asserts elsewhere, both extratextual correspondence (i.e., real-world referentiality) and intratextual coherence (i.e., narrative consistency)— "history is no less a form of fiction than the novel is a form of historical representation" ("The Fictions of Factual Representation," 23). Form and content are reciprocally influential in the writing of history—an uncontroversial point in postmodern criticism but one that continues to inspire hot debate among historians and philosophers of history. The narrativist school of historiography—and we can count Danto, Dray, Gallie, and White among its more prominent members—emphasizes the *fictional* quality of all history.[5] *History* only begins when the historian, having sifted through a plethora of "facts," gives shape to them through the processes of selection and storytelling. And, as White points out, all narrative discourse projects value:

> If every fully realized story, however we define that familiar but conceptually elusive entity, is a kind of allegory, points to a moral, or endows events, whether real or imaginary, with a significance that they do not possess as mere sequence, then it seems possible to conclude that every historical narrative has as its latent or manifest purpose the desire to *moralize* the events of which it treats. ("The Value of Narrativity," 17–18)

A Sorrow Beyond Dreams is a very self-conscious exercise in narrativist historiography. Handke accepts, indeed celebrates, the view that the creation of narrative discourse brings one into a personal, highly individuated relationship to event. It remains the ethical responsibility of the writer to determine a mode of discourse appropriate to the phenomena under review. In *A Sorrow Beyond Dreams*, he ruminates on the narrative strategies open to him. *A Sorrow Beyond Dreams*, as metahistory, as metafiction, discards the traditional fact–fiction dichotomy. Through its halting, often pointillistic description, through essayistic digressions on language and narrative form, the novella portrays the capacity of verbal constructs to at once defile and define the human condition.

In *A Sorrow Beyond Dreams*, Handke, perhaps the most Gallic of prominent German-language writers today, extends the French tradition of the memoir novel. Proust's *À la recherche du temps perdu* and Céline's *Voyage au bout de la nuit* are, stripped bare of certain novelistic conventions, essentially autobiographical. Sartre's sainted Genet, as a function of his radically antinomian ethics, discards the minimal illusionism of Proust and Céline in *The Thief's Journal (Journal du voleur)*. Fact–fiction distinctions are no longer of any import. Declares Genet in a metafictional aside in his *Journal:*

> We know that our language is incapable of recalling even the pale reflection of these bygone, foreign states. The same would be true of this entire journal if it were to be the notion of what I was. I shall therefore make clear that it is meant to indicate what I am today, as I write it. It is not a quest of time gone by, but a work of art whose pretext-subject is my former life. It will be a present fixed with the help of the past, and vice versa. Let the reader therefore understand that the facts were what I say they were, but the interpretation that I give them is what I am— now. (71)

The distinctions formerly apparent between memoir and prose fiction no longer hold sway. Burroughs in *Junkie* and the more subjective of the "New Journalists"—Mailer and Hunter S. Thompson, for example—similarly ignore traditional generic distinctions that separate fact and fiction, historical narrative and imaginative literature.

In contrast to those metafictionists who boast of their cleverness to the reader—an inclination apparent from time to time, for instance, in the work of Sukenick and Federman—Handke remains considerably less self-assured and, in his own view, less conforming. Notes Handke,

> I'm sick of those passages in our work that refer however suavely to how the work is being made or how it should be made although in a broader sense I still deal with the self-referential condominiums. The former seems to be at this point like nothing more than another dull literary convention to be purged. (Quoted in Klinkowitz, "Aspects of Handke: Fiction," 416)[6]

Through canonization and overuse (the same thing, Handke would probably argue), self-reflexivity has, to some degree, lost its intellectual resonance, has become faddish and mannered. As a narrative convention, it threatens to become a cliché. Handke, of course, has been long devoted to the denigration of accepted norms. His famous attack on the *Gruppe 47* at Princeton in 1965 served notice that he would not be influenced by the realist aesthetics and *engagement* that had dominated German literature since the end of the war.[7] Handke's Princeton speech established him as an early exponent of *neue Subjektivität* ("new subjectivity") in German language and letters.[8] Heavily influenced by existentialism, Handke has maintained, with doctrinaire rigidity, the primacy of the individual. Though his alteration of generic conventions, especially in his drama, leaves him open to the charge of formalism, the entirety of Handke's corpus aims at real-world referentiality, at achieving the intersubjectivity necessary for the moral education of the reader. Handke refuses, however, to see his writings as oracular discourse. The plays, the novels, even his essays, reveal the tentative probings of an inquisitive mind struggling to make *personal* sense of life. Literature provides Handke, first and foremost, an opportunity for self-discovery. Thus, in *Der Hausierer* (1967), Handke, exploring the limits of the detective novel, takes himself (and the reader) into the hidden recesses of human consciousness where sense perceptions are recorded and appraised. The plays extend the Brechtian program of audience alienation—not, however, in the interests of political agitation but in those of increased self-awareness. In *Offending the Audience* (*Publikumsbeschimpfung*), an early *Sprechstück*—an undramatized audience dialogue devoid of "theatricality"—the players openly bait the audience, demanding that every individual viewer take on an active posture, both as theatergoer and *Mensch:*

> No actions take place here. You feel the discomfort of being watched and addressed, since you came prepared to watch and make yourselves comfortable in the shelter of the dark. Your presence is every moment explicitly acknowledged with every one of our words. Your presence is the optic we deal with from one breath to the next, from one moment to the next, from one word to the next. Your standard idea of the theatre is no longer presupposed as the basis of your actions. You are neither condemned to watch nor free to watch. You are the subject. You are the play-makers. (*Offending the Audience*, 19–20)

Auto-Bio-Graphy as metafiction

Though metafictionality advances a critique of literary form, its ramifications are not confined to the purely formal or the purely literary.
Metafictionality, in its more profound forms, questions the grounds
we have for claiming *to know* and *to understand*. Not unexpectedly, in
our highly self-conscious postmodern age, epistemological inquiry
has not remained the concern of a small group of experimental novelists. The roll of contemporary metafictionists continues to grow and
includes writers working in such diverse traditions as science fiction—
Ursula Le Guin (*The Left Hand of Darkness*) and Samuel Delany (*Tri-
ton*)—the socialist novel—Ulrich Plenzdorf (*Die neuen Leiden des jungen W.*) and Jurek Becker (*Jakob der Lügner* and *Irreführung des Behörder*)—and, with Handke, both biography and autobiography.[9]

Language has long served as a means to epistemological insight for
Handke. In an autobiographical essay, Handke acknowledges that, as
a schoolboy writing descriptive essays, he first became aware of the
formative role language plays in our construction of a world view:

> When I was supposed to describe an experience, I didn't write
> about the experience as I had experienced it. Rather the expe-
> rience about which I was writing changed itself or often came
> into existence for the first time through the writing of sentences
> about it, and certainly through the sentence models that people
> had taught me: Even a specific experience seemed to me differ-
> ent when I had written a sentence about it. (*Ich bin ein Bewohner
> des Elfenbeinturms*, 13–14; my translation)

Through language, one (re-)negotiates one's subjectivity. For Handke,
one only understands after one has constructed a narrative, after one
has told a story about an event or experience. Narrative construction,
when proceeding according to collective views of language usage and
storytelling, yields a meaning consonant with that of the collectivity.
The effacement of self becomes an unavoidable consequence for
those who fail to shape their experiences in *personally* meaningful
ways. Handke accepts a proposition fundamental to existentialist ethics—one must choose oneself for oneself. In *A Sorrow Beyond Dreams*,
Handke manipulates the classical narratorial perspectives of *mimesis*
and *diegesis*. At the level of biography and memoir, the author illus-

trates or *shows* his response to his mother's life and death; at the level of metafiction and meta-auto-bio-graphy, he delineates or *tells* the operation of self-choice that leads to the particular meaning he assigns to his mother's tragic existence.

In Handke's view, the construction of narrative must be a highly self-conscious act if one is to avoid the tyranny of "mass-speak" and "mass-truth." Since, as Werner Thuswalder rightly points out in his Handke study, language embodies the interests and biases of a culture, the cultural critic must also be a critic of language (79). The investigation of language and literary form is an investigation of collective attitudes. The formal novelty of Handke's work (the above "influences" duly noted) merely attests to the novelty of life. Old forms remain insensitive to the novelty of quotidian phenomena. Writing in his by now famous essay "Ich bin ein Bewohner des Elfenbeinturms," Handke describes the significance literature holds for him:

> I expect from the literary work some news for myself, something that changes me, if only a little, something that makes me aware of a not yet thought, a not yet conscious *possibility* of reality, that makes me aware of a new possibility to see, to speak, to think, to exist. (*Ich bin ein Bewohner des Elfenbeinturms,* 19–20; my translation)

Through questioning traditional patterns of storytelling (e.g., Aristotelian illusionism in drama, objective biography, the bildungsroman), Handke sets an example for the reader who, though probably not an imaginative writer, must, like Handke, involve himself or herself imaginatively in his or her own personal experiences if they are to have personal significance and personal appeal. All of Handke's literary efforts are autobiographical, are acts of self-exploration:

> I have only one theme: to become clear, clearer about myself, to get to know myself or not get to know myself, to learn what I am doing falsely, what I am thinking falsely, what I say without reflection, what I say automatically, also what others do, think, speak without reflection: to become attentive and to make attentive: to make and to become more sensible, sensitive, and exact so that I and also others can exist more exactly and sensibly, so

that I can communicate better with others and interact better with them. (*Ich bin ein Bewohner des Elfenbeinturms,* 26; my translation)

Through narrativization, Handke comes to terms with his own existence.

Narration is, for Handke, a way to humanize human being. It is not primarily a literary event but rather a primordial response to being. When language and literary conventions are appropriated self-consciously and critically, they allow one to define and assert one's identity. In *A Sorrow Beyond Dreams* Handke establishes the living relationship that exists between *fictional* and *historical* narratives. Notwithstanding the highly personal, even private, subject matter, despite his frequent essayistic digressions on narrative aesthetics, *A Sorrow Beyond Dreams* has broadly relevant social and philosophical implications.[10] The novella exceeds the apparent solipsism of Handke's very personal family portrait; it is more than a purely "literary" enterprise, though its dissections of narrative praxis and genre theory are, in themselves, important. His narrative aesthetics concurs with that of Ricoeur, which asserts that "the work-world of narratives is always a temporal world. In other words, time becomes human time to the extent that it is articulated in a narrative way, and narratives make sense to the extent that they become conditions of temporal existence" ("Narrative and Hermeneutics," 149).

A Sorrow Beyond Dreams: *The story of a life, the life of a story*

As metafiction, *A Sorrow Beyond Dreams* gives two essential issues—one literary, one epistemological—a problematic cast. What are the grounds of human knowledge? How effective is language in conveying such knowledge? Actually, the two issues do not exist separately but together as aspects of humanity's ceaseless inquiry into the nature of truth. A statement by Handke early in the novella echoes these two concerns: "I experienced moments of extreme speechlessness and needed to formulate them—the motive that has led men to write from time immemorial" (245/11). For Handke, a verbalizing talent serves as the necessary adjunct of knowledge and understanding. This is hardly new, of course; phenomenologists such as Heidegger and Gadamer have long asserted that language molds our powers of conceptualization and shapes our thoughts—in the words of Edmond Jabès, "You are the one who writes and the one who is written" (quoted in Kawin, 233). This awareness of language's partial dominion over us accounts, in part, for Handke's interest in verbal and generic experimentation. An ironic attitude toward language is, then, characteristic of Handke (and of many other postmodernists, one might add), who realizes that language must at once serve as midwife to his thoughts as well as the agent of the conformity and intellectual lassitude that he loathes. Writes Frank Kermode, "Hence for Handke language is what prevents us from being in the world as it is, a set of debilitating fictions. . . . Attack language, Handke seems to be saying, and you attack the root of evil" (21).

The capacity of language to enslave has three major reference points in *A Sorrow Beyond Dreams:* first, there is the moral bankruptcy that the instrumentalization of language has occasioned in Austrian and German society; second, there is the role language plays in the reification of Handke's mother; and, lastly, of most interest here, there are the problems of language and generic convention that the author himself wrestles with in the novella. Let us reflect upon each of these in turn to appreciate the full range of Handke's ironic metafictional perspective and to see how the author is capable, finally, of escaping the straitjackets of "mass-speak" and traditional literary form as he fashions a work of originality and compassion.

A Sorrow Beyond Dreams is a telling critique of middle-class values, both as practiced by the bourgeoisie and as imitated by the urban and rural poor. Except for brief membership in the Berlin working class, Frau Handke lives out her life among the poor craftsmen and peasantry of provincial Austria. Notwithstanding obvious differences, both social groups share an important feature—an intolerance of individuality. Despite short periods of individuation, of personal blooming, Frau Handke returns again and again to the "zero degree" of personality that social integration requires of her. In such a society, religious practice has become pure ritual, the mouthing of catechismal truths and pious phrases. Handke writes that "little remained of the human individual, and indeed, the word 'individual' was known only in pejorative combinations" (267/48). Language is reduced to mere instrumentality. In instrumentality, it gives up its expressive, individuating capacities; it becomes the tool of a culture's social and po-

litical self-reinforcement. The media manipulate this dehumanizing
potential in language. With the *Anschluss*, the rape of language becomes programmatic. The "Sieg Heil" becomes mandatory. The press
comes to embody more fully Benjamin's characterization of it as "the
theatre of the unbridled debasement of the word" (225). The radio,
as a major propaganda organ, markets as news the tired phrases of
fascist optimism; it inculcates in the populace an acceptance of Nazi
horrors, rendering injustice palatable through the artful marriage of
circumlocution and euphemism. And the people, never aware of language's ability to critique itself, its power to peel back the layers of
rhetoric and moral cant to expose a barren core, fall in line, beguiled
by the Sirens' song. And what was "politics"? asks Handke rhetorically.

> A meaningless word, because, from your schoolbooks on, every-
> thing connected with politics had been dished out in catchwords
> unrelated to any tangible reality and even such images as were
> used were devoid of human content: oppression as chains or
> boot heel, freedom as mountaintop, the economic system as
> a reassuringly smoking factory chimney or as a pipe enjoyed
> after the day's work, the social system as a descending lad-
> der: "Emperor-King-Nobleman-Burgher-Peasant-Weaver/Car-
> penter-Beggar-Gravedigger." (252–53/23–24)

The reduction of social praxis to schematized relations, to sentimental
role-playing, leaves a social organism devoid of vitality and inimical to
the interests of the individual. These, then, the Austrian *Dorf* and
postwar Berlin are the social ambiences in which Frau Handke moves.

Frau Handke's biography is the history of an individual's submission to the imperatives of the group. Ebullient and curious by nature,
she has allowed personal weakness and overpowering circumstance to
blunt her nobler instincts. The moral mediocrity of her social setting,
its chauvinism, its disdain for idiosyncrasy—all slowly stifle her spontaneity. Such a milieu consumes individuality. Frau Handke conforms; she dons the mask of anonymity. In Berlin, she mimics the
speech and manners of the hardened locals although she herself is
gentle and sensitive. She becomes typical, construing life in typical
terms, freeing herself "from her own history" (261/38). In her rela-

tionship with men, for example, "clichés are taken as binding rules and any *individual* reaction, which takes some account of an actual person, becomes a deviation" (261/39).

Frau Handke emulates the petty proprieties of the bourgeoisie, but, as Handke points out, bourgeois values do not insulate her from despair because she, being poor, lacks the material resources that give a hollow succor and some distraction to the middle-class matron. No, the life of the narrator's mother is founded on disjunctions. Her world view does not correspond to the material circumstances of her life. Her verbal address does not match her actual concerns and feelings. She does not live her own life but that of a socially determined mean; the question of *happiness* becomes for her, as for Auden's "unknown citizen," beside the point, absurd even. Menial tasks give her life what meaning it has and, in the long run, leave it quite devoid of all real meaning. For Frau Handke, time exists only as a ceaseless repetition of tedious routine:

Today was yesterday, yesterday was always. Another day behind you, another week gone, and Happy New Year. What will we have to eat tomorrow? Has the mailman come? What have you been doing around the house all day? (275/61)

The search for self-expression within the bounds of the socially permissible becomes Frau Handke's irresolvable dilemma. Ultimately, she becomes a person alienated both from self and society. Misery, mental illness, and suicide all come to characterize what Handke, in an ironic inversion of a common expression ("wunschlos glücklich sein"), calls her "sorrow beyond dreams."[11]

It is Handke's expressed objective in the novella to detail the existential failure of a noble woman, the causes of that failure, and its consequences. However, a measure of his honesty and sophistication, the author is very much aware of the pitfalls open to the biographer. There must exist, for example, a delicate balance between the description of particular aspects of his subject's life and generalizing statements that synthesize and render typical and symbolic these particularities. Handke as ironic narrator, as metafictionist, acknowledges in his reflexive commentary that literature invariably points in one of two directions—toward the concrete and descriptive or toward the abstract and symbolic. The former risks losing its reader when a welter of detail detracts from narrative interest, as every reader of Beckett knows. The author promises the reader more than purely local verisimilitude when taking up the pen. Conversely, and a point of special concern for Handke, a largely symbolic rendering of one's subject matter may leave a rather vapid *Tendenzroman* that may well have little to do with anything other than the author's philosophical speculations. The most serious problem connected with a symbolic-allegorical approach for Handke is that it would replicate, if in a different manner, the reification his mother suffers among her family and friends:

> The danger of all these abstractions and formulations is of course that they tend to become independent. When that happens, the individual that gave rise to them is forgotten—like images in a dream, phrases and sentences enter into a chain reaction, and the result is literary ritual in which an individual life ceases to be anything more than a pretext. (263/42)

The point of perfect equilibrium between the particular detail and the general truth becomes, in itself, an abstract impossibility, one that Handke himself is aware of. He admits as much to the reader, suggesting to the latter the careful scrutiny of the author's narrative aesthetic. Handke's discussion of narrative problems dispels the illusion put forth by much nonreflexive fiction—that fiction is not made but simply materializes out of thin air. Reflexivity is, of course, as much a matter of theme as one of form and certainly only one theme among many. It is, however, an important one for the postmodernist who is intent upon instilling in the reader a root suspicion of all that appears inevitable and "objective" in the literary work (and, indeed, in life itself). Handke demands that the reader subject his novella to the kind of critical awareness that he himself applies to the circumstances of his mother's life and to the circumstances surrounding his literary depiction of that life.

The limits of language and form

Handke admits to no Olympian perspective. He finds himself existentially involved as he writes. His "prejudice" cannot be overcome, nor is this desirable. It can, however, be acknowledged. His writing is first and foremost a project of self-discovery and only secondarily a commodity for vicarious appreciation. *A Sorrow Beyond Dreams* is as much his story as his mother's, as much autobiography as biography:

> I am only a *writer* and can't take the role of the *person written about,* such detachment is impossible. I can only move myself into the distance; my mother can never become for me, as I can for myself, a winged art object flying serenely through the air. She refuses to be isolated and remains unfathomable; my sentences crash in the darkness and lie scattered on the paper. (265/44)

Here, writing is necessarily ironic, a dissimulation of truth—a dissimulation that is not willed but fated. Humanity may be more than a collection of monads but its powers to penetrate into the deepest recesses of one another's souls have perceptual and verbal limits. But Handke, like many other twentieth-century writers, realizes that language is all there is, or, as a pop song has it, "words are all we have." So, as with Hofmannsthal in his Lord Chandos letter and Musil in *Törless,* who both actually extend language in their discussion of its limits and imperfection, or like Hemingway who, seeing "more" in "less," achieves a new range of expressivity through precision and economy, the narrator of *A Sorrow Beyond Dreams* enjoys a conditional victory over what might otherwise remain genuinely "speechless moments of terror" in his imperfect portrayal of them.

To extend the limits of language, to defer its tyranny over the individual, Handke resorts to various ploys. His dissection of bankrupt concepts has been explored briefly with reference to "politics." We might also consider the manner in which he ironically manipulates clichés.[12] Setting them off in uppercase print or inverted commas, he exposes their pretensions and vacuity. At the conclusion of the novella, he cites a trite graveside remark, placing it in quotation marks— " 'She took her secret to the grave' " (297/97). The narrator mocks this pious statement and its reluctance to penetrate into the tragic circumstances of his mother's life, its willingness to dispatch her to the realm of nonidentity with the wave of a colloquial wand. Handke himself must stand on guard against such an easy sentimentality. Curiously, something strange and vital occurs when the author disfigures the disfigurement language accomplishes through clichés and worn pieties.[13] His ironic verbal play liberates language, if only briefly, from the squalor of "mass-speak." As Karsten Harries points out, a cliché "functions as cliché only as long as it lulls the spectator into taking for granted what is presented. In recognizing a cliché for what it is we are already beyond it" (*Meaning*, 140).

Handke's suspicion of language is mirrored by his distrust of generic convention. *A Sorrow Beyond Dreams* eludes succinct generic definition. The novella, through Handke's self-reflexivity, merges a number of generic strains into a highly original pattern of discourse. Most obviously biography, the text shifts toward metabiography when the narrator takes up the problems connected with that genre. The novella, as mentioned earlier, is also an essay in autobiography and self-definition; yet, its self-reflexivity points beyond all conventional autobiography to an analysis of the possibilities of the autobiography form. Handke manipulates auto-bio-graphy (not to mention social and political history); he does, however, give little credit to two premises basic to "nonfictional" genres—that, one, objective exegesis is their legitimate goal and, two, that this goal is realizable. Echoing the thoughts of many postmodernists, the narrator wonders, "Isn't all formulation, even of things that have really happened, more or less a fiction?" (253/24). What the narrator says of Marlow in *Heart of Darkness* might be applied with equal justification to Handke. Truth has become insubstantial, less the "light" that generates illumination than the faint penumbra that enshrouds it.[14] Handke's only recourse is infinite description. The book ends with the promise to write something more on these themes at a later date.[15]

In the absence of apodictic truths, given the opacity of language, the author can only be an ironic metafictionist, a conscious dissimulator, a teller of incomplete truths at best. Handke's novella is, then, necessarily episodic and incomplete. It scrutinizes, with varying concentration, the circumstances of Frau Handke's life and the author's own concerns. *A Sorrow Beyond Dreams* is sometimes expansive, sometimes curt. Given its lack of measure and formula, its halting progression, the novella resembles a home-movie with Handke, the anxious projectionist, never quite managing to get everything in focus. And yet, notwithstanding this "homemade" quality, the author conveys the horror of his mother's life with sensitivity and conviction and perhaps

even accuracy. Handke purports a vague phenomenological awareness that "truth" resides more in an endless dialectical preoccupation
with formal and ontological possibilities than in traditional claims to
objective representation. Or, as Heidegger expresses it somewhat
more succinctly, "The work's becoming a work is a way in which truth
becomes and happens" (*Poetry, Language, Thought,* 60).

7

Intertextuality and *Mulligan Stew:*
In and (Never) Out of the Labyrinth

AT THE END OF *MULLIGAN STEW,* Sorrentino draws up a list of gifts to his friends. He does not neglect the reader: ". . . to all you other cats and chicks out there, sweet or otherwise, buried deep in wordy tombs, who never yet have walked off the page, a shake and a hug and a kiss and a drink. Cheers!" (445). There are easier ways to earn a beer but few as instructive for the student of the modern novel as staying the course with *Mulligan Stew.* A novel-within-a-novel, *Mulligan Stew's* metafictionality is enhanced by Sorrentino's wholesale appropriation of the conventions of the twentieth-century novel and his profanation of that great tradition. His major sources are, among very many other minor ones, Joyce, Fitzgerald, the long overlooked Flann O'Brien of *At-Swim-Two-Birds,* Nabokov, and, indeed, himself. In *Mulligan Stew* the reader confronts a complex and at times inscrutable array of cross-referencing—a kind of inter-/intratextual web—that threatens to trap him or her within a realm of "pure text," unable to draw out from the text the cognitive or mimetic significance that it, as a fine satire, contains. It is my purpose here to illustrate how its status as text—really, an intertextual system—allows the reader to infer something meaningful about the postmodern age in which we live.

Mulligan Stew, *intertextuality, and the lived-world*

Sorrentino establishes the theme of intertextuality even before the beginning of the fictional narrative. Between cover and title page, the reader finds a number of reviews and rejection letters that *Mulligan Stew* has purportedly inspired. Physically set off, this section is further distinguished from the main body of the novel by the color—blue, Sorrentino's favorite—and quality of its paper. The rejection letters reveal the capacity of text to generate new text, to found new intertextual relationships. Initially, the letters themselves seem to be actual responses from publishers. However, because the letters are signed by such luminaries of the fictional canon of characters as Yvonne Firmin (*Under the Volcano*), Flo(rence) Dowell (*The Good Soldier*), and Claude Estee (*The Day of the Locust*), the well-read reader discerns through the pretense of "pretext" the early rumblings of *intertextuality*, what Sorrentino calls "the mortal sin of bookishness" (*Mulligan Stew*, n. pag.). Before taking up a discussion of intertextuality as an organizing principle in *Mulligan Stew*, its usefulness as a methodological premise merits brief consideration.

Broadly defined, "intertextuality" collates nothing more than a number of critical commonplaces. Text, whether literary/fictive or expository/nonfictive, responds to an ever evolving system of conventions. Texts do not arise *ex vacuo*. Notwithstanding the most radical experimentation, no verbally expressive phenomenon can claim absolute originality, i.e., the status of an *Ur-text*. Language is always social, and hence contractual. Eliot addresses these issues in "Tradition and the Individual Talent" when he writes:

> No poet, no artist of any art, has his complete meaning alone. His significance, his appreciation is the appreciation of his relation to the dead poets and artists. You cannot value him alone; you must set him, for comparison and contrast, among the dead, I mean this as a principle of aesthetic, not merely historical, criticism. (784)

Conceptually, intertextuality presents few problems for the contemporary critic skilled in genre theory, thematic exegesis, influence studies, and semiotics. Each of these critical orientations posits intertextual relations. Each, at its best, sheds light on correspondences and oppositions among texts. A recurring drawback of each, however, has been a frequent incapacity or unwillingness to discuss the relationship of the literary artifact to the lived-world. The critic who valorizes intra-literary studies, who ignores the intentionality of literary representation and the implicit epistemological and ethical claims of literary form, maintains, whether by program or default, the autonomy of art.

Culler, in summarizing the critical strategies of intertextuality, suggests the need for a synthesis of various critical approaches. As he points out, while the linguistic interests of Kristeva, Bloom's "misreading" thesis, and Barthes' concept of text as "infinite and anonymous citations" all have something to contribute to the study of intertextuality, none in itself is particularly concerned with the broader extraliterary, extralinguistic implications of intertextuality as a literary theme ("Presupposition and Intertextuality," 100–18).[1] *Mulligan Stew* is, as one reader puts it, "a primer for the reading of novels," and an ability to identify even a few of Sorrentino's many intertextual references would certainly indicate a kind of technical competence on the part of the reader (J. O'Brien, "Every Man," 63). It is important, however, to go beyond the mere identification of influences and sources. Certainly Bakhtin, to whom I shall presently turn for methodological insight, successfully links narrative strategies to both the author's moral and social concerns.

Quite obviously *Mulligan Stew* is more than a mere formal exercise in which Sorrentino recapitulates the narrative conventions of other twentieth-century novelists. In bringing together facets of this tradition, Sorrentino at once confirms and extends it. Though the importance of *Mulligan Stew* as critical commentary on novel-writing should not be overlooked, the novel, like others that make intertextuality a major theme—*Ulysses, Ada, Die neuen Leiden des jungen W., If on a winter's night a traveler,* for example—has a satirical bent that extends beyond matters of a purely literary ken. In their concern for charting literary influences and tropological play, in themselves entertaining in *Mulligan Stew,* critics have frequently ignored the cognitive import borne by the novel's satire—its critique of literary reception in the consumer, publishing, and academic domains, notably.

The limited response that Sorrentino's work has generated is characterized by formalistic preoccupations and a strong publicistic bent. There are several reasons for this kind of reception. Readers have been legitimately concerned with making the technical virtuosity of Sorrentino's work better known. This, in itself, is constructive. Clearly, the very intricate patterns of Sorrentino's intertextual tapestry deserve patient study. Such scholarly efforts contribute to canon revision, an important task when considering materials as rich and variegated as postmodern fiction. However, the early reception of Sorrentino's work has largely neglected its satirical commentary.[2] Sorrentino himself has on occasion abetted a critical reading that divorces his work from its cultural context. Indeed, the internal contradictions we found prevalent in the ontologies of the literary work put forward by Gass and Sukenick are all present in Sorrentino's notion of what a literary work *is*.

The radical rhetoric of the early O'Brien interview is perhaps the understandable self-indulgence of a man aggravated by the appreciation and acclaim many of his by-no-means-superior contemporaries have received:

> The work of a novelist such as John Gardner or William Styron or James Baldwin is clotted, thick, and graceless . . . it's intent upon getting a story across to you so that you will be moved or warmed, it's clearly rubbish. . . . when you come across a Styron, a Baldwin, a Mailer, the popular writers of our time, your expectations are fulfilled. You are being given the wisdom of Norman Mailer's enormous experience of the world; you are not being given literature. ("An Interview," 21–22)

Claims such as these, when not integrated with some of Sorrentino's more socially engaged self-commentary, give the impression of a solipsistic creative will spinning out nonrepresentational prose. An opinion offered in another interview, this time with Dennis Barone, undermines these autonomist sentiments:

> Artists must confront the fact that they live in this particular world. They should use the very materials of this terrifying world in order to make an art which replies to this world. You cannot make the world any better for yourself or for anyone else by harking back to the time of the glorious primitive. (236–37)

Here, of course, Sorrentino emphasizes the social role of the artist as well as the real-world referentiality of his work. This statement suggests, unambiguously enough, that the writer is not socially superfluous in Sorrentino's view. The obvious implication here is that, notwithstanding the degree to which one's writing ameliorates the human condition, it is important to try.

Perhaps the clearest articulation of his ontology of the literary work—though not entirely free of ambiguity—comes in Sorrentino's William Carlos Williams essay where he claims the following:

> The novel must exist outside of the life it deals with; it is not an imitation. The novel is an invention, something that is made; it is not the expression of "self"; it does not mirror reality. If it is any good at all it mirrors the processes of the real, but, being selective, makes a form that allows us to see these processes with clarity. (*Something Said*, 26)

Here, Sorrentino both denies and corroborates the view that fiction has any links with the world. Without clearly identifying the dialecticality of his position, Sorrentino suggests, correctly in my view, that the novel is both imitative and performative, that it at once "mirrors" reality or, better, the "processes of the real" and shapes them. Clearly, the "processes of the real" refers not to some obvious empirical reality but to discernible constituents of a Schützian lived-world, to modes of knowledge for example, to patterns of behavior, to language itself.

As a linguistic construction, Sorrentino's fiction responds positively and negatively to the "prejudices" that language and, more to the point here, the conventions of genre manifest. The manner in which Sorrentino develops language and structure in the novel presupposes personal ethical and epistemological codes. While his narrative strategies may obscure these codes, a careful analysis of their operation reveals a rather trenchant cultural critique at the heart of the novel. By wrapping itself securely, hyperbolically, in conventionality, *Mulligan Stew* points out the artistic and philosophical pretensions of various "better" authors as well as the sterility of the highly schematized genres of *Trivialliteratur*. In *Mulligan Stew*, through a *reductio ad absurdum*, Sorrentino shows how an endless shuffling and reshuffling of dated viewpoints can only produce intellectual and aesthetic malaise. Like the author in his or her fiction, the reader, in life, must fashion a world view. If the reader chooses to emulate the standards and values of others uncritically, he or she stands the risk of constructing a slapdash, antiquated view of the world on the model of *Mulligan Stew*, a work that rejects immediacy for the comfort of established norms. For Sorrentino, there is an ethical imperative to be true to oneself. In choosing to construct a parody that mocks all notions of proportion and balance, he fixes his own antinomian course through the world of generic convention. Analogously, the reader should rely upon personal insight and intuition in shaping a response to his or her own existential condition.

In the labyrinth

Mulligan Stew is a highly imaginative satire on the conditions of artistic production in a market economy. Catering to unrefined mass tastes, editors promote literature that has narrative interest, charismatic characterizations, and pornographic appeal.[3] In *Mulligan Stew*, these are the key features of the commercially successful fiction of Dermot Trellis, a principal foe of the protagonist, Antony Lamont. Further, these are features that Lamont, his highbrow pretensions notwithstanding, apes in his pursuit of popular acclaim. The New York publishing world (with certain obvious exceptions such as Grove, the publisher of *Mulligan Stew* and for whom Sorrentino has worked as an editor) often chooses to meet the minimal demands of the "average" reader (and the major demands of the shareholder) rather than promoting interest in genuinely creative literature.[4] The indulgence of crude literary tastes only further retards the possibility that serious literature will have a serious impact on any but a narrow coterie of readers. This indeed has been Sorrentino's fate. *Mulligan Stew* masterfully manipulates the hackneyed, outdated narrative strategies that hack authors and their profit-motivated editors continue to foist upon an all too innocent public.[5] Generally, publishers promote works that most fully satisfy the expectations of a mass, generally unlettered readership. And, it is worthy of mention, *Mulligan Stew* and Coover's *The Public Burning*, arguably two of the more significant novels of the seventies and authored by mature, well-known writers, had difficulty finding publishers.

By the time the reader—suspecting or not—reaches page one of *Mulligan Stew*, he or she is well within Sorrentino's intertextual labyrinth. I have mentioned the letters that introduce the reader both to the novel and to the critical acuity of Flo Dowell, Claude Estee, et al. Sorrentino dedicates his novel to Brian O'Nolan, a master intertextualist, an author whose experimental fiction forms a bridge between the high modernism of *Ulysses* and the mature postmodernism of *Mulligan Stew* itself.[6] Prefatory quotations from Flann O'Brien (a Brian

O'Nolan *nom de plume*) and Joyce presage further appropriations in the novel. The title at once suggests Stephen Dedalus's friend, Buck Mulligan, and mimes the accent and syllabification of *Finnegans Wake* (though the Saxon genitive is suppressed).[7]

A "Chinese box" structure, *Mulligan Stew* starts off with two Chapter 1's—the first untitled, the second called "Fallen Lucifers." The untitled Chapter 1 introduces the reader to a variety of texts, fictional and documentary. In a halting, awkward manner, one Martin Halpin narrates a short passage of fictional prose. In addition to this borrowed, footnoted personage from *Finnegans Wake*, the emergent love triangle involves none other than Daisy Buchanan—here, as elsewhere, the flighty wife of the very masculine Tom Buchanan—and Ned Beaumont (of Dashiell Hammett's *The Glass Key*).[8] The narrator further suggests Fitzgerald through the choice of phrases and diction that bring to mind the titles of the latter's major fiction: "tycoon," "beautiful in an unearthly way" (i.e., "paradise"), the repeated "a damned soul," and the counterpointing of "damned" and "beautiful" (1–3). To the intertextual chords that are struck through his various borrowings, Halpin contributes an intratextual echo by mentioning Horace Rosette, the author of one of the pre-textual reviews. The section concludes with a sentence that employs a parenthetical aside in the manner of Nabokov: "It was Corrie Corriendo and Berthe Delamode, implausible names (implausible women!) if I ever heard them . . ." (3).

In addition to the fictional text, the untitled Chapter 1 includes letters from Antony Lamont (author of the above-noted Halpin narrative) to his sister Sheila, wife of Dermot Trellis, and to a Professor Roche in addition to an excerpt from "Lamont's Notebook" that discusses narrative strategies for his as yet unnamed novel. The notebook excerpt includes more "textuality" in the form of an excerpt from an earlier Lamont novel, *Baltimore Chop*. The letter to Roche details Lamont's willingness to have his works included in the professor's course in the "American experimental novel," a literary tradition that, Lamont assumes, includes himself and that he characterizes as "a kind of elaborate jigsaw puzzle, whose image does not appear whole until the entire history of such novels is traced meticulously" (4). The letters themselves bear out Lamont's assertion. They refer to texts such as an earlier Lamont "classic," *Fretwork* (suggestive of Sorrentino's *Steelwork*), that in one way or another serve as intertextual reference points for the reader, however vague. Clive Sollis, more booty from the *Wake,* figures as a character in *Fretwork.* Clearly, Sorrentino's novel covers a good deal of ground in its first eight pages. One sees in the first chapter the "layering" of texts that characterizes the novel as a whole and induces in the reader a strong sense of displacement, even vertigo. Text invariably refers to text; text compels the reader to share in its retrospections on its textual antecedents. The reader receives no "baseline" information by which to assess the claims made in the various documentary texts, e.g., notebooks, letters, excerpted materials. The text compels the reader to reflect upon the act of reading, to become self-critical in the interpretation of the text.

In his second letter to Professor Roche, Lamont offers an autocritique of his "work-in-progress":

> . . . I'm at work on a new novel, another first-person narrative, but this one with a real *persona,* a man who doesn't know what he is doing, or, for that matter, what he *has* done. I'm afraid that I'm having trouble with it, and am casting about for the correct "tone" to give this voice. The working title is *Guinea Red,* the vulgarity of the same being rescued by the ambiguity that the structure of the book will ultimately lend to it. (7)

His reflections bring to mind the problems Sorrentino confronts. Should he include an authorial persona, a positive figure to draw back the opaque curtains of intertextuality occasionally for the reader? And what about tone? Will a consistently parodic pitch ultimately dull the reader's sensitivity to the issues at hand, i.e., slavery of the intellect and philistinism? Will the allusion to Joyce in the title suggest to the reader the importance of the book's structure? Will it become clear that, while Sorrentino's montage necessarily mimes the hack's techniques, the self-consciousness of its mimicry separates it from pulp fiction? The parodist does indeed play with fire. One can easily be consumed by the shortcomings one seeks to parody. Or, if not properly keynoted, one's parody may pass for "straight" writing. Of *Mulligan Stew,* Sorrentino notes:

> You have to read a while to see that "I" am not writing this; it's the bad prose of somebody else. Also, it can be bad prose written in such a way that it can become good; for instance, mis-

takes made in order to make the line comic or ludicrous. Bad
prose, however, that is intended to be serious is usually identifiable, maybe not in a line, but in a page. (J. O'Brien, "An Interview," 21)

Here, quite clearly viewing his parody from a production point of
view, Sorrentino assumes the competence of his parody (an assumption I shall qualify in my conclusion). The reader's task remains to
identify the parodic elements of the novel and to draw out their mimetic significance. Where successful, parody permits the reader to
meet this challenge; where not, it declines into an unconscious self-
travesty. Sorrentino does, like Antony Lamont, rely upon a persona in
Mulligan Stew, three in fact—two traditional personae who, in the
form of characters, walk the pages of the novel and another less obvious persona who haunts the prose of Lamont and his peers. We turn
to a master of intertextual studies, Mikhail Bakhtin, to his "hidden
voice" concept of parody, in a tentative effort to find our way out of
the novel's labyrinth of intertextuality, out of its "pure textuality."

Intertextuality as coded value: The personae

i) Profanation and the hidden voice
In his famous study of Dostoevsky's poetics, Bakhtin discerns in the
carnival spirit of pre-Lenten celebrations the primary catalyst of generic change in Western literature. During the annual pre-Lenten festival, Westerners rebel against the restraints and inhibitions imposed
upon them by the mores of society. A "syncretic pageant," carnival
brings together a myriad of opposing impulses (100). The marriage
of these impulses, or "attitudes" as Bakhtin calls them, produces a po-
lyphony of individual voices. Though each contends the priority of
his or her own "voice," the laissez-faire ambience of the festival allows
none precedence. As common qualities of each individual's antinomian rite, Bakhtin lists freedom, eccentricity, familiarity, and profanation (100–108). And, although Bakhtin's attribution of generic
change to a carnival spirit may seem an overgeneralization, i.e., "un-
polyphonic," his concept of the "carnivalization of literature" is a useful heuristic design when exploring *Mulligan Stew* and, in particular,
the operation of the author's personae. It is through the latter that the

judgments and biases of Sorrentino's intertextuality most clearly develop.

The carnival, as Bakhtin suggests, has major philosophical, even
political import. Unlike "official feasts"—ecclesiastical, feudal, royal—
that valorize permanence, being, and the status quo, the pre-Lenten
festival proclaims the sovereignty of the unofficial, of the unsanc-
tioned:

> . . . it marked the suspension of all hierarchical rank, privileges,
> norms, and prohibitions. Carnival was the true feast of time, the
> feast of becoming, change, and renewal. It was hostile to all that
> was immortalized and completed. (*Rabelais,* 10)[9]

Through parody, burlesque, travesty, and inversion, the carnival spirit
invests literature. In Rabelais, we find parodies of contemporary ideologies, e.g., religious liturgies and rites, and arid scholasticism. The
stylistics of laughter—sanctioned by the carnival tradition—provides
a critical perspective on the hegemonic status of church and state.
(Censorship, enforced by the state and church through such means as
coercion, imprisonment, excommunication, and even capital punishment, does not allow critical practice to develop in "serious" literary-
cultural forms, e.g., the political pamphlet, the newspaper, the poster,
the history/chronicle.) Essentially an oral tradition, the carnival spirit
critiques the status quo by establishing a relationship—one based on
ridicule—between its own parodic "texts" and the solemn liturgies of
church and state. The carnival reveler—and the writer taken by the
latter's spirit—evaluates power structures by establishing new intertextual relations. For his part, Sorrentino is perhaps more concerned
with criticizing the aesthetic hegemony of the editor, the publisher,
the reviewer, the scholar than, strictly speaking, with the broader
sociopolitical implications of publishing world politics. In any event,
he, like the carnival reveler, evaluates the status quo by developing a
parodic intertextual relationship between his own and accepted strategies of narrative construction; he, like the carnival reveler, promotes
freedom and change.[10]

Intertextuality concerns itself, quite obviously, with texts, with the
generic conventions that govern them, with textual evaluation. As was
noted above, intertextuality is a condition of language's status as a social and historical phenomenon. Every text mobilizes a strategy that

brings together certain texts in certain measure and ignores other texts. Whether they occur through reflex or reflection, acts of exclusion and inclusion take place in writing. These acts project value. In the view of Bakhtin, and later endorsed for example by Kristeva (*Le texte du roman*) and others, generic change is a positive force. Change occurs through the articulation of new intertextualities, of new combinatory gestures. It seems clear that Antony Lamont has not articulated new designs and that his current "boss," Gilbert Sorrentino, has. But how? If we accept Bakhtin's closely argued thesis that generic change is a consequence of attitudinal change, then a discussion of Sorrentino's manipulation of generic conventions in *Mulligan Stew* should permit us to deduce the attitudes of the author and to show how these attitudes are responses to his (and our) lived-world. The task becomes, then, to establish the relationship between Sorrentino's aesthetic codes and his own axiology, and thereafter to extrapolate a "significance" or "cognitive import" relevant to an informed reader.

At the beginning of *Mulligan Stew,* Gilbert Sorrentino and Antony Lamont, author and protagonist, stare across the shadowy line that separates the realms of fact and fiction in the postmodern novel; they are drawn together by common professional interests—creative writing, the novel, its tradition, its experimental limits, the vagaries of editors. Yet, by novel's end, the inestimable gulf that separates the virtuoso's performance from the hack's has intervened. Each of the authors, real and fictive, respectively, has activated the four cardinal attitudes of the carnival but with radically different results. Antony Lamont has turned to a systematic recuperation/plagiary of the classical canons of fiction and poetry in an effort to produce a serious work of stylish *Angst.* Sorrentino, using a similar strategy at an ironic remove, has succeeded in writing a humorous novel with serious implications. *Mulligan Stew* critiques, specifically, the culture industry; by implication, it denigrates those autocratic structures that aim to define our attitudes—moral, political, epistemological.

Profanation, writes Bakhtin, blasphemes against sacred texts and proverbs (*Dostoevsky's Poetics,* 101). It is an outrage directed at the spirituality of reproduction and fertility. Notwithstanding its pretensions to high-mindedness, Lamont's profanation of the literary tradition is accomplished unintentionally. His profanation of the literary canon reflects timidity, not boldness, a yielding to the pressures of tradition.

Genuine experimentation profanes a tradition through the calculated reduction and extension of its standards. Lamont, on the other hand, profanes tradition through an unconscious trivialization. He writes unintended travesties of techniques and genres that, in abler hands, have advanced the expressive range of language, e.g., stream-of-consciousness narration in "She is the Queenly Pearl," Eliot's objective correlative in "Burst Loveletters," flashback (passim), and the epistolary novel (passim). In taking up such dated issues of aesthetic production as diegesis versus mimesis and aesthetic distance, Lamont reveals that his own standards are prosaic and unadventurous (125–26). An author of fading, if not extinct, creative energies, Lamont's vanity and desire for self-promotion lead him to appeal to the formulas of others. The intertextuality Lamont sets up in *Guinea Red* (renamed *Crocodile Tears* at novel's end) profanes the tradition from which it borrows/steals. This profanation does not occur, however, as a result of a conscious effort. Rather, it is the unintentional product of Lamont's ungainly adaptations. "What does it matter," he asks himself in his journal, "if the ambiguity [of *Guinea Red/Crocodile Tears*] is intentional or not?" (125). Of course it matters a great deal. Lamont's mechanistic appropriation of past masters leaves his literary work a vulgar, lifeless exercise.

In contrast to the involuntary profanation of Lamont's accidental burlesques and parodies, Sorrentino blasphemes tradition with a studied intentness. A number of things have excited Sorrentino's contempt: the status of editors and publishers as arbiters of literature for the masses; the status of scholars and professors as arbiters for informed readers; the *roman à thèse;* the novel of moral platitudes; and, above all, creative writers who allow external pressures to influence their writing. Sorrentino has always refused to become an author-for-hire. He addresses the issue in an interview:

I've always had the idea that I could be an enormously wealthy and honored writer if I wanted to be because I have all the abilities to be one of the great slick writers of all time. But that is an unbearably boring thing to do; to figure out a formula and then run the formula over and over again, merely dropping Judy in place of Sally, and Bill instead of Tom. . . . It's an utterly boring conception. (J. O'Brien, "An Interview," 26)

Of course Antony Lamont has resorted to formula. Repeating the narrative strategies of successful writers, e.g., Fitzgerald, Hammett, and Nabokov, *Guinea Red/Crocodile Tears* is extended pastiche. Typically a means to satire, pastiche, here, is no more than a careless collocation of styles—in short, *kitsch*. Clement Greenberg points out that kitsch is only possible where there is available "a fully matured cultural tradition" from which it can borrow "devices, tricks, stratagems, rules of thumb, themes" (102). Twentieth-century literature is the tradition that Lamont consciously plagiarizes in an effort to achieve celebrity.

"Painful Digests," chapter 3 of Lamont's novel, is a lengthy parody of Nabokov. Through the fiction of Lamont and other "documentary" texts, Sorrentino projects what Bakhtin calls a "hidden" or "foreign" voice. "The element of the so-called reaction to the foregoing literary style which is present in every new style is," writes Bakhtin, "also in its way an inner polemic or, so to speak, a hidden anti-stylization of the other style, and often combines with an obvious parody of that style" (*Dostoevsky's Poetics*, 163). The "hidden voice" expresses itself through what Bakhtin refers to elsewhere as the "indirect word" (*Dialogic Imagination*, 61). *Mulligan Stew* stylizes fictional narrative in a spirit of anti-style, of disrespect. In Lamont's stylization of Nabokov, Sorrentino is able, through the "hidden voice" of parody, to satirize both Lamont's appropriation of Nabokov as well as the latter's highly affected style. In Bakhtinian language, such discourse is "heteroglossic." It presents not only the values and opinions of Lamont/Nabokov but those of the author as well. A dialogue occurs between the former and the latter, a dialogue that points out the tired aestheticism of Lamont (as well as, to some degree, that of Nabokov). "Painful Digests" isolates and mimics the themes and stylistic nuances of Nabokov. Lamont transposes the masturbation scene of *Lolita* from a family drawing room to an elegant New York restaurant. Ned Beaumont is engaged in a discussion with Martin Halpin, a crotchety elitist for whom democracy is a "virulent and pandemic virus" (53). Orgasm occurs for Beaumont as the climax of an absurd discussion that is marked by non sequiturs borrowed from the lexicon of Escoffier.

In addition to the parody of Nabokov in "Painful Digests," there is also the interview "Chats with the Real McCoy." Taken from the journal of Martin Halpin (the latter, like certain figures of *At-Swim-Two-Birds,* is both a fictional character and an independent, reflective individual), the McCoy interview is a documentary text paralleling Lamont's "Notebook." Through his journal reflections and the documents he reproduces therein, Halpin serves as an important authorial persona, providing the reader an acerbic commentary on Lamont's abortive efforts in *Guinea Red/Crocodile Tears*. In the absence of an omniscient narrator, Halpin's journal allows Sorrentino to introduce a critique of Lamont and Nabokov surreptitiously. The interview opens with the "heralded" author making the following enigmatic comment: "There is a complex *jeu d'esprit* of a novel in progress to be engaged under the usual enormous pressure" (36). At quick glance there might appear to be an elusive profundity in McCoy's remark, but a closer reading does not bear out this suspicion. The foreign idiom, the familiar (even arrogant) "usual," the ponderous transition from subjective completion to the adverbial phrase, all summon up an image of a finely tuned intellect gone slightly awry—an image Nabokov cultivates in his protagonists. The interview is highly entertaining, isolating as it does key features of Nabokov's philosophy on life and letters. McCoy's estimations of Dante ("a ridiculously overrated author") and Joyce ("that greatest of literary frauds") recall similarly dubious evaluations Nabokov has made, for example, of Faulkner and Mann.[11] McCoy, like Nabokov, is an elitist aesthete: "One wishes," he opines, "to create characters who will speak directly to the minds of comparative literature professors and intelligent book reviewers" (38). McCoy's claim to authenticity is Nabokovian: Interviewer: "What are the problems posed for you by other authors?" McCoy: "You are confusing me with someone else" (40). McCoy regards Soterroni's, i.e., Sorrentino's, work as inferior. He will not read *At-Swim-Two-Birds* because Joyce has praised it.

The hidden voice of Sorrentino speaks over the campy narrative of Lamont in "Painful Digests" and the bête noire judgments of McCoy. Both Lamont and McCoy lack authenticity. Each apes a value structure that is held a priori to be "estimable"—Lamont the affectation of a Nabokovian narrative, McCoy the dandy-aesthete stereotype. Sorrentino profanes a tradition that unreflexively valorizes aesthetic and philosophical codes that are bound to superficiality. Notwithstanding Lamont's technical skill as an imitator, his work lacks integrity and creative vision.

Sorrentino's "hidden voice" persona operates throughout the novel—in Lamont's fiction, in his "Notebook" and correspondence, as well as in the other "texts" that Lamont incites others to create, e.g., reviews, rejection letters, and miscellaneous correspondence (from professors, editors, family, etc.). In identifying the hidden voice of the author, the reader can discern, as we have with "Painful Digests" and the McCoy interview, Sorrentino's attitude toward the moral responsibility of the writer. Formalistic criticism has, in general, failed to plumb beyond the surface of Sorrentino's rich intertextuality to the moral implications of his work. *Mulligan Stew* is not "pure art," drained of all mimetic import. "Pure art" is, of course, "affirmative culture." It supports the status quo by refusing to cast doubt on the latter's legitimacy. In contrast, the satirical invective of *Mulligan Stew* points to the operation of a critical consciousness, to what Adorno calls "negative aesthetics." Kenneth Burke asserts the need for a didactic function in art:

> . . . it [pure art] tends to become a social menace in so far as it assists us in tolerating the intolerable. And if it leads to a state of acquiescence at a time when the very basis of moral integration is in question, we get a paradox whereby the soundest adjunct to ethics, the aesthetic, threatens to uphold an unethical condition. For this reason it seems that under conditions of competitive capitalism there must necessarily be a large *corrective* or *propaganda* element in art. (321)

In an age of confused priorities, where profit margins—a function of advertising and mass approbation—determine a publisher's approval or rejection, commercial interests alienate, as Burke says, the naturally conjunctive—ethics and aesthetics. *Mulligan Stew* is a response to this situation. Sorrentino's hidden voice articulates the author's values: the importance of self-accountability and, as the existentialists so often put it, self-choice.

ii) Antony Lamont and Martin Halpin
As Bakhtin points out, it is not always easy to know where the indirect authorial word ends and the direct authorial word begins, where, in short, the author ceases to parody and starts to give his views in a straight way, devoid of parodic refraction (*Dialogic Imagination,* 77). Yet, the reader must often contend with such a shift in the novel, and such is clearly the case in *Mulligan Stew.* The moral implications of

Sorrentino's intertextual strategies are not solely apparent through profanation and his "hidden voice" persona. Both Lamont and Martin Halpin serve as personae, the latter more obviously than the former. However, Halpin, like Lamont, is not a spokesman throughout the novel. Like Lamont's, his status shifts. In his role as a character in Lamont's novel, Halpin is wholly dependent upon the latter's bizarre narrative stratagems. By "day" an "employee" engaged in the enterprise of Lamont's novel, Halpin is a creation of the author's fantasy. But, as in *At-Swim-Two-Birds,* Halpin's "evenings" are his own.[12] After a hard day on the "set" (the actor analogy comes most readily to mind), Halpin returns to his lodgings to ruminate with his colleague, Ned Beaumont, on the progress of Lamont's novel and to record their thoughts in his journal. Halpin's journal allows Sorrentino to interject both a running critique of Lamont's self-styled avant-garde novel and, at the same time, a parody of the fashionably experimental in contemporary letters.

Halpin, an experienced character (he worked for "Mr. Joyce" who, he notes, used him "fairly and with kindness"), criticizes the conventionalities that mar much fiction-making. He quotes the opinions of another *Finnegans Wake* conscript, Clive Sollis:

Sollis is convinced that boring and philosophical asides, ruminatory interludes, and endless descriptions of nature, buildings, interiors, and the like, all occur in novels because the author has returned to "work" and is unable to find his character where he left him. Hence, the descriptive or philosophical tripe is brought in desperately in order to push the creaking narrative along. He is also convinced that background material of a psychological nature, brought in to make a character's actions understandable, is all trash as well. (154)[13]

Sollis reacts to the simplistic empiricism and naive morality of much literature that, with its labored litany of surface description, supports a crude reflectionist view of literary representation. For Sorrentino, "meaning" is rarely obvious. In the same journal entry, again referring to Sollis, Halpin notes:

. . . he seems to think the better the author, the more difficult he is toward his workers. He pointed out that he had yet to meet a malcontent from the pages of a "commercial" novel or slick-magazine short story. "They live in a world of kisses, nice clothes, and happy divorces, with plenty of polite sex thrown in," he said. (155)

"Truthful" writing will, of necessity, replicate the opacity of life; "truthful" writing will avoid the reductive epistemologies of, for example, social realism and the psychological novel. Through the commentary of Martin Halpin, Sorrentino confirms that the postmodern era is indeed one of suspicion.

Lamont, hack imitator and author of *Guinea Red/Crocodile Tears*, is quite obviously not an authorial persona. It is in other guise—that of the righteously indignant author, the victim of an insensitive readership—that Lamont fulfills this latter function. There are then two Lamonts: Lamont the writer and Lamont the victim of editorial ill will and publishing-world politics. For one reason or another, reviewers, editors, and publishers have not responded enthusiastically to Lamont's work. There is of course a certain justice to the jilting of a hack. With this, Sorrentino is in obvious concurrence. However, the author's point is something quite other. It is less an issue of Lamont's rejection than of the acceptance that kindred hacks enjoy. Dermot Trellis, for example, Lamont's brother-in-law, has received considerable acclaim, both critical and editorial. He is a commercial success. For his course on the American experimental novel, Professor Roche has elected to replace a Lamont work with a selection from the Trellis corpus. Trellis's novel *Red Dawn and Blue Denim* succeeds in marrying the Western adventure novel and pornography (just as earlier work has brought together detective fiction and smut). A brief passage from the nine-page excerpt will suffice to show the work's inferiority:

Flinging then from his ice-blue eyes the tell-tale moistures, Big Cal next flung from his brain the form and voice of Patience, blushing at the bewildering sensations her memory evoked in his loins. Then he leaped from his blankets with the celerity of a maverick whose rump had just been branded by the cruel, yet kind, iron. Eager now to be on his way, his lynx eyes darted about through the clearing mists that swirled about the boulders among which he had made his camp. (133)

The outrage Lamont expresses over Trellis's aesthetic-moral compromise and his consequent celebrity and commercial success is Sorrentino's as well.[14]

Writing to his sister, Trellis's wife, Lamont reflects:

> He [Dermot Trellis] looked for easy money and accolades . . .
> Dermot *deliberately* wrote in that weary, bankrupt vein so beloved
> by the corps of geniuses who fire their salvos of praise or dam-
> nation from the fortress of *ignorance,* God knows they didn't
> make him into an overnight Great Writer. . . . They (also) took
> pains to run that review along side a long essay on Miller and
> Borges . . . And it was that review that prompted the re-issue of
> the book as a "fad" item. You of course know that. What I am
> trying to get at is that Dermot *very consciously* took apart the fab-
> ric of his inspiration and put it back together again to match his
> conception of what was fashionable. (58)

In the context of Lamont's maudlin, self-pitying letter, this passage does not immediately stand out as the commentary of a persona. However, isolated, it reminds one of some of the more acerbic judgments that Sorrentino makes in interviews. Not unexpectedly, personal experience colors Sorrentino's opinions of the publishing world. As Burke points out (and de Tocqueville long ago implied), "Under capitalism this basic integration between work-patterns and ethical patterns is constantly in jeopardy, and even frequently impossible" (316). For Sorrentino, the supplanting of personal convictions by material interests is a highly reprehensible moral compromise. Though more often a foil and buffoon, Lamont occasionally serves as Sorrentino's spokesman.

Lamont has quite as little respect for the literary establishment as does Sorrentino himself. As persona, he enumerates the moral failings of those who prop up writers of negligible talent. Professor Roche, lionizer of Dermot Trellis's "cash trash" novels, hitches his own star to the ascending celebrity of a rank pornographer. Unfortunately, the opinions of what Lamont calls "the publisher-retailer-critical-academic machinery" do, in large measure, control the reading patterns of both professional and casual "consumers" of literature (252). Lamont's final letter to Roche trains its colorful philippic against the critical misjudgments of the professional reader. Sorrentino gives

vent to his frustrations through Lamont. Lamont criticizes a number
of professorial shortcomings: his petty careerist preoccupations, his
narcissism, his lack of critical acuity (Roche regards *The Centaur* as a
"breakthrough" novel), the stylistic dullness of professional criticism,
and, foremost, the reluctance of academics to deal with contemporary
experimental literature. Lamont makes the latter point with some ve-
hemence: "My dear old bumbling Roche, I suspect that you would not
know an avant-garde work were it to grasp you by your academic tool"
(321). Similarly vituperative letters to other "writers" make an obvious, yet important point—not only does the serious experimental
writer fail to reach "the (wo)man in the street," he or she in general
fails to engage the interest and respect of both those ensconced in the
ivory towers of academe and those resident in the great steel-glass
houses of the publishing world.[15] As Sorrentino notes, gifted experimental writers like Sorrentino and his friends Robert Creeley and
Jack Kerouac suffer the same fate as the *poseurs:*

> . . . in the fifties there was quite literally no place to publish if
> you did not either know those people or write the way they
> thought you should write. . . . Editors know what the spirit of the
> age tells them. Editors are probably among the dullest of all hu-
> man beings. Enormously incompetent. (Barone, 237–38)

Interestingly, *Mulligan Stew* apparently only saw print because of the
author's contacts at Grove.

In the labyrinth (still)

To shift, briefly, from a descriptive mode of criticism to one of prescription here in the conclusion, we might consider some of the more
obvious flaws in Sorrentino's intertextual epic. In his monograph on
reflexive fiction, Robert Alter points out a weakness common to the
experimental novel (and indeed to innovative art in general)—liberty
frequently runs the risk of becoming license and self-indulgence (*Partial Magic*, 224). Of the latter, Sorrentino is not completely innocent.
The lists alluded to above often degenerate into an endless litany of
"one-liners." Like the "life" of the party, Sorrentino frequently persists
in telling one or, more usually, one hundred jokes too many. In its
early stages, a list of fictive books and periodicals are moderately hu-

morous: "*Sexual Fulfillment in the Woods* by Birch Humpper," "*Come in Your Trunks: Entertaining at the Shore* by Buffie Whitestone," "*Fire Pails* by Vladimir Papilion," "*Bitter and Vicious* by Gilles de Sorentain." While the sexual *doubles entendres*, the veiled allusions to himself, and the comical characterizations of other writers are entertaining at the outset, the cumulative effect of a five-page catalogue is one of boredom and impatience (*Mulligan Stew*, 31–35). An obvious penchant for self-caricature does not completely excuse the author's excesses. Recreation and instruction are the two primary attributes of good literature. Sorrentino's preoccupation with "text" (and his own cleverness) frequently fails to advance the novel on either front. Likewise, the lengthy "Flawless Play Restores: The Masque of Fungo" (published under that title by Black Sparrow Press in 1974) is devoid of major interest—its inclusion a gesture perhaps significant to the author but not, regrettably, to the reader. In an early notebook on *Mulligan Stew*, Sorrentino admits that the book should be short "so as not to exhaust the idea with repetition" (J. O'Brien, "An Interview," 18). In several places over the course of its four-hundred-plus pages, the novel exhausts both idea and reader.[16] While it is important to acknowledge these shortcomings, they do not, in any event, obscure or overwhelm those parts of the novel that effectively parody the production and consumption of contemporary literature.

"Much of literary competence," writes Robert Scholes, "is based upon our ability to connect the worlds of fiction and experience" (*Semiotics and Interpretation*, 32). My reading of *Mulligan Stew* aims at meeting this requisite of reading competence. It has focused on the role intertextuality plays in the novel—its capacity to satirize the production and reception of contemporary experimental fiction as well as its intention (implicit but unmistakable) to promote alternative values, aesthetic and ethical. As I asserted at the outset, highly inventive intertextual play is not emblematic of purely literary or aesthetic concerns. Rather, in fact, intertextuality conveys considerable cognitive import in the novel; it suggests the opinions and values of the author. In this case, specifically, Sorrentino asserts the priority of creative sovereignty and, therein, repudiates a publishing industry that accepts and promotes only with great reluctance the noncanonical work. Clearly, a publishing policy that is responsive only (or largely thereof) to formulaic texts neutralizes literature, making of it a "good," an object for quick and carefree consumption.

I have characterized Sorrentino's novel as an intertextual labyrinth that threatens to entrap the unwary reader in a world of pure text. However, by emphasizing the ethical implications of a parodic manipulation of intertextuality, I have sought to chart a readerly course through and beyond the intertextual maze. There remains, however, something of an interpretive reduction here. *Mulligan Stew* is not reducible to a *roman à thèse*, a form that Sorrentino denigrates without reserve. While didactic and critical in the measures outlined at length above, the novel does, at the same time, remain the ludic enterprise of the author (and of the reader). The great lists, the interpolation of previously published material, the author's ongoing allusions to himself, the extended pastiches—all suggest the performative element common to postmodern fiction, whatever their mimetic value. Students of experimental fiction fail to avail themselves of the full power of the work under consideration when they neglect its value as entertainment *and* socially responsive statement.[17]

Mulligan Stew remains labyrinthine in the end. No reading can reconfigure the twisting, involuted paths of the novel's intertextuality. I have merely discerned a few coordinates in the maze—those places in the text that analogize conditions in the lived-world, here specifically, the politics of literary reception and the belletrist's social milieu. Satire has always had to establish such coordinates in the reader's mind to be efficacious. And it has been precisely the satirical elements of postmodern fiction that formalists tend to overlook. It has been my aim here to vitalize the discussion of postmodern intertextuality by extending the range of the debate beyond the purely formal to embrace problems of axiology and social critique.

Conclusion

THE EXPERIENCE OF READING a postmodern novel is obviously unsettling. Yet, however disagreeable or *angstvoll* we find the encounter, we can learn a good deal from postmodern fiction. In its nervousness, in its arbitrary patterning, postmodern literature brings us far closer to the sensibilities of our time than do the great epics of the twenties or their contemporary emulations. The modernists were of course experimenters too, shapers of novel forms, but they manifested a faith in their shaping vision that postmodern writers find hard to imitate. The mythopoeticism of Joyce, Eliot, Döblin, of Faulkner even, outlines with relative confidence an integrated world view where antinomies resolve themselves with time's passage, where the torch passes from one family to another, one class to another, one generation to another, with a defiant inevitability. The reader, standing without the novel, surveying the action, evaluates the motives and moralities of the players. Responding to different pressures and impetuses, the modernist novel reflects progressions and energies unapparent in postmodernism. Curiously, aiming at a critique of bourgeois mores, at a critique of the empiricist preoccupation of high realism, modernism nonetheless embraced so many features of bourgeois realism: the positive hero (though in diluted form), transparent typologies, the unifying myths of Western culture. In postmodern fiction, categories become mixed: the factual and the fictional, the ontic and the ontological, the historical and the imagined, the heroic and antiheroic.

179

Though interested in myth as well, the postmodernist deals with highly privatized mythic patterns, or with parodic treatments of public myths. In postmodern fiction, nothing, except perhaps ambiguity, seems necessary or ineluctable.

It is not surprising that many readers are dismayed with postmodern narratology. Traditionally, writers have sorted through their narrative choices, their epistemological possibilities, before committing themselves to telling a story. It was possible formerly—and still possible for those who yield to nostalgic yearnings—to construct a metaphysics that *guaranteed* effective moral action in the world. Installing one's star within a divine or divinely human cosmology, one could locate truth and apodicticity. But, as Foucault points out, the murder of *God* made the murder of *Man* inevitable (*The Order of Things*, 383). Once able, like Pope's divinity, to *pro*pose and *dis*pose, humankind is now bound to supposition. In postmodernism, we find the operation of a politics of finitude. Fiction has caught up to Nietzsche's radical skepticism. Frailty marks the behavior of characters in the fiction of Coover, Vonnegut, Handke, Calvino, Heissenbüttel, and Pynchon. Contrasted with the heroic praxis, however muted, of K., Jimmy Herf, Bloom, with the long-suffering nobility of the Faulknerian heroine, of Woolf's Mrs. Ramsay, the efforts of Abish's Ulrich, of Coover's maid, of Vonnegut's Billy Pilgrim are indeed very inadequate. Superior morality—whether stoic or vitalistic—is not easily purchased. Humankind cannot transcend its existential condition through purity of vision. A critical orientation that presumes heroic transcendence will fail to see the merit of postmodern "negative aesthetics."

Postmodern fiction does not herald, as many have claimed, the loss of our subjectivity in a world propelled by mammoth institutional forces, in a world that no longer offers the reassurances tendered formerly by religion or classical humanism. Rather, we find in each of the postmodern fictions considered here a renegotiation of human subjectivity that at once accepts *and* rejects the seemingly insuperable influences to which we are exposed in the late twentieth century. In this respect, the postmodernist retraces the worn path of Sisyphus, though often this journey is comic or tragicomic, rather than tragic. Malcolm Bradbury calls the postmodern age one of "epistemological redefinition" (162). In postmodern fiction, the protagonist lives out this philosophical quandary through worldly interaction; there is in short an "existentializing" of epistemological critique, as well as of moral choice. The problem of knowledge, once the concern of the professional philosopher, has become topical for us all.

We in the late twentieth century are highly suspicious and skeptical. There are obvious reasons for this skepticism. Perhaps the most notable is what Lyotard calls the "mercantilization of knowledge" (5). Certainly, the accumulation/manufacture and use of "information" by a variety of constituencies—pollsters, political pundits, politicians, civil servants, advertisers, "industry spokespersons"—to advance often venal ends do not inspire trust in what others posit, however sincerely or zealously, as the "truth." The various fictions discussed here analyze narrative conventions and in so doing effectively critique the validity of truth claims made by more conventional forms, whether fictional or nonfictional. These works demonstrate that all narrative strategies reveal moral and epistemological biases. As literary exercises, postmodern fictions liberate the novel from canonical tyranny. They do much more, however; they instill in the reader a sense of self-accountability. In their interrogation of narrative practices they encourage the reader to bring suspicion to his or her own enterprise of world construction. The general antinomianism of postmodern fiction promotes, as many have noted, readerly activity. Its self-consciousness and self-referentiality encourage circumspection in the reader, not only when in the act of interpreting literature but also while in the act of understanding the events of life.

Many postmodern fictions are baldly allegorical. Now construed in more general, more fundamental terms, morality becomes a function of epistemology. To fashion a truly individuated response to life, the individual must, like the postmodernist and the postmodern protagonist, confront those axiological structures that aim to impose upon us a world view, such structures as unreflective patriotism, technocracy, literary tradition, social millennialism, official history, to cite a few. Critics of postmodernism, those who see in it only nihilism and aestheticism, refuse for whatever reasons to participate in the revisionist project that this literature encourages. In an age of social fragmentation and ideological zealotry, one either remains precritically committed to dogma—whether political or religious or commercial— or one moves beyond such modern, "contemporary" truths to a point of critical awareness that is atypical, that is, in a sense, *postmodern, post-contemporary*. The postmodernist criticizes the unreality of a world view that conceptualizes current problems in terms of the nineteenth century or early twentieth century.

Postmodern fiction is a *representation* of this questioning of the values and preoccupations of our epoch; in this lies its mimesis, its mimetic function. The literary ramifications of this questioning include the thematization of uncertainty, ambiguity, indeterminacy and a consequent concern for *form* that emphasizes the latter as a potentially liberating phenomenon. Many contemporary philosophers—well-known thinkers like Kuhn, Feyerabend, and Foucault—have succeeded in casting doubt on the integrity of methodological objectivity. Though paradigms, methods, epistemes were once thought inviolable by either time or revision, we now view them as historically conditioned, as value-laden, as arbitrary to some greater or lesser degree. Through its formal involutions postmodern fiction works out this same suspicion of objective methods and incontrovertible truths. What E. D. Hirsch derogates as "cognitive atheism"—an outlook that denies the existence of a unitary, transhistorical truth—is really the claim that truth can exist in many places, not just one (*The Aims of Interpretation*, 36). The postmodernists no longer view their medium—language—as transparent, a pure communicative instrument. Their suspicion of language has spawned a suspicion of all formative structures, whether moral or conceptual or aesthetic. Though few will argue that it can save the world, postmodern fiction, seen in this light, is afforded the potential at least of a social function; it becomes, in a transvalued sense, a kind of "critical realism" that depicts, however paradoxically, foibles of contemporary life. And, as I have sought to demonstrate throughout here, we can learn a good deal from our readerly (re-)construction of this depiction, this representation, this *mimesis*.

I would like to end with a digression on the political foundations of postmodernism and postmodernity, a subject that has been largely neglected in this study but one that I plan to investigate in future work. (Consistent with the growing practice, I will use "postmodernism" to refer to cultural forms and "postmodernity" to refer to all phenomena—cultural, political, etc.—pertaining to the period.) The "politics" of postmodernism/postmodernity has become a topic of interest in recent years, with Western Marxists, neo-Marxists, and post-Marxists putting forward the most ambitious and thought-provoking analyses. To a very large extent, given their contrasting views of history and political economy, Rortian postmodern bourgeois liberals and Marxists argue at cross purposes when debating and theorizing postmodernity and its cultural forms. In the view of Rortian liberals, and in my own, postmodern fiction feeds upon, and contributes to, the pluralistic energies of Western liberal democracy. While not a dominant voice in contemporary society, postmodern fiction nonetheless contributes to important dialogues. And, of course, it is the philosophical tolerance and economic prosperity of liberal democracy that allow this voice to enunciate itself and allow it to be heard. Western postmodern fiction will always fall short of the expectations of Marxists and neo-Marxists. In failing to promote profound social reorganization, such fiction can for them rarely rise above aestheticism and false consciousness. Marxists see in postmodernity generally just another stage in the inexorable teleological march of history where every minor and major cultural or social event becomes an illustration of some profound historical circumstance that is in itself a part of a larger historical drama.

Fredric Jameson has attempted the most encompassing reading of postmodernism as the cultural reflection of late twentieth-century capitalism. Until the release of his forthcoming book on postmodernism, the long essay, "Postmodernism, or The Cultural Logic of Late Capitalism," will remain his primary position paper on this issue. This essay manifests many of the strengths of Jameson's earlier work on Marxist and narrative theory. In it we find the same extraordinary range of erudition and imaginative analysis as well as the willingness and fortitude to define and maintain a clearly nuanced position. Jameson investigates five key aspects of postmodernism: depthlessness; the replacement of "personal style" by pastiche and the loss of historical consciousness; the breakdown of communication; the causal relations between technology and contemporary culture; and, finally, postmodern architecture. Jameson's estimation of postmodern culture is not much different from that offered by Lukács of literary modernism and, of course, Jameson has long served as both explicator of and apologist for Lukácsian aesthetics. Like Lukács's, Jameson's aesthetics is a totalizing one, predicated on the close and total linkage of economic and cultural history. Jameson draws from a plethora of cultural phenomena in an effort to demonstrate that postmodern cultural forms have *en masse* failed to move beyond triviality to achieve the "critical distance" necessary to question the foundations of our

politico-economic system. Such cultural forms are not resistant or op-
positional; they do not identify the problems emphasized by the
grand Marxist metanarrative and naturally do not propose ameliorative courses of action. In his veiled valorization of modernism, Jameson, like Habermas, remains one step behind cultural developments.
(Lukács, in favoring realism over modernism, exhibits a similar kind
of *mal de siècle* sensibility.) Jameson's views on postmodernism have
softened a little since the 1984 "Postmodernism" essay. Presumably in
deference to dialecticality, Jameson does, in a 1988 interview, identify
positive aspects of postmodernism—its emphasis on storytelling, its
accessibility, and its democratization of forms (Stephanson, 12). Yet,
given the overall bleakness of his diagnosis, one gets the feeling that
these represent very small redemptions.

Marxists like Jameson understand postmodernism "better" than
postmodern bourgeois liberals who generally do not see history as a
structured progression, who have no privileged view of futurity. The
Marxists' metanarrative allows/compels them to identify postmodernity as, in the words of Marx, "the closing chapter of the prehistoric
stage of human society" (or subchapter in the case of Jameson) (Marx,
634). Consequently, Jameson can, with the intrepidity typical of a neo-
Lukácsian, reduce the postmodern period (with all of its variegations)
to simple "cultural imperialism," to the "superstructural expression"
of worldwide "American military and economic domination" (Stephanson, 16; "Postmodernism," 57). The only solace that a Marxist
can take in this generally lamentable situation lies in the realization
that capitalism's failings and internal contradictions hasten its own
collapse. Given this view, postmodernism—the "cultural logic of late
capitalism"—is, when seen dialectically (or "paradoxically" as a postmodernist might say), at once "catastrophe" and "progress," as Jameson tells us ("Postmodernism," 86). Postmodernity represents both
history as trauma and history as herald of better things to come.

While one can (and should) readily admit the horrors of American
militarism, particularly in the postwar period, as well as the outrages
perpetrated by multinational companies on the public and even their
own employees, military aggression and ecological crimes are not the
monopoly of any "side" or constituency as, for example, recent Af-
ghan history and industrial practices in Chernobyl and the Soviet Bal-
tic states show us. Jameson's judgments court reductionism and a narrow tendentiousness. In my view, there is reason to question the very

attempt to identify the central premises of postmodern culture or postmodernity generally. There is no single defining characteristic or relationship or theme, or cluster of characteristics or relationships or themes, that somehow unites all aspects of postmodernity. Not class struggle, not colonialism, not ecology, not gender or race politics, not religious fundamentalism, not militarism, and not ("late") capitalism. I readily admit that many Marxist constructs—ideas like hegemony, reification, subalternity, and commodity fetishism—can yield very useful insights. Yet, generally, the reliance on a monocausal explanation of history is disabling. The monocausal explanation misses too much. Further, much of what is going on today is not even "postmodern" in any obvious sense, but rather the recuperation of past possibilities or even the projection of future ones, ones we have not yet identified with the appropriate "-ism." Jauss, building on an insight of Siegfried Kracauer, calls this condition "the noncontemporaneity of the contemporaneous" (*Toward an Aesthetic of Reception,* 36). If Jameson wishes to seek a totalizing critique of postmodernism, "noncontemporaneity" must be fully acknowledged and engaged. Postmodernism cannot be discussed simply in isolation in terms of its internal pressures; it must also be discussed in relation to nonpostmodern societies generally, East and West, North and South, developed and developing nations alike. Such a project would offer a more dialectical reading of the strengths *and* weaknesses of various political and cultural forms and move more vigorously to the new "internationalism" that Jameson advocates in the "Postmodernism" essay and in the more recent article, "World Literature in an Age of Multinational Capitalism."[1]

In my view, twentieth-century history is the product of a myriad of influences and interests, not all of which pursue the same developmental trajectories, not all of which can be explained as the product of, or reaction to, a lupine capitalism. I believe our colleagues in the sciences have a better shot at discovering a Unified Field Theory of the Universe (and claiming their Nobel prize) than we do of writing a Unified Field Theory of Postmodernity. In any event, both projects are fashionable today. With respect to understanding postmodernity, I think that, for the foreseeable future, the important work will be done in the area of "case studies," what we used to call in our own discipline "practical criticism," i.e., the analysis of given works. In any event, though I deny the possibility of a foundational ontology/cri-

tique of postmodernism and its politics, there remains a strong temptation to characterize the latter, if only in a provisional, vague way.
Andrew Britton defines postmodern politics as "essentially Stalinist
popular frontism under a different name" (9). Britton objects to the
divorcing of various movements—gay, "green," black, women's—
from the class struggle and the pursuit of the Marxist millennium.
There are a couple of problems in all of this. The social pluralism that
has enabled the founding and (limited) advancement of these movements is more common in Western liberal democracies than it is in
Marxist societies (even as one acknowledges, for example, Gorbachev's halting attempts to *liberalize* Soviet politics and economics
through *glasnost* and *perestroika,* respectively). But, Britton informs us,
we must be cautious here in using these popular movements "as an
alibi for McCarthyist jeremiads against Marx, Marxist theory and the
Soviet Union" (9). The jeremiad is of course an unsavory, discomfiting
business, indeed often no more than self-indulgent tirade—such as,
for example, the assigning of Stalinist motivations to free and noble
democratic movements. He and I agree that McCarthyism and jeremiads, not to mention their union, are to be avoided.

   Still, one wonders who might have valid grounds for judging the
totalizing politics of Marxism (and, implicitly, therein, for legitimizing
the liberal pluralistic politics of postmodernity). Does First Secretary
Gorbachev have such grounds in promoting his unprecedented reforms? Do Solidarity activists? What about the friends and relatives of
Imre Nagy and his colleagues (who were executed after the Hungarian revolution as "counter-revolutionaries" and whose "rehabilitations" were finally coerced from party authorities in 1989)? What
about those who complained in Tiananmen Square about party privilege? What about those who have survived to complain anew even as
the prospects of a new "Cultural Revolution" loom large in China?
What about the brave citizenry of Timişoara? Perhaps these varied
constituencies have valid reasons for denouncing totalizing politics.
Perhaps these are all postmodern voices who, in different registers,
are promoting pluralism. Perhaps these voices are crying out for the
dispersion/decentralization of power that, as Stanley Aronowitz tells
us in a lucid essay, is a distinguishing feature of postmodern politics.[2]
Events around the world in the late eighties suggest that totalizing
politics are not working very well, either in terms of economic progress or safeguarding fundamental human rights. Surely that is the

lesson of 1989, our own century's "year of revolution." And, while the Britton article prompts me to cite leftist examples of political totalization, we can hardly overlook that racism, religious sectarianism, monarchism, and rightist fascism all have as their goal a similar unitary politics.

Pluralism comes up a lot when discussing postmodernity though more fashionable proximate synonyms are often used by academicians, e.g., dialogicality, plurivocity, plurisignification, indeterminacy, overdetermination, polysemy, etc. Pluralism is the opposite of dogmatism. It produces a great deal of anxiety and insecurity. Like most things, political pluralism can be good or bad. It can result in anarchy and paralysis, or it can result in, quite simply, pragmatism and liberal democracy. But it cannot by definition result in totalitarianism, nor has it historically resulted in totalitarianism (except perhaps in times of war or other extreme national crisis). It is time for cultural historians to put away the rhetoric and dogma of the Cold War, and the barren binary reductions the latter entail. The politicians are doing it; we should too.

Two contemporary political scientists, both independently and in collaboration, have offered some suggestive remarks about current and future political pluralism. In essays and in their jointly authored *Hegemony and Socialist Strategy,* Ernesto Laclau and Chantal Mouffe talk about "radical and plural democracy" (*Hegemony,* 167). "Radical democracy" rejects the concentration of power and defines society as a host of antagonisms. Social change occurs when particular groups achieve relative ascendancy. Yet, ascendancy is always contingent and malleable, and cannot be legitimated on absolute transcendental grounds. This political philosophy rejects a number of traditional views of how society is constituted and changed. It denies "classism," the position that the working class is the "privileged agent" of social change; it rejects "statism," the belief that big government can solve all problems; and, finally, "economism," a mechanical-deterministic view positing a necessary link between economic measures and political effects (177). The subject can no longer be defined as a "unified and unifying essence" (181). Rather, subjects belong to given social entities and take their identity from these.

"Radical democracy" posits political and social life as a field with diverse and contingent meanings. Though neither Mouffe nor Laclau thinks we have achieved this condition yet, each seems to believe we are moving toward it. I think this is true of Western nations today, and in the future may be true of other countries of the world, especially those who are now working their way through the various stages of postcolonial national self-definition. In its concurrent promotion of canon revision and moral reflection, postmodern fiction *may* contribute in some measure to the formation of a more radically heterogeneous and democratic world. That, at least, is one contingent reading of its prospects.

Notes

Chapter 1

1. Audience response is also mentioned in *Politics* where Aristotle identifies three effects of music (*mousike*): education for the young; catharsis as defined in the *Poetics;* and entertainment and relief from stress. See Grube for the relevant passages and a brief analysis of these (66–69, 132–33).

2. Stefan Morawski describes the inductive bias of Aristotelian aesthetics as an "active process of perception . . . which generalizes through particulars, compressing complex processes into concrete situations and a multiplicity of social types into a single exemplar" (221). Gadamer is less inclined than I (and Morawski) to deny relativity to the Aristotelian view of aesthetic perception. See *Truth and Method,* especially 115–17 and 314–20.

3. "The virtues . . . are acquired by first giving them expression in actual practice, and this is true of the arts as well. To learn an art (*techne*) it is first necessary to perform those actions that pertain to it" (*The Nicomachean Ethics, Aristotle,* 181–82).

4. Extrapolating from the Lukácsian argument, we can see several antitheses developing out of the mimesis versus expressionism juxtaposition— objectivity and subjectivity, content and form, life and art, society and the individual, whole and part. Most aestheticians have not endorsed such a schematic view of art and its production. They have rather, while perhaps emphasizing them unequally, developed aesthetic theories that in effect synthesize the above oppositions. Where doctrinaire Marxists have clung to their narrow mimetic theories and some, like Croce, have regarded the creative act as au-

tonomous and purely self-expressive, others have attempted to avoid such extreme positions. (The following is characteristic of the Crocean intuitionist view of artistic production: ". . . intuitive knowledge is expressive knowledge. Independent and autonomous in respect to intellectual function; indifferent to later empirical discriminations, to reality and unreality, to formations and apperceptions of time and space, which are also later. . . . To intuit is to express . . ." [731].) To mollify the rigid determinism of his own theory of artistic production, Taine (recalling Pope and his "ruling passion") introduced his *faculté maîtresse*. The Russian formalists, for their part, firmly located literature and its study in historical time, recognizing for literature "both analogies with other kinds of cultural development and proof of the independence of the phenomena of literary evolution" (Eichenbaum, 844). To these who have sought to collapse the categorical oppositions, we can add progressive Marxists such as Marcuse and Sartre, and the Heideggerian school of phenomenology.

5. See also Lukács, "Realism in the Balance," 57.

6. Of these critics, only Graff, so far as I know, has acknowledged a formal, self-conscious application of Lukácsian values in his reception of postmodern fiction, though I maintain for all a neo-Lukácsian bias. The contemporary endorsement of Lukácsian narrative aesthetics is not, in any event, confined to Gerald Graff. Though more concerned with the twentieth-century novel generally than with postmodern fiction, and hence not germane to the present discussion, both Michel Zeraffa, in his *Fictions: The Novel and Social Reality*, and J. M. Bernstein, in his *The Philosophy of the Novel: Lukács, Marxism and the Dialectics of Form*, offer Lukácsian readings of the novel and its social relevance. For a summary consideration of the Bernstein work, see my review of it.

7. Writing in the early 1970s, Hassan cites, among others, as "Modernist" readers Frye, Howe, Kazin, Kermode, Leavis, Pritchett, Tate, Trilling, Warren, Wellek, and Schorer (*Paracriticisms*, 44). To this list, I contend, we can add Graff, Aldridge, and Newman.

8. Though I will not discuss his views here—they have been fully considered by many others elsewhere—John Gardner's definition of "moral fiction" is, like Aldridge's, simply too narrow to be useful when reading noncanonical literature.

9. This Humanism, of course, dates from the Renaissance, a period to which we owe our love of mathematical precision and empirical truth. Copernicus's validation of the heliocentricity thesis put humanity at the center of all things, not the sun. Our mental energies no longer co-opted by shamans and deities, we were now able to meditate on the hidden but determinate meaning of all things. We could now pose and resolve questions through methods and technologies, without appeal to grace or superstition.

10. While I agree with Graff that Gass, as we will presently see, maintains fiction's autonomy in his essays, Federman's position is actually more equivocal than Graff allows. Federman calls fiction "an autonomous reality whose only relation with the real world is to improve that world" ("Surfiction—Four Propositions in the Form of an Introduction," *Surfiction: Fiction Now . . . and Tomorrow*, 8); here, the relative clause vitiates the seeming radicality of its antecedent. In any event, the claims of Gass and Federman notwithstanding, it is by no means certain that their imaginative works and those of their peers support the contention. Certainly, the paradox of writers using a communal medium—language itself—to make intersubjective the claim that intersubjectivity is unavailable needs to be examined. Pynchon is of course little heard from. However, the autobiographical comments found in the introduction to *Slow Learner*, a collection of early (1958–1964) short works, suggest one genuinely concerned with the militarism and avarice that have helped to shape American history throughout Pynchon's adult life.

11. In a candid, self-critical introspective published in *Partisan Review* on the occasion of its fiftieth anniversary, Graff categorizes his views in the sixties and seventies as "heterodox Marxist" and acknowledges an intellectual debt to the critiques of "romantic irrationalism" put forward by Lukács and Yvor Winters. Only the debt with respect to the former is of interest here.

12. Graff equates postmodernism not only with post–World War Two experimental fiction in the vein of Mailer, Burroughs, and Pynchon but also with such noninnovative (and accomplished) fiction as *The Catcher in the Rye, The Invisible Man,* and *Herzog.* A prominent essay by Irving Howe, "Mass Society and Postmodern Fiction," (written in 1959 and cited by Graff) attributes postmodernity to the more progressive (if only moderately innovative) of contemporary writers. The earliness of the essay perhaps accounts for Graff's and others' use of "postmodernism" as broadly descriptive of a literature preoccupied with "narcissistic isolation" or "escapist gamesmanship" (*LAI,* 215). I would, on the other hand, confine postmodernism to only the most innovative fiction since the early or mid-sixties. This is not totally arbitrary. Current critical practice tends to differentiate strongly between the essentially traditional fictions of Bellow, Roth, Heller, Updike, and even Mailer with their neurotic middle-class milieus and updated "psychological realisms" and the reflexive, deconstructive forms worked by Barth, Coover, Barthelme, and Peter Handke, among others. In the present context, such problems of definition and taxonomy are of little interest. One can always arrive at a definition that approaches real coherence within the frame of one's own discussion. As a comparatist, I am content to focus equally on difference and similarity rather than confining myself to determinations of genre and period in the traditional manner of literary scholarship. Postmodernism remains for me posited on a general innovative inclination, and I am not concerned with establishing an

"innovation index" although such could, with greater or lesser difficulty, be arrived at.

13. Lukács says much the same thing in *Studies in European Realism* where he characterizes his method as a search for "the material roots of each phenomenon, regards them in their historical connections and movement, ascertains the laws of such movement and demonstrates their development from root to flower, and in so doing lifts every phenomenon out of a merely emotional, irrational, mystic fog and brings it to the bright light of understanding" (1). Both the botanical and chiaroscuro metaphors underscore Lukács's yearning for the clarity and order of the Enlightenment.

14. See Heidegger's "On the Essence of Truth" for a discussion of his notion of truth as "freedom" (*Basic Writings*, 117–41).

15. John Gardner is similarly critical of Barthelme's fiction but for a different reason. Admitting its referentiality, Gardner mourns the absence of a positive agenda in Barthelme's work; for Gardner, the latter's "satire of despair" is born of "weariness" and "New York stylishness" (*On Moral Fiction*, 79–80).

16. It may be asked what constitutes irrelevant opinions. Gadamer talks of *incorrect questions* that lead nowhere, but, consistent with his suspicion of "method," he refuses to outline a hermeneutic procedure that would guide and confirm one's interpretive speculations (*Truth and Method*, 325–41). In the absence of such a procedure, I can only (with Gadamer) suggest that a willingness to engage in genuinely open and protracted dialogue with the text is the best route to understanding. See E. D. Hirsch's *Validity in Interpretation* for a more structured view of interpretive validation, especially 173–98.

17. *The Post-Modern Aura* first appeared in *Salmagundi* nos. 63–64 (1984); representative responses to it and a rejoinder by the author are collected in *Salmagundi* no. 67 (1985): 163–97.

18. Incidentally, as I observe above, a distinction needs to be made between what Gass claims for his fiction in his essays and the interpretations the fictions themselves yield. Newman overlooks this point. Certainly, as Gass tells us in "The Death of the Author," the author's intention is "only occasionally relevant" (*Habitations of the Word*, 283).

19. Collected in *After the Great Divide*, "The Search for Tradition: Avant-garde and Postmodernism in the 1970s" first appeared in *New German Critique* 22 (1981): 23–40.

20. Terry Eagleton makes this same point (though resorting to hyperbole to do so): "What is parodied by postmodernist culture, with its dissolution of art into the prevailing forms of commodity production, is nothing less than the revolutionary art of the twentieth-century avant-garde. It is as though postmodernism is among other things a sick joke at the expense of such revolutionary avant-gardism" ("Capitalism, Modernism and Postmodernism," 385). Quite clearly, I reject a basic premise of Eagleton's argument—that

(neo-) Marxist *revolution* is necessary today in Western liberal democracies to ensure the liberties of the individual. Strategic reformation, rather than revolution, strikes me as a more appropriate course, a position shared, appropriately enough I think, by most postmodern fictionists.

21. We might also remark that modernism is marked by gloomy sentiments. See Lunn (46–52).

22. See Schücking's classic essay, "Literarische 'Fehlurteile'," for a helpful overview of the problem of "arbitrary valuation," particularly in early nineteenth-century German criticism.

23. Collected in *After the Great Divide,* "Mapping the Postmodern" first appeared in *New German Critique* 33 (1984): 5–52.

24. The Emersonian echo in Sukenick's essays is loud. Compare the following, the first taken from Emerson's "The Poet," the second from Sukenick's "Thirteen Digressions": "The sign and credentials of the poet are that he announces that which no man foretold. He is the true and only doctor; he knows and tells; he is the only teller of the news" (546); "We [writers] live in language, and only writers are free—only they know how to move into a more and more spacious syntax" (32–33). Sukenick's postulation of an unattenuated freedom is of course decidedly un-postmodern.

25. Sukenick's Fiction Collective colleague Raymond Federman puts forward a very different view of the reader's interaction with the postmodern text: "No longer being manipulated by an authorial point of view, the reader will be the one who extracts, invents, creates a meaning and an order for the people in the fiction" ("Surfiction," 14). While I agree that postmodern fiction admits the prominence of the reader, I think Federman overstates his case when he claims that the reader will be beyond authorial manipulation. While we might legitimately concern ourselves more with the implied author(s) of a text and/or its fictive author(s) than with the historical author, I would suggest that an "unmanipulative" text is a contradiction in terms. There is always some kind of manipulation invested in a text though the nature of the manipulation, and our response to it, will certainly vary. See Link's *Rezeptionsforschung: Eine Einführung in Methoden und Probleme* for a discussion of a work's various "authors" (39–41, 52–64).

26. While in my view self-contradiction weakens Sukenick's arguments, Klinkowitz praises Sukenick for establishing a "coherent literary theory" (*Literary Subversions: New American Fiction and the Practice of Criticism,* 189). In his review of *In Form,* Brian McHale is also laudatory (801).

27. Both Jonathan Baumbach—author of two Fiction Collective titles— and Gene Lyons have written essays on the early history and aesthetics of the Fiction Collective. Lyons is critical of the group's self-congratulatory attitudes and what are for him specious claims of novelty (642–47).

28. The search for a special method of inquiry for, what Mill calls, the

"moral sciences" (and Dilthey the *Geisteswissenschaften*) has inspired perhaps the most rigorous critique of epistemology. Dilthey's notion of *Verstehen* attempts to define the basis of human understanding in nonmethodological, nonepistemological terms. *Verstehen,* an essentially intuitive drive, works within the confines of fundamental existential categories, e.g., part-whole, inner-outer, and value, among others, and equally fundamental social ones such as nations and cultural systems. It pursues a knowledge of the lived-world (*Lebenswelt*) that is neither scientific nor reductive. Though Dilthey's project is rife with contradiction and susceptible to charges of "scientism," it serves as a useful point of departure for later hermeneutic theory, e.g., Gadamer's and Ricoeur's.

29. In an insightful remark, in a gently reproachful essay, Hassan suggests the influence of New Criticism in *The World Within the Word,* the second essay collection ("Wars of Desire, Politics of the Word," 53). Of course, as Hassan points out, Gass attended Kenyon College, from where John Crowe Ransom helped shaped English studies in the United States. For a brief discussion of Gass's respect for the methods of New Criticism, see the interview included in Arthur Salzman's Gass study (171–74).

30. Gass continues to assert the separation of word and world in later essays. The following is taken from "Representation and the War for Reality": ". . . the large, lazy, slop-about novel, whose representations of the world no more *resemble* it than the models of science and philosophy do, and whose weapons are the cast-off equipment of the sophist—the esthetic grammar of the language, of course, and then the schemes, tropes, figures and fancy forms of rhetoric and oratory, table talk and kitchen gossip" (*Habitations of the Word,* 93–94).

31. The passage goes on to observe that the storyteller "will avoid recording consciousness since consciousness is private—we do not normally 'take it down'—and because no one really believes in any other feelings than his own" (*FFL,* 32). This sounds a little like Thomas Kuhn's idea that communication between paradigms is not possible. Gass implies that "your emotions are yours and mine are mine and ne'er the twain shall meet." Surely, however, your emotions are relevant to me if I can reach some kind of understanding of them, if empathy and/or imagination allow me to appropriate them in some personally significant way. What else is communication?

32. In his Gass study, Arthur Salzman asserts that "Gass himself recognizes that creative activity must ultimately lead to a repossession of the world" (22). While Salzman's critical readings of Gass's fiction ably illustrate this "repossession," Salzman neglects the point that I make, along with Bruss and Hassan, that Gass's essays are burdened by a self-conscious aestheticism. I maintain that one can claim for Gass a recognition of the *worldliness* of the literary text only by reading his essays "against the grain."

33. Notwithstanding nuances of method and emphasis, recent studies that include Theo D'haen's *Text to Reader: Fowles, Barth, Cortázar and Boon,* Allen Thiher's *Words in Reflection: Modern Language Theory and Postmodern Fiction,* Linda Hutcheon's *Narcissistic Narrative: The Metafictional Paradox,* Alan Singer's *A Metaphorics of Fiction: Discontinuity and Discourse in the Modern Novel,* and Dina Sherzer's *Representation in Contemporary French Fiction* number among those concerned with the referentiality issue. Though not concerned specifically with postmodern fiction, Thomas Pavel's *Fictional Worlds* examines literature's ability to represent.

34. Cited by Ihab Hassan ("Wars of Desire, Politics of the Word," 48), "de-define" is the coinage of Harold Rosenberg.

Chapter 2

1. Mentioned in Geoffrey Green's *Literary Criticism and the Structures of History: Erich Auerbach and Leo Spitzer,* 21. In the present discussion of Auerbach, I rely a good deal upon Green's study for critical insight and biographical data.

2. Of Auerbach's ongoing preoccupation with the historicity of human understanding, W. W. Holdheim writes: "Knowledge is not a detached and 'objective' adherence to a methodologically preestablished pattern; rather, it is *Wirkungsgeschichte,* radiation, living appropriation, dependent upon an *esprit de finesse* that cannot be predetermined or codified. If Auerbach proceeds as he does, it is not because he cannot do any better but because this is the way history should be apprehended if it is to remain history. And this is why his work is a model even now—especially now—no matter how this or that specialist may evaluate this or that particular literary analysis" (224).

3. For an early and insightful consideration of mimesis and postmodern fiction, see Myron Greenman's article. Though Greenman considers mimesis from the point of view of production, rather than from that of reception, he, as I do, regards the representation of a "reality" as the constant, inevitable goal of literature: "although the mimetic effort, the apparent need to imitate or represent reality in literature, may be and probably is a constant in the artistic process, the reality imitated shifts, diffuses, reassembles itself, discloses itself now variously, now obscurely; so that to speak of new [i.e., postmodern] fiction not only as a break with the traditional view of reality . . . but also as a departure from the mimetic tradition itself, becomes absolutely erroneous" (311).

4. Interestingly, a key element of Hirsch's theory has undergone recent revision/refinement and, consequently, it can be argued that his theory *in toto* has been called into question. Hirsch has long held that textual *meaning* is authorially determined and impervious to change while textual *significance* is

defined by the individual reader and therefore malleable. While reiterating this position in a 1984 essay, "Meaning and Significance Reinterpreted" (204), Hirsch goes on to define *meaning* in new, more expansive terms, suggesting that there are variable "extensions" of fixed, authorially intended meaning. In uniting the contrary notions of change and permanence, a "meaning extension" is a paradoxical concept that seems to enfranchise at once both author and reader, past and present. While the implications of this essay for the overall theory need to be interrogated, this is not an appropriate context.

5. While working out the transvalued, "reader-centered" view of mimesis I offer here, I was unaware of any similar effort to reconstitute mimesis. I have since come across an article with a similar project in mind. In "Social Representation and Mimesis," Luiz Costa Lima aims at "rethinking mimesis." Though my debt is primarily to twentieth-century phenomenology—in addition to the latter Costa Lima also considers speech-act theory and Goffman's concept of "frame analysis"—we both agree that mimetic significance is temporally conditioned and emerges only through a collaborative process involving text and reader. The following is taken from the conclusion of "Social Representation and Mimesis": "the only thing that can be said about the universality of the products of mimesis is that they are not universal due to some essential quality but rather become so for communities, and, within these, for those recipients who are able to carry out a peculiar keying, the one that discloses to them a kind of play which is not merely playful, a play that involves both pleasure and estrangement, a play in which pleasure prompts estrangement and the latter demands a return to the former" (463).

6. Traditional hermeneutics actually discerns three separate, separable levels or modes of interpretation: the "understanding" of authorially intended *meaning (subtilitas intelligendi)*; the reader's "interpretation" of the authorially intended meaning *(subtilitas explicandi)*; and the use or "application" the text affords the reader *(subtilitas applicandi)*. Embracing a position already found in Ernesti's *Institutio Interpretis Novi Testamenti* of 1761 and, with slight modification, in Schleiermacher's aphorisms of 1805 and 1809–10, Hirsch's hermeneutics maintains the separability of the three levels (Schleiermacher, *Hermeneutics*, 41; Hirsch, *Validity in Interpretation*, 129). Calling the three levels a "triadic unity," Hans Robert Jauss also promotes the "separability" thesis ("Literature and Hermeneutics"). Gadamer, with whom I agree in this regard, conflates the three in *Truth and Method*. See Hoy's *The Critical Circle: Literature, History, and Philosophical Hermeneutics*, 51–55, for a comparative overview of the Hirsch and Gadamer positions.

7. In addition to the "Appropriation" essay, from which the above quotes are taken, Ricoeur's "What is a text?" has also been helpful to me in understanding the issue of appropriation. In the latter essay, Ricoeur's "structuralist hermeneutics" emphasizes the collateral importance of structural analysis and

appropriation (*Hermeneutics and the Human Sciences*, 45–64). The relational model of mimesis which I put forward here corresponds to *mimesis₃*, that Ricoeur discusses in *Time and Narrative*, especially 1:70–87.

8. Charles Newman puts forward a grimly different view of what literature has to offer us as readers: "When it [literary experimentation] doesn't work we are reminded that innovation in and of itself is not only tedious but ultimately self-cancelling, that what we finally want from literature is neither amusement nor edification, but the demonstration of a real authority which is not to be confused with sincerity, and of an understanding which is not gratuitous" (173). While I fully endorse the first part of the statement, the second half seems at best self-indulgently nostalgic, at worst Orwellian (in the unhappiest of the term's significances).

9. Harry Levin, unable to portend the literary developments of the last twenty years, says much the same thing in "What Was Modernism?" (*Refractions*, 272–73).

10. I will in any case readily admit that some of my own undergraduate students have put forward convincing readings of such postmodern works as *Slaughterhouse-Five* and *The Crying of Lot 49;* both of these works have of course gone through numerous paperback reprintings—as of 1982, thirty-seven and nineteen, respectively.

Chapter 3

1. Lukács's *The Theory of the Novel* remains one of the most important analyses of the novel's history and its ethico-social importance, and one that clearly influences my own understanding of the genre. In *Theory*, Lukács feels that existential tension is normal and that the novel, the "epic" of the age, is preoccupied with it. I agree with him on both points.

2. While I find Rorty's distinction between the two liberalisms helpful, his views on twentieth-century literary history are open to question. See Norris for a lucid critique of Rorty's views on literary modernity (*Contest*, 154–61).

3. I consider Jameson's views further in my conclusion.

4. Whether Christian, Christian-Marxist, or Marxist of one stripe or another, Terry Eagleton's political and literary views have always been characterized by millennialist yearnings. See Bergonzi for an analysis of Eagleton's intellectual development that is generally unsympathetic, though fair in my judgment (188–209).

5. An interesting and illuminating exercise would be to compare the formalistic biases evident in the essays of William Gass and Ronald Sukenick to the mimetic significance of their fictions. Although there would be a place for such an inquiry in the present context, I have opted to look at authors and works I find more important.

6. It is of course Plato, a major villain in the late twentieth century, who first

promotes this specialization of function. We see this in his *Republic* where he arrogates extraordinary powers to the professional sage, the "Philosopher King." Similarly, in "Ion," Socrates argues that the rhapsode cannot speak knowledgeably about thematic elements in literature but only about form and artistic inspiration.

Chapter 4

1. For brief analyses of *Alphabetical Africa,* a work I will not discuss here, see Martin (230–33) and my review essay "Walter Abish."

2. Though brief, Messerli's discussion of Abish's seemingly objective point of view in *How German Is It* is helpful (298–300).

3. On this same subject of language's capacity to shape personal ethics Adorno writes: "Fascism was not simply a conspiracy—although it was that—but it was something that came to life in the course of a powerful social development. Language provides it with a refuge. Within this refuge a smoldering evil expresses itself as though it were salvation" (*The Jargon of Authenticity,* 5).

4. I mostly agree with Holdheim, though one might regard Melville's "Benito Cereno," for example, contrary to Holdheim's view, as a case in which, arguably, an author has delineated with some acuity the relationship between morality and plain stupidity. I am thinking particularly, of course, of Captain Delano.

5. Incidentally, William Kowinski cheerfully speculates that the amalgamation of malls and condominiums, i.e., "the Mallcondo Continuum," may well be the way of the future: "The new challenge is to create the ever-beckoning Eden of the frontier within the internal worlds of the planned town, the megastructure, the dome, the mall. It's enclosing time in the Garden of the West" (388). Many will find this vision of Fortress Suburbia "post-Edenic," even dystopian. Are we approaching the day when an entire life will be lived within an emporium? The thought gives chilling new meaning to the notion of a "captive clientele."

6. In the McCaffery/Gregory interview, Abish cites the influence of Godard's early films on his fiction. Bontemps appears to be modeled on Godard, whose films, Abish notes in the interview, develop an "uneasy relationship between his revolutionary fervor and his aesthetic concern," though the two never quite "merge" (24). Incidentally, like Bontemps' film, Godard's *Vent d'Est* also involves the physical destruction of shopping malls and their patrons. Throughout Abish's fiction we find the same themes that pervade Godard's films: gratuitous violence, materialism, and the exploitation of women. Political extremism also figures prominently in many of Godard's films as it does in "This Is Not a Film" and *How German Is It.*

7. A paraphrase of this same statement appears in *How German Is It,* but, strangely, Whitehead is introduced there as an "American thinker" (15).

8. The many recent films and literary works dealing with this subject are well known. In world affairs, Nazi atrocities continue to be a focal point. One can cite, for example, Wiesel's receipt of the 1986 Nobel Peace Prize as well as the ongoing efforts of various national and international bodies to identify and prosecute Nazi war criminals. In recent years, in unrelated cases, two Canadian anti-Semites, Jim Keegstra and Ernst Zundel, have been prosecuted for violation of Canadian hate laws (Quinn; Aikenhead). (Both Keegstra and Zundel were initially convicted; an appellate court threw out the former's conviction on a legal technicality while Zundel's conviction was upheld by an Ontario Appeal Court ruling, with both appellate judgments occurring coincidentally in June 1988.) And, of course, there is the 1985 Bitburg incident when Ronald Reagan visited a West German cemetery to honor 1,900 German war dead among whom were 49 soldiers of the infamous Waffen-SS. Reagan rankled many people by suggesting that members of Hitler's armed forces were also victims of a "vicious ideology" (quoted in Rentschler, 88). Rentschler's article provides an excellent analysis both of the Bitburg incident and of current attitudes toward Nazism, particularly as presented by the news media and film.

9. Formal English gardens are mentioned recurrently in the novel, e.g., Munich's Englischer Garten (16), Geneva's Jardin Anglais (47), and the Englischer Garten of Egon's city (127).

10. The principal formal differences between the story and the novel are, first, that the former has a first person narrator and the latter a third person, and, second, consistent with the necessary economy of the form, the action of the short story is brisker and more concentrated. The suppression of historical truth is, of course, the primary theme of both. Brumhold, Durst, and the Holocaust's victimized Jewry are emphasized more in "The English Garden" than in the novel. See Arias-Misson for a discussion of "The English Garden" (117–18).

11. In "On Aspects of the Familiar World as Perceived in Everyday Life and Literature," an unpublished conference paper from 1981, Abish emphasizes the disruptive purposes of experimental fiction: "The innovative novel is, in essence, a novel of disfamiliarization, a novel that has ceased to concern itself with the mapping of the 'familiar' world" (quoted in Martin, 238).

12. In fairness to Heidegger, it should be noted that, in contrast to those of the fictitious Brumhold, his "reckless speeches" are confined to a brief ten-month period. His 1933 Rector's address at Freiburg, "The Self-Assertion of the German University," is of course the most famous and noteworthy exemplar in this particular genre. Heidegger offers a spirited defense of himself in the 1966 *Spiegel* interview, published posthumously in 1976, in which, while

acknowledging a brief infatuation with Nazism, he depicts himself as the victim of "slander," misinformation, malice, and misquotation. As Heidegger admits in the interview, it was his view in 1933 that, given the "general confusion of opinions and of the political trends of twenty-two parties," Hitler would bring national political cohesion (270). Published first in 1933, the *Rektoratsrede* was not republished until 1983 at which time it was accompanied by a foreword by Heidegger's son Hermann. The first (and only, so far as I know) English translation of the address is Karsten Harries's in 1985. In addition to his remarks in the *Spiegel* interview, Heidegger's "The Rectorate 1933/ 34: Facts and Thoughts," written in 1945 after the collapse of the Third Reich, also serves as self-apology. (The latter was first published in the early eighties; Harries's translation of it accompanies the translation of the *Rektoratsrede*.)

Predictably, Heidegger's involvement with the Nazis has inspired much commentary. See Gillespie for an overview of the various positions up until the early eighties (198–99n.38). We are entering a new period of investigation with the recent appearance of Victor Farias's highly critical study, *Heidegger et le Nazisme* (1987). See Wolin for an analysis of the Farias book and reactions to it. *New German Critique* has recently published translations of other public political statements Heidegger made in 1933 and 1934; the same issue provides translations of two essays by Heidegger's former student, Karl Löwith. Neither Harries nor Löwith accepts Heidegger's claims, and those of later apologists, that his embracing of Nazism was a temporary, politically expedient move. Harries's "Heidegger as a Political Thinker" argues convincingly that, far from being a philosophical aberration, Heidegger's political views in the thirties build on notions developed in *Being and Time:* "Once we recognize that authenticity demands the subordination of the individual to a common destiny, it becomes impossible to see the *Rektoratsrede* as diametrically opposed to *Being and Time*" (651). Löwith also sees an organic link between Heidegger's ontology and politics: "The possibility of a Heideggerian political philosophy was not born as a result of a regrettable 'miscue,' but from the very conception of existence that simultaneously combats and absorbs the 'spirit of the age' ("Political Implications," 132). Indicative of renewed interest in Heidegger's political views, *Critical Inquiry* devoted much of its Winter 1989 issue to the subject of "Heidegger and Nazism."

13. Heidegger has not been flatteringly characterized in imaginative literature. In Borges's "Guayaquil" (1970) and Grass's *Dog Years* (*Hundejahre* [1963]), Heidegger is depicted as a Nazi apologist and irrational idealist, respectively. In his lengthy essay *The Jargon of Authenticity* Adorno emphasizes both these points. In Bellow's *Herzog* (1964), the protagonist includes Heidegger in his gallery of intellectual foes. Rebuking the philosopher for his denigration of the "quotidian," Herzog claims that every person's moral worth is centered in quotidian behavior and quotidian values, not in learned abstrac-

tion: "Dear Doktor Professor Heidegger, I should like to know what you mean by the expression 'the fall into the quotidian.' When did this fall occur? Where were we standing?" (49; 106). Heidegger discusses the falling of *Dasein* and its causes—"idle talk," "curiosity," and "ambiguity"—in *Being and Time* (210–24).

14. Heidegger's most explicit statement regarding the promise and historical destiny of the Nazis occurs at the very end of the rectorial address. The conclusion of the speech is unmistakably supportive of the Nazis though in it Heidegger makes his familiar claims about the imminent collapse of Western culture and the exemplarity of the classical Greek tradition: "But no one will even ask whether we do or do not will [the centrality of the German university in German society], when the spiritual strength of the West fails and the joints of the world no longer hold, when this moribund semblance of a culture caves in and drags all that remains strong into confusion and lets it suffocate in madness. Whether this will happen or not depends alone on whether or not we, as a historical-spiritual people, still and once again will ourselves. Every individual *participates* in this decision, even he, and indeed especially he, who evades it. But we do will that our people fulfill its historical mission. We do will ourselves. For the young and the youngest strength of the people, which already reaches beyond us, *has* by now *decided* the matter. But we fully understand the splendor and the greatness of this setting out only when we carry within ourselves that profound and far-reaching thoughtfulness that gave ancient Greek wisdom the word: 'All that is great stands in the storm' (Plato, *Republic*, 497 d, 9)" (479–80).

15. And, we should note, the very name "Brumhold," drawing as it seems to from *brume*, a French term for heavy fog, is in itself an authorial judgment on Brumhold's views, which are arguably "fogbound."

16. Obviously, the German belief that language shapes national consciousness and, consequently, national values predates the twentieth century. Herder, Fichte, and Humboldt, among others, make the same claim much earlier. See Stambrook for a discussion of the language issue in the context of German nationalism in the nineteenth century (16–28).

17. Curiously, Adorno, not unlike Brumhold, maintains that German is uniquely suited to philosophical meditations, that "there is a specific, objective quality of the German language" ("On the Question: 'What is German?'" 130). I am ill-equipped to say if this is simple chauvinism or an exile's nostalgia for the *Vaterland* or the truth of the matter.

18. In Abish's story, "I Am the Dust Under Your Feet," Rainer, a gamekeeper, is a reassuring presence: "Even his twill knee-length trousers, his leather vest, his broad leather belt, his worn bone-handle hunting knife, his heavy socks, scuffed resoled boots, were a means of mapping the topography" (8).

19. In Karl Löwith's view, Heidegger, for his part, mastered the art of rhetorical equivocation well in his political addresses, which, Löwith observes, left

his auditors unsure whether they should take up the study of the pre-Socratics or enlist in the Storm Troopers (quoted in Megill, 130). Megill provides a succinct overview of Heidegger's political texts from the thirties (128–36).

20. "Just When We Believe That Everything Has Changed" and "I Am the Dust Under Your Feet," two excerpts from Abish's next novel, continue his discussion of the "New Germany."

21. Though its emphasis is entirely different, Toni Morrison's *The Bluest Eye* also investigates the signifying practices of the material world. In that novel, black children learn racial self-loathing through the models of perfection offered by a dominant white culture. A number of images promote their self-loathing: the domestic harmony of a white household as represented in the "Dick and Jane" reading primers; the sheer "cuteness" of child film star Shirley Temple whose visage decorates a cup; blue-eyed Caucasian dolls; and even the picture of a pretty little white girl on a candy wrapper.

22. Here, it seems to me, Abish's position is very similar to Sartre's when the latter says that there is no such thing as a *good* anti-Semitic novel or a *good* novel that oppresses workers or blacks or colonial peoples (*What Is Literature?* 58).

23. The relationship between skepticism and the "forgetting" of history is a topic of some concern today in critical circles given the recent (1987) de Man disclosures ("Yale Scholar's Articles"). For early contributions to the de Man debate, see articles by David Hirsch, Wiener, Hartman, and Barbara Johnson. See also the various essays in *Critical Inquiry* 15.4 (Summer 1989).

Chapter 5

1. The Grove edition of *Spanking the Maid* that I am using appeared in 1982, a year after Bruccoli Clark brought it out in a limited edition.

2. Larry McCaffery establishes a parallel between certain stories in *Pricksongs and Descants* and cubism. In his view, Coover's creation of a "deliberate ambiguity of event" is similar to the cubists' development of "spatial ambiguity" (*The Metafictional Muse,* 72). McCaffery's analogy is apt in that it illustrates the many-sidedness of both cubistic representation and Coover's short stories, particularly the early ones. However, the analogy is of limited applicability because the cubists posit space less in ambiguous terms than in inclusive, holistic ones.

3. In what was the first article on *Spanking the Maid,* my "Another Exemplary Fiction: Robert Coover's *Spanking the Maid*" emphasized, like Pieiller's review, paradox, ambiguity, and skepticism, in short, the theme of epistemological breakdown. While I continue to believe the latter to be of central importance, the reading I offer here is not confined to this interest.

4. To call attention to the well known, Grove publishes a rather extensive line of erotica—most of which is authored anonymously, purportedly in the last century—in order at least in part, one assumes, to finance the publication of such "serious" authors as Coover. One wonders how many readers of such literature have purchased *Spanking the Maid* and had their expectations radically disappointed. I have noticed that in at least one metropolitan bookstore such confusion has been encouraged (strategically? accidentally? ambiguously?) by the shelving of *Spanking the Maid* among Grove's erotica. Incidentally, in the late sixties and early seventies, Grove distributed *I Am Curious, Yellow*, the first mass-circulated pornographic film. Citing *Life* magazine figures, Edward Mishan notes that Grove had made $5 million up to 1970 in the United States alone in this venture (36).

5. Other of his fictions indicate Coover's own preoccupation with the female posterior. See, for example, *Gerald's Party*, "You Must Remember This" (*A Night at the Movies*, 172–73), and "Charlie in the House of Rue" (*A Night at the Movies*, 90–92, 99).

6. Hegel, of course, investigates the paradox peculiar to the master-slave relationship wherein the master cedes his own independence in the very attempt to curtail another's; see chapter 4 of *Phenomenology of Spirit*. See Girard for both an exploration of the master-slave theme and a discussion of sadomasochism (96–112; 176–92).

7. Incidentally, the Neoplatonists' typology of love might be profitably applied to the study of *A Farewell to Arms* wherein, it seems to me, the priest promotes an asexual divine love, Catherine an exemplary human love, and, of course, Rinaldi bestial love. Admittedly, the identification of Catherine as a positive character contradicts the standard and often overwrought claim that Hemingway is *always* misogynistic. While the latter is frequently the case, it is not invariably so. For a typical feminist reading of *A Farewell to Arms*, see Fetterley (46–71). I would cite the recently published *The Garden of Eden* as the most virulently misogynistic of Hemingway's work, both in its depiction of Catherine *and* Marita.

8. Toward the end of *Vita Nuova*, Dante defines this dichotomy: ". . . the two divisions of my thoughts. The one I call Heart, that is, appetite; the other, I call Soul, that is, reason" (103). The passage in which this appears provides commentary for a sonnet in which Heart and Soul are in dialogue.

9. Not only peers, there is another marked similarity between the two. Like Sade, Rousseau had a taste for the whip, as a recipient thereof. In *Les Confessions*, he notes the sexual stirring he felt when whipped upon the buttocks by his matron, Mlle. Lambercier (44–45).

10. See Gorer (27–30) for a detailed description of the "Affaire Keller." Gorer is strangely, even perversely skeptical of Mme Keller's claim that she

was an *unwilling* participant in the Sadeian rite (flagellation). In passing, we might note that Sade whipped Rose Keller with a martinet—a knotted whip— an instrument also used by the master in *Spanking the Maid*.

11. Coover undertakes a similar phonetic manipulation in *The Public Burning* wherein the fourth word of the agitprop slogan, "AMERICA IS THE HOPE OF THE WORLD," undergoes considerable semantic shift for satirical effect: "hope" becomes dope, rope, rape, rake, fake, fate, hate, nate, nite, bite, bile, pule, puke, juke, joke (36–41). Incidentally, in *Spanking the Maid* the playful offsetting of similarity and difference is not confined to that found in homonymity; repetition is also important as a structural device where the repeated scenario in the bedroom undergoes slight changes as the work progresses.

12. In a self-reflexive comment in one of his earlier stories, "The Magic Poker," Coover notes that, like Zeno's turtle, he is always with us, the readers. In fact, he asserts, his readers, like his fictions, are his own creations. Referring to the fictive setting of this story he writes: "Who invented this map? Well, I must have, surely . . . Yes, and perhaps tomorrow I will invent Chicago and Jesus Christ and the history of the moon. Just as I have invented you, dear reader, while lying here in the afternoon sun" (*Pricksongs and Descants*, 40).

13. Of the several interviews I have read, the Bigsby piece presents Coover's most expansive statement on his moral intentions, intentions that are successfully realized in his works, in my view; see especially 86–89.

Chapter 6

1. Manheim's translation of *Wunschloses Unglück, A Sorrow Beyond Dreams*, is collected in *Three by Peter Handke*. All references to the novel will be to the Manheim translation and the original 1972 German edition; the second page number given refers to the German edition. (A stage adaptation of *A Sorrow Beyond Dreams* has been produced off-Broadway.) *Three by Peter Handke* also includes Michael Roloff's translation of *Die Angst des Tormanns beim Elfmeter* (*The Goalie's Anxiety at the Penalty Kick*) and Manheim's translation of *Der kurze Brief zum langen Abschied* (*Short Letter, Long Farewell*).

2. For Manheim's translations of *Die linkshändige Frau* (*The Left-Handed Woman*) and *Die Stunde der wahren Empfindung* (*A Moment of True Feeling*), see *Two Novels by Peter Handke*. For Roloff's translations of *Der Ritt über den Bodensee* (*The Ride Across Lake Constance*) and *Kaspar* (*Kaspar*), see *The Ride Across Lake Constance and Other Plays* and *Kaspar and Other Plays*. Roloff has also translated *Die Innenwelt der Aussenwelt der Innenwelt* (1969), Handke's best-selling (plus 75,000 copies) poetry collection: *The Innerworld of the Outerworld of the Innerworld*.

3. While her death is volitional, I do not agree with those readers who, uncritically and without qualification, accept as valid the narrator's implica-

tion that Frau Handke's suicide is an act of strength. Ursula Love, for example, writes: "The narrator sees it not as an act of desperation but rather as a decision which the mother makes with a clear head upon recognizing that it is her only alternative. Her suicide is, in his view, actually a 'freely elected death' [Freitod] and not only an understandable act but an admirable one as well. As represented by the narrator, it is the sensible conclusion to a senseless life and illustrates how the mother, despite everything, comes to acknowledge herself after all even if self-realization is possible for her only in self-destruction" (141; my translation). At the time of her suicide, Handke's mother is quite as subject to the machinations of her physical and psychical maladies as she has been to the oppressively conformist ideals of her culture. Her suicide is a "concession" to her illness(es) and is no more self-individuating than her concessions to petty bourgeois ideals have been. To assert the contrary is to assign to the novella the sentimentality it strives to avoid.

4. Not all readers concede that the writing of the novella is for Handke a therapeutic act. Rainer Nägele and Renate Voris, for example, state in their Handke monograph that "writing here is not, in the vulgar psychological sense, a liberation from a trauma" (60; my translation). For my part, I rely upon remarks made in an interview with Heinz Ludwig Arnold where Handke asserts that writing has helped him to become unashamed of himself and his background. On more than one occasion in *A Sorrow Beyond Dreams*, Handke claims that writing is a means to overcoming the horrors of "those speechless moments."

5. In addition to White's *Metahistory*, see his *Tropics of Discourse*, as well as the following: Danto's *Analytical Philosophy of History*, Dray's *Laws and Explanation in History* and *Philosophy of History*, and Gallie's *Philosophy and the Historical Understanding*.

6. Klinkowitz does not cite his source for this quote.

7. Of the *Gruppe 47* writes Handke: "One has the impression that these writers . . . could spare themselves a lot of time and trouble by using a camera and yet achieve much better results" (*Ich bin ein Bewohner des Elfenbeinturms*, 32; my translation).

8. In an article devoted to the subject, Hans-Gerhard Winter lists as prominent features of *neue Subjektivität* the following: a personal perspective (whether *Er*- or *Ich-Erzähler*), conflation of inner and outer world, self-referentiality, identity crisis, the demand for active readerly involvement, and partial resolution (109–10).

9. For a discussion of metafictionality in Delany's novel, see Ebert's article; see Manger for a discussion of the metafictionality theme in Becker's work.

10. Peter Horn is of the opinion that Handke's self-professed egocentricity effectively preempts any possibility of a meaningful social praxis for his work: "Alienation can never be overcome through alienated literature anymore

than it can be overcome through individual actions or passions" (my translation); see 45–64, especially 61–62. Horn's critique advances the conservative leftist view—what Karl Popper calls "methodological holism"—that social change can only occur through collective gestures (rather than personal or private ones). I maintain that the individual can meaningfully influence events even as I concede that major social change can only be effected through mass response. In the long run, innovative fictions are far more likely to breed in their readers a liberated, more genuinely democratic sensibility than are formulaic fictions.

11. For a discussion of his *Wortspiel* see Bohn's article (370). "Wunschlos glücklich sein" means, literally "to be happy beyond one's wishes (dreams)." Frau Handke is, of course, "unhappy" ("unglücklich") beyond her wishes.

12. Donald Barthelme and Robert Coover also denigrate the use of "automatic" language though, usually, in a more humorous, less somber manner than Handke. See, for example, Barthelme's *Snow White* and Coover's *The Public Burning*.

13. An unironic use of clichés can also serve the interests of greater understanding. In her discussion of the fiction of the Latin American writers Manuel Puig and Luis Rafael Sanchez, Lois Zamora points out that popular language can "make us aware of the self-imposed limitations of literary language during this century by implicitly rejecting the cerebral self-consciousness of much advanced contemporary fiction" (434). It is of course important to note that the two writers in question, Puig and Sanchez, strive for, in the interests of raising political awareness, the broadest possible appeal. Handke's audience, better educated and better politically informed, is less likely to be confused by the relative novelty of auto-bio-graphy as metafiction.

14. To Marlow, "the meaning of an episode was not inside like a kernel but outside, enveloping the tale which brought it out only as a glow brings out a haze, in the likeness of one of these misty halos that sometimes are made visible by the spectral illumination of moonshine" (5).

15. A later work, *Die linkshändige Frau,* does, in fact, take up the problems attendant on being a mother-housewife, though no direct reference is made to Handke's mother or *A Sorrow Beyond Dreams.* In this instance, the heroine forsakes her husband and reduces her commitment to her son in the interest of establishing a personal identity. As for later autobiographical works, *Das Gewicht der Welt* (1977) is a *Tagebuch* full of intimate reflections upon life.

Chapter 7

1. Peter Zima is similarly critical of such French semioticians as Kristeva and Greimas who, in his view, through their efforts to codify intertextual re-

lationships, often lapse into a rigorously technical critique (*eine technizistische Ideologie*) that ignores the role played by subjective praxis (82).

2. Though their emphasis is formalistic, overview essays by Klinkowitz and O'Brien's reading of *Mulligan Stew* are valuable introductions (Klinkowitz and Behrens, *The Life of Fiction*, 7–15; Klinkowitz, *Literary Disruptions*, 154–67; O'Brien, "Every Man"). Klinkowitz's bibliography of primary and secondary Sorrentino materials is also useful (*Literary Disruptions*, 286–89). Incidentally, the inaugural issue of *The Review of Contemporary Fiction*, under the editorship of O'Brien, deals solely with Sorrentino's work.

3. In his *The End of Intelligent Writing*, a scathingly critical study of publishing politics in the United States, Richard Kostelanetz cites another key determinant for many publishers when deciding whom and what to publish—the capacity of the benefiting writer to return in some way the blessing bestowed upon him or her. Kostelanetz implies that many literary reputations are made and sustained largely by virtue of one's membership in the "New York [literary] mob." Writing in the early seventies, he suggests that Jason Epstein's *The New York Review of Books* should in fact be called *The New York Review of Each Other's Books* because of its cliquish reviewing policies (64–65). For an earlier fictionalized depiction of the New York literary world—similarly critical—see William Gaddis's *The Recognitions* (1955).

4. For a brief (and affectionate) description of Sorrentino the editor, see the comments of Stephens (97–98).

5. Perhaps polarization of aesthetic values is an inevitable consequence of liberal democracy. De Tocqueville, with characteristic insight, commented on the issue a century and a half ago: In democracies, he writes, "the production of artists are more numerous [than in aristocracies], but the merit of each production is diminished. . . . In aristocracies a few great pictures are produced; in democratic countries, a vast number of insignificant ones" (54). Today, the public consumes more fiction than ever before, yet, to all appearances, sympathy for innovative fiction has not increased. Of the top ten bestsellers of the seventies—ranging from *The Godfather* (13.5 million copies) through *Jaws* (9.4 million) to Jong's *Fear of Flying* (5.8 million)—none is formally experimental (though Jong's is *thematically* novel) ("A Decade's Top Ten," 4). Notwithstanding the increased complexity of the avant-garde work, its neglect is not so inevitable as many would claim. Promotion (even annotated editions) could help alleviate the perception of abstrusity that many have of noncanonical literature.

6. Of the novel's relationship to modernism Sorrentino has remarked the following: "The novel is, or was meant to be, the end of that process we call modernism; and its ultimate roots are in *Bouvard and Pécuchet*. Edward Sapir, in his brilliant 1931 paper 'Fashion,' notes that 'a specific fashion is utterly unintelligible if lifted out of its place in a sequence of forms.' If I substitute

'literary work' for 'fashion,' I might say, then, that *Mulligan Stew* is *only* intelligible when in place in the sequence of forms known as the modernist movement" (*Something Said*, 263).

7. *Mulligan Stew* also happens to be the title of a forties film. I have been unable to unearth details but infer from its absence in film indices that it is a "B" class production or worse.

8. Martin Halpin's only appearance in *Finnegans Wake* occurs in a footnote which describes him as "an old gardener from the Glens of Antrim who used to do jobs for my god father, the Rev. B. B. Brophy of Swords" (266). Adaline Glasheen's index of characters in *Finnegans Wake* has proven very helpful for tracking down and elucidating the Joycean allusions in *Mulligan Stew*. For the identification of the Hammett plagiarism, I am indebted to Donald Greiner's "Antony Lamont in Search of Gilbert Sorrentino" (107).

9. Michael Holquist sees strong similarities between the Rabelaisian age and that of Bakhtin. Political autocracy dominates each's culture: "Like Rabelais, Bakhtin is throughout his own book exploring the interface between a stasis imposed from above and a desire for change from below, between old and new, official and unofficial" (10).

10. Bakhtin claims that modern parody, unlike its medieval counterpart, is "solely negative" and devoid of "regenerating ambivalence" (*Rabelais*, 21). This is certainly not true of *Mulligan Stew* and postmodern parody generally. Sorrentino's self-caricature throughout the novel suggests his own understanding of the paradox of every creative project. One can claim originality only where one violates accepted norms, yet one's originality can only be adduced through reference to these very norms. To a major extent, norms control the non- or abnormative. Sorrentino, quite obviously, does not propose to abandon the tradition but to evaluate it continually, reshaping it into a more potent medium of expression. In "From the Prehistory of Novelistic Discourse," Bakhtin also claims for parody progressive historical decline: "In modern times the functions of parody are narrow and unproductive. Parody has grown sickly, its place in modern literature is insignificant. We live, write and speak in a world of free democratized language" (*Dialogic Imagination*, 71). While it is true that language today is open and eclectic, and that traditional distinctions between high/sacred and low/vernacular modes of discourse are largely overlooked, language nonetheless manifests a natural tendency to ape (and reinforce) hierarchies whether social or political or economic or aesthetic, a claim with which Bakhtin would obviously not disagree. Consequently, while Holy Writ and classical languages are no longer the targets of parody as they were in the late Middle Ages and the Renaissance, new targets have come into being for modern parodists. Among these "new targets"—actually old targets that are "newly" fashionable—we might

mention various kinds of specialized, stylized discourse, e.g., bureaucratese, journalese, "press conference" language, and, as we see most obviously in *Mulligan Stew,* belletristic discourse.

11. Nabokov expresses his low opinion of Mann and Faulkner repeatedly in correspondence and interviews. A letter to Edmund Wilson (Nov. 21, 1948) details his contempt for Faulkner's *Light in August,* an opinion Wilson did not share (Karlinsky, 212–13). In another letter to Wilson (April 17, 1950), Nabokov writes that Mann (like T. S. Eliot) is "a fraud and a fake" (237). Sorrentino's McCoy interview appears to borrow from those collected in Nabokov's *Strong Opinions.*

12. A brief outline of O'Brien's neglected metafiction will perhaps prove helpful to those unfamiliar with the work. The unnamed protagonist of O'Brien's *At-Swim-Two-Birds* is at work on a novel in which his protagonist, Dermot Trellis, is at work on a novel that features one Antony Lamont as well as a Sheila Lamont, Antony's sister. A primary conceit of *At-Swim-Two-Birds* holds that author, Dermot Trellis, and characters, e.g., the Lamonts, have equal ontic status. Dermot Trellis not only "creates" Sheila Lamont but *physically* rapes her. Orlick Trellis is the illegitimate issue of their union. *At-Swim-Two-Birds* is a novel (Dermot Trellis's) within a novel (the unnamed young writer's) within a novel (Flann O'Brien's). In addition to the novel-within-a-novel format, Sorrentino also borrows from O'Brien the technique of adapting the characters of other authors for his own fictions.

13. We might compare this evaluation with Sorrentino's own declared "artistic necessities": ". . . an obsessive concern with formal structure, a dislike of the replication of experience, a love of digression and embroidery, a great pleasure in false or ambiguous information, a desire to invent problems that only the invention of new forms can solve, and a joy in making mountains out of molehills" (*Something Said,* 265).

14. A major contrast remains between Sorrentino's aesthetic practice and that of Lamont—the latter will, in an effort to secure critical esteem, imitate the vulgar narrative of Trellis. Sorrentino has not, as far as I know, taken this course. David Lodge would perhaps maintain that Sorrentino has "sold out" in a recent work, *Aberration of Starlight.* In a review of the latter work, he condemns Sorrentino for having retrogressed. *Aberration of Starlight* is, as Lodge points out, decidedly modernist and, appearing in 1980, a year after *Mulligan Stew,* may suggest to some an aesthetic recidivism of sorts (774). While strongly suggestive of early twentieth-century fiction, Faulkner's *The Sound and the Fury* in particular—*Aberration of Starlight* offers four different points of view on a narrow range of events—the novel remains an evocative representation of the thirties and, in places, a sensitive psychological study of the four principal figures. Yet, and a point overlooked by Lodge, its obvious intertex-

tual self-consciousness makes it more than just a "straight" neo-modernist work. For a reading of *Aberration* dissimilar to both mine and Lodge's see Messerli's, which regards the novel as "an indictment of the modernist novel and the vision inherent in its narrative approaches"; Messerli claims that an author cannot simultaneously serve objectivist and metafictional points of view (296–97). In short, Lodge regards *Aberration* as (unfortunately) "modernist," while Messerli identifies it as (laudably) "postmodernist" or, to use his own formulation, "nonmodernist." In my view it is both. As I point out at the conclusion of "The Last Fictions: Calvino's Borgesian Odyssey," citing Hutcheon's theory of parody, the schizoid tendency in much postmodern parody allows the latter to mock and praise, *simultaneously*.

15. As many people have observed, it seems peculiar that most literary critics intent on applying new theoretical insights tend to focus their attentions on traditional canonical works and not on contemporary experimental literature.

16. Kenner, in a review of *Mulligan Stew*, claims for the novel another shortcoming: "His [Sorrentino's] parodies of silly rhetoric depend more on silly ideas than on inappropriate tropes" ("Traffic," 89). I would counter that the primary weakness of Sorrentino's parodies lies in their length and repetitiveness and not in the author's inclination to parody tropes that have become, through excessive quotation, both silly and inappropriate.

17. See Thielemans's article for a more detailed discussion of the *pleasure Mulligan Stew* affords the reader. Otherwise a sound reading of the novel, this essay is too quick to accept statements found in *Mulligan Stew* and *Splendide-Hôtel* on the purported superfluity of the contemporary writer. I also reject the notion put forward by Thielemans that postmodern fictions are nonmimetic (117). As I argue throughout, and particularly in chapter 2, postmodern fiction provides the reader with a glimpse of his or her own lived-world through its depiction of a fictional one.

Conclusion

1. Jameson's views on postmodernism and postmodern politics deserve patient, systematic analysis, something my brief remarks here do not claim to offer. I am not aware of any detailed discussion of Jameson's position on these particular matters though his concern with contemporary culture is a relatively new development, as he notes in the 1982 *Diacritics* interview (L. Green et al., 74). For brief considerations of his analysis of postmodern culture see, variously, Arac (284–87, 305–7), Chabot (11–17), Kearney (383–86), and Sarup (141–46). Presumably, the appearance of Jameson's book (Duke University Press, forthcoming) will inspire more detailed inquiries.

2. Aronowitz outlines seven features of postmodern politics and briefly illustrates their operation in contemporary global history. Aronowitz's fine essay appeared in a special issue of *Social Text* (7.3 [1989]). His piece and other contributions to the same issue are collected in *Universal Abandon? The Politics of Postmodernism,* a volume I strongly recommend.

Works Cited

Abish, Walter. *Alphabetical Africa*. New York: New Directions, 1974.

———. "The Fall of Summer." *Conjunctions* 7 (1985): 110–41.

———. *How German Is It*. New York: New Directions, 1980.

———."I Am the Dust Under Your Feet." *Conjunctions* 10 (1987): 7–33.

———. *In the Future Perfect*. New York: New Directions, 1977.

———. "Just When We Believe That Everything Has Changed." *Conjunctions* 8 (1985): 125–31.

———. *Minds Meet*. New York: New Directions, 1975.

———. "Self-Portrait." In *Individuals: Post-Movement Art in America*, edited by Alan Sondheim, 1–25. New York: Dutton, 1977.

———. "The Writer-To-Be: An Impression of Living." *Substance* 27 (1980): 101–14.

Adams, Hazard, ed. *Critical Theory Since Plato*. New York: Harcourt, 1971.

Adams, Hazard, and Leroy Searle, eds. *Critical Theory Since 1965*. Tallahassee: Florida State University Press, 1986.

Adorno, Theodor. *The Jargon of Authenticity*. Translated by Knut Tarnowski and Frederic Will. Evanston: Northwestern University Press, 1973.

———. "On the Question: 'What Is German?'" Translated by Thomas Y. Levin. *New German Critique* 36 (1985): 121–31.

Aikenhead, Sherri. "An outcast in eclipse." *Maclean's* (31 March 1986): 8.

Aldridge, John. *The American Novel and the Way We Live Now*. New York: Oxford University Press, 1983.

Alter, Robert. "Mimesis and the Motive for Fiction." *TriQuarterly* 42 (1978): 228–49.

————. *Partial Magic: The Novel as Self-Conscious Genre.* Berkeley: University of California Press, 1975.

Arac, Jonathan. *Critical Genealogies: Historical Situations for Postmodern Literary Studies.* New York: Columbia University Press, 1987.

Arias-Misson, Alain. "The Puzzle of Walter Abish: *In the Future Perfect.*" *Substance* 27 (1980): 115–24.

Aristotle. *Aristotle.* Translated and edited by P. Wheelwright. Indianapolis: Bobbs-Merrill, 1951.

Arnold, Heinz Ludwig. *Als Schriftsteller leben: Gespräche mit Peter Handke, Franz Xaver Kroetz, Gerhard Zwerenz, Walter Jens, Peter Rühmkorf, Günter Grass.* Reinbek bei Hamburg: Rowohlt, 1979.

Arnold, Matthew. "The Function of Criticism at the Present Time." In Adams, *Critical Theory Since Plato,* q.v., 583–95.

Aronowitz, Stanley. "Postmodernism and Politics." In *Universal Abandon? The Politics of Postmodernism,* edited by Andrew Ross, 46–62. Minneapolis: University of Minnesota Press, 1989.

Auerbach, Erich. *Mimesis: The Representation of Reality in Western Literature.* Translated by Willard R. Trask. Princeton: Princeton University Press, 1953.

Bakhtin, Mikhail. *The Dialogic Imagination: Four Essays.* Translated by Michael Holquist. Edited by Caryl Emerson and Michael Holquist. Austin: University of Texas Press, 1981.

————. *Problems of Dostoevsky's Poetics.* Translated by R. W. Rotsel. Ann Arbor: Ardis, 1973.

————. *Rabelais and His World.* Translated by Helene Iswolsky. Cambridge, Mass.: MIT Press, 1968.

————. *Speech Genres and Other Late Essays.* Translated by Vern W. McGee. Edited by Caryl Emerson and Michael Holquist. Austin: University of Texas Press, 1986.

Balakian, Anna. "Relativism in the Arts and the Way to the Absolute." In *Relativism in the Arts,* edited by Betty Jean Craige, 75–98. Athens: University of Georgia Press, 1983.

Barone, Dennis. "An Interview with Gilbert Sorrentino." *Partisan Review* 48 (1981): 236–46.

Barth, John. "The Literature of Exhaustion." *Atlantic* (August 1967): 29–34.

————. "The Literature of Replenishment: Postmodernist Fiction." *Atlantic* (January 1980): 65–71.

Barthes, Roland. "The Death of the Author." In *Image-Music-Text,* translated and edited by Stephen Heath, 142–48. Glasgow: Fontana/Collins, 1977.

————. "The Eiffel Tower." In *A Barthes Reader,* edited by Susan Sontag, 236–50. New York: Hill and Wang, 1983.

Baudrillard, Jean. *For a Critique of the Political Economy of the Sign.* Translated by Charles Levin. St. Louis: Telos, 1981.

Baumbach, Jonathan. "Who Do They Think They Are? A Personal History of the Fiction Collective." *TriQuarterly* 43 (1978): 625–34.

Baxandall, Lee, and Stefan Morawski, eds. *Marx and Engels on Literature and Art.* St. Louis: Telos, 1973.

Bellow, Saul. *Herzog.* Harmondsworth: Penguin, 1976.

Benjamin, Walter. *Reflections.* Translated by Edmund Jephcott. Edited by Peter Demetz. New York: Harcourt, 1978.

Bergonzi, Bernard. *The Myth of Modernism and Twentieth-Century Literature.* Brighton: Harvester, 1986.

Bernstein, J. M. *The Philosophy of the Novel: Lukács, Marxism and the Dialectics of Form.* Minneapolis: University of Minnesota Press, 1984.

Bigsby, Christopher. "Robert Coover." In *The Radical Imagination and the Liberal Tradition: Interviews with English and American Novelists,* edited by Christopher Bigsby and Heide Ziegler, 79–92. London: Junction, 1982.

Bohn, Volker. "Später werde ich über das alles genaueres schreiben." *Germanisch-Romanisch Monatsschrift* 26 (neue Folge) (1976): 356–79.

Booth, Wayne. *The Rhetoric of Fiction.* Chicago: University of Chicago Press, 1961.

Borges, Jorge Luis. "Guayaquil." Translated by N. T. di Giovanni. In *Borges: A Reader,* edited by Emir Rodriguez Monegal and Alastair Reid, 311–16. New York: Dutton, 1981.

Bradbury, Malcolm. *The Modern American Novel.* Oxford: Oxford University Press, 1983.

Brenkman, John. "Theses on Cultural Marxism." *Social Text* 7 (1983): 19–33.

Britton, Andrew. "The Myth of Postmodernism: The Bourgeois Intelligentsia in the Age of Reagan." *CineAction!* (Summer 1988): 3–17.

Bronowski, Joseph. "The Act of Recognition." In *The Visionary Eye: Essays in the Arts, Literature, and Science,* edited by Piero Ariotti, 114–27. Cambridge, Mass.: MIT Press, 1978.

Bruss, Elizabeth. *Beautiful Theories.* Baltimore: Johns Hopkins University Press, 1982.

Burke, Kenneth. "The Nature of Art under Capitalism." In *The Philosophy of Literary Form: Studies in Symbolic Action,* 2d ed., 314–22. Baton Rouge: Louisiana State University Press, 1967.

Butler, Christopher. "Scepticism and Experimental Fiction." *Essays in Criticism.* 36 (1986): 47–67.

Calvino, Italo. *If on a winter's night a traveler.* Translated by William Weaver. New York: Harcourt, 1981.

Carter, Angela. *The Sadeian Woman and the Ideology of Pornography.* New York: Pantheon, 1978.

Chabot, C. Barry. "The Problems with Postmodernity." *New Literary History* 20.1 (1988): 1–20.

Conrad, Joseph. *Heart of Darkness*. Edited by Robert Kimbrough. New York: Norton, 1971.

Coover, Robert. *Gerald's Party*. New York: Plume, 1987.

———. *In Bed One Night*. Providence, R.I.: Burning Deck, 1983.

———. "The Kid." In *A Theological Position: Plays*, 11–75. New York: Dutton, 1972.

———. "Love Scene." In *A Theological Position: Plays*, 77–98. New York: Dutton, 1972.

———. *A Night at the Movies Or, You Must Remember This*. New York: Linden; Simon and Schuster, 1987.

———. *Pricksongs and Descants*. New York: New American Library, 1969.

———. *The Public Burning*. New York: Viking, 1977.

———. *Spanking the Maid*. New York: Grove, 1982.

———. "A Theological Position." In *A Theological Position: Plays*, 121–72. New York: Dutton, 1972.

Cope, Jackson I. *Robert Coover's Fictions*. Baltimore: Johns Hopkins University Press, 1986.

Costa Lima, Luiz. "Social Representation and Mimesis." Translated by J. Laurenio de Mello. *New Literary History* 16 (1985): 447–66.

Croce, Benedetto. From *Aesthetic*. In Adams, *Critical Theory Since Plato*, q.v., 727–35.

Culler, Jonathan. "Presupposition and Intertextuality." In *The Pursuit of Signs: Semiotics, Literature, Deconstruction*, 100–118. Ithaca: Cornell University Press, 1981.

———. *Structuralist Poetics: Structuralism, Linguistics and the Study of Literature*. London: Routledge and Kegan Paul, 1975.

Dante. *Vita Nuova*. Translated by Frances de Mey. London: George Bell, 1902.

Danto, Arthur. *Analytical Philosophy of History*. Cambridge: Cambridge University Press, 1965.

———. "The Appreciation and Interpretation of Works of Art." In *Relativism in the Arts*, edited by Betty Jean Craige, 21–44. Athens: University of Georgia Press, 1983.

"A Decade's Top Ten." *Critique: Studies in Modern Fiction* 23.1 (1981): 4.

Derrida, Jacques. *Of Grammatology*. Translated by Gayatri Chakravorty Spivak. Baltimore: Johns Hopkins University Press, 1976.

D'haen, Theo. *Text to Reader: Fowles, Barth, Cortázar and Boon*. Amsterdam: John Benjamins, 1983.

Dilthey, Wilhelm. *Wilhelm Dilthey: Selected Writings*. Translated and edited by H. P. Rickman. Cambridge: Cambridge University Press, 1976.

Dray, William H. *Laws and Explanation in History.* London: Oxford University Press, 1957.

———. *Philosophy of History.* Engelwood Cliffs, N.J.: Prentice-Hall, 1964.

Eagleton, Terry. "Capitalism, Modernism and Postmodernism." *New Left Review* 152 (1985): 60–73.

———. "Last Post." Review of *Post-Structuralism and the Question of History,* edited by Derek Attridge, Geoff Bennington, and Robert Young. *Textual Practices* 2 (1988): 105–11.

Ebert, Teresa L. "The Convergence of Postmodern Innovative Fiction and Science Fiction." *Poetics Today* 1 (1980): 91–104.

Eichenbaum, Boris. "Literary Environment." In *Readings in Russian Poetics: Formalist and Structuralist Views,* edited by Ladislav Matejka and Krystyna Pomorska, 56–65. Cambridge, Mass.: MIT Press, 1971.

———. "The Theory of the 'Formal' Method." In Adams, *Critical Theory Since Plato,* q.v., 829–46.

Eliot, T. S. "Tradition and the Individual Talent." In Adams, *Critical Theory Since Plato,* q.v., 784–87.

———. "The Waste Land." In *The Waste Land and Other Poems,* 27–54. New York: Harcourt, 1962.

Emerson, Ralph Waldo. "The Poet." In Adams, *Critical Theory Since Plato,* q.v., 545–54.

Enzensberger, Hans Magnus. *The Consciousness Industry.* Edited by Michael Roloff. New York: Seabury, 1974.

Farias, Victor. *Heidegger et le Nazisme.* Translated by Myriam Benarroch and Jean-Baptiste Grasset. Paris: Editions Verdier, 1987.

———. *Heidegger and Nazism.* Translated by Paul Burrell and Gabriel R. Ricci. Edited by Joseph Margolis and Tom Rockmore. Philadelphia: Temple University Press, 1989.

Federman, Raymond. "Surfiction—Four Propositions in Form of an Introduction." In *Surfiction: Fiction Now . . . and Tomorrow,* edited by Raymond Federman, 2d ed., 5–15. Chicago: Swallow, 1981.

Fetterley, Judith. *The Resisting Reader: A Feminist Approach to American Fiction.* Bloomington: Indiana University Press, 1978.

Feyerabend, Paul. *Against Method.* London: Verso, 1974.

Fokkema, D. W., and Elrud Kunne-Ibsch. *Theories of Literature in the Twentieth Century: Structuralism, Marxism, Aesthetics of Reception, Semiotics.* London: C. Hirst and Company, 1979.

Foucault, Michel. *The History of Sexuality.* Vol. 1. Translated by Robert Hurley. New York: Pantheon, 1978.

———. *The Order of Things: An Archeology of the Human Sciences.* New York: Vintage, 1973.

———. "What Is an Author?" In *Language, Counter-Memory, Practice,* translated by Donald F. Bouchard and Sherry Simon, edited by Donald F. Bouchard, 113–38. Ithaca: Cornell University Press, 1977.

Gadamer, Hans-Georg. *The Relevance of the Beautiful and Other Essays.* Translated by Nicholas Walker. Edited by Robert Bernasconi. Cambridge: Cambridge University Press, 1986.

———. *Truth and Method.* New York: Continuum, 1975.

Gaddis, William. *The Recognitions.* Harmondsworth: Penguin, 1985.

Gado, Frank. *First Person: Conversations on Writers and Writing.* Schenectady: Union College Press, 1973.

Gallie, W. B. *Philosophy and the Historical Understanding.* New York: Schocken, 1964.

Gardner, John. *On Moral Fiction.* New York: Basic Books, 1978.

Gass, William. *Fiction and the Figures of Life.* New York: Knopf, 1970.

———. *Habitations of the Word: Essays.* New York: Simon and Schuster, 1985.

———. *The World Within the Word: Essays.* New York: Knopf, 1978.

Genet, Jean. *The Thief's Journal.* Translated by Bernard Frechtman. New York: Grove, 1973.

Gilbert, Stuart. *James Joyce's* Ulysses*: A Study.* New York: Vintage, 1955.

Gillespie, Michael Allen. *Hegel, Heidegger, and the Ground of History.* Chicago: University of Chicago Press, 1984.

Girard, René. *Deceit, Desire, and the Novel: Self and Other in Literary Structure.* Baltimore: Johns Hopkins University Press, 1965.

Glasheen, Adaline. *Third Census of* Finnegans Wake*: An Index of Characters and Their Roles.* Berkeley: University of California Press, 1977.

Gorer, Geoffrey. *The Life and Ideas of the Marquis de Sade.* 2d ed. London: Panther, 1965.

Graff, Gerald. *Literature Against Itself: Literary Ideas in Modern Society.* Chicago: University of Chicago Press, 1979.

———. "Teaching the Humanities." *Partisan Review* 51 (1984): 850–52.

Grass, Günter. *Dog Years.* Translated by Ralph Manheim. New York: Harcourt, 1965.

Green, Geoffrey. *Literary Criticism and the Structures of History: Erich Auerbach and Leo Spitzer.* Lincoln: University of Nebraska Press, 1982.

Green, Leonard, Jonathan Culler, and Richard Klein. Interview with Fredric Jameson. *Diacritics* 12.3 (1982): 72–91.

Greenberg, Clement. "Avant-Garde and Kitsch." In *Mass Culture: The Popular Arts in America,* edited by Bernard Rosenberg and David Manning White, 98–110. Glencoe, Ill.: Free Press, 1957.

Greenman, Myron. "Some Experimental Modes." *Modern Fiction Studies* 20 (1974): 307–16.

Greiner, Donald. "Antony Lamont in Search of Gilbert Sorrentino: Character and *Mulligan Stew.*" *The Review of Contemporary Fiction* 1 (1981): 104–12.

Grube, G. M. A. *The Greek and Roman Critics.* London: Methuen, 1965.

Habermas, Jürgen. "Modernity versus Postmodernity." *New German Critique* 22 (1981): 3–14.

Handke, Peter. *Across.* Translated by Ralph Manheim. New York: Farrar, Straus and Giroux, 1986.

———. *Ich bin ein Bewohner des Elfenbeinturms.* Frankfurt am Main: Suhrkamp, 1972.

———. *The Innerworld of the Outerworld of the Innerworld.* Translated by Michael Roloff. New York: Continuum, 1974.

———. *Kaspar and Other Plays.* Translated by Michael Roloff. New York: Farrar, Straus and Giroux, 1969.

———. *Offending the Audience.* Translated by Michael Roloff. London: Methuen, 1971.

———. *The Ride Across Lake Constance and Other Plays.* Translated by Michael Roloff. New York: Farrar, Straus and Giroux, 1976.

———. *Three by Peter Handke.* Translated by Ralph Manheim and Michael Roloff. New York: Bard, 1977.

———. *Two Novels by Peter Handke.* Translated by Ralph Manheim. New York: Bard, 1979.

———. *Wunschloses Unglück.* Salzburg: Residenz, 1972.

Harries, Karsten. "Heidegger as a Political Thinker." *The Review of Metaphysics* 29 (1976): 642–69.

———. *The Meaning of Modern Art: A Philosophical Interpretation.* Evanston: Northwestern University Press, 1968.

Hartman, Geoffrey. "Blindness and Insight: Paul de Man, Fascism, and Deconstruction." *The New Republic* (7 March 1988): 26, 28–31.

Hassan, Ihab. "Making Sense: The Trials of Postmodern Discourse." *New Literary History* 18 (1987): 437–59.

———. *Paracriticisms.* Urbana: University of Illinois Press, 1975.

———. *The Right Promethean Fire: Imagination, Science, and Cultural Change.* Urbana: University of Illinois Press, 1980.

———. "Wars of Desire, Politics of the Word." In *Representation and Performance in Postmodern Fiction,* edited by Maurice Couturier, 47–55. Montpellier, France: Delta, 1982.

Heidegger, Martin. *Being and Time.* Translated by John Macquarrie and Edward Robinson. New York: Harper and Row, 1962.

———. *Discourse on Thinking.* Translated by John M. Anderson and E. Hans Freund. New York: Harper, 1966.

———. "Letter on Humanism." Translated by Frank A. Capuzzi and J. Glenn

Gray. In *Basic Writings,* edited by David Farrell Krell, 193–242. London: Routledge and Kegan Paul, 1978.

———. "Martin Heidegger: Political Texts, 1933–34." Translated by William S. Lewis. *New German Critique* 45 (1988): 96–114.

———. "'Only A God Can Save Us': *Der Spiegel*'s Interview with Martin Heidegger." With Rudolph Augstein and Georg Folff. Translated by John D. Caputo and Maria P. Alter. *Philosophy Today* 20 (1976): 267–84.

———. "On the Essence of Truth." In *Basic Writings,* edited by David Farrell Krell, 117–41. New York: Harper and Row, 1977.

———. *Poetry, Language, Thought.* Translated by Albert Hofstadter. New York: Harper and Row, 1971.

———. "The Self-Assertion of the German University: Address, Delivered on the Solemn Assumption of the Rectorate of the University of Freiburg"; "The Rectorate 1933/34: Facts and Thoughts." Preface by Hermann Heidegger. Translated by Karsten Harries. Introduction by Karsten Harries. *The Review of Metaphysics* 38 (1985): 467–502.

Hirsch, David H. "Paul de Man and the Politics of Deconstruction." *The Sewanee Review* 96 (1988): 330–38.

Hirsch, E. D. *The Aims of Interpretation.* Chicago: University of Chicago Press, 1976.

———. "Meaning and Significance Reinterpreted." *Critical Inquiry* 11 (1984): 202–25.

———. *Validity of Interpretation.* New Haven: Yale University Press, 1967.

Holdheim, W. W. *The Hermeneutic Mode: Essays on Time in Literature and Literary Theory.* Ithaca: Cornell University Press, 1984.

Holquist, Michael. "Bakhtin and Rabelais: Theory as Praxis." *Boundary 2* 11 (1982/83): 5–19.

Horkheimer, Max. "The Social Function of Philosophy." In Adams and Searle, *Critical Theory Since 1965,* q.v., 687–96.

Horn, Peter. "Die Sprache der Vernünftigen und die Sprache der Unvernünftigen." In *Handke: Ansätze - Analysen - Anmerkungen,* edited by Manfred Jurgensen, 45–64. Bern: Franke, 1979.

Hoy, David Couzens. *The Critical Circle: Literature, History, and Philosophical Hermeneutics.* Berkeley: University of California Press, 1978.

Hutcheon, Linda. *Narcissistic Narrative: The Metafictional Paradox.* New York: Methuen, 1984.

———. *A Theory of Parody: The Teachings of Twentieth-Century Art Forms.* New York: Methuen, 1985.

Huyssen, Andreas. *After the Great Divide: Modernism, Mass Culture, Postmodernism.* Bloomington, Indiana University Press, 1986.

Iser, Wolfgang. *The Act of Reading: A Theory of Aesthetic Response.* Baltimore: Johns Hopkins University Press, 1980.

Jameson, Fredric. "Beyond the Cave: Modernism and Modes of Production." In *The Horizon of Literature*, edited by Paul Hernadi, 157–82. Lincoln: University of Nebraska Press, 1982.

———. "The Politics of Theory: Ideological Positions in the Postmodernism Debate." *New German Critique* 33 (1984): 53–65.

———. "Postmodernism, or The Cultural Logic of Late Capitalism." *New Left Review* 146 (1984): 53–92.

———. "World Literature in an Age of Multinational Capitalism." In *The Current in Criticism: Essays on the Present and Future of Literary Theory*, edited by Clayton Koelb and Virgil Lokke, 139–58. West Lafayette: Purdue University Press, 1987.

Jardine, Alice. "Gynesis." *Diacritics* 12 (1982): 54–65.

Jauss, Hans Robert. *Aesthetic Experience and Literary Hermeneutics*. Translated by Michael Shaw. Minneapolis: University of Minnesota Press, 1982.

———. "Literature and Hermeneutics." In *What Is Criticism?* translated by Timothy Bahti, edited by Paul Hernadi, 134–47. Bloomington: University of Indiana Press, 1981.

———. "Theses on the Transition from the Aesthetics of Literary Works to a Theory of Aesthetic Experience." In *Interpretation of Narrative*, edited by Mario J. Valdés and Owen J. Miller, 137–47. Toronto: University of Toronto Press, 1978.

———. *Toward an Aesthetic of Reception*. Translated by Timothy Bahti. Minneapolis: University of Minnesota Press, 1982.

Johnson, Barbara. "Preface to the Paperback Edition. A Note on the Wartime Writings of Paul de Man." In *A World of Difference*, xi–xviii. Baltimore: Johns Hopkins University Press, 1989.

Joyce, James. *Finnegans Wake*. New York: Viking, 1944.

Karlinsky, Simon, ed. *The Nabokov-Wilson Letters: Correspondence between Vladimir Nabokov and Edmund Wilson, 1940–1971*. New York: Harper and Row, 1979.

Kavanagh, James M. "'To the Same Defect': Toward a Critique of the Ideology of the Aesthetic." In *Literature and Ideology*, edited by Harry R. Garvin, 102–23. Lewisberg: Bucknell University Press, 1982.

Kawin, Bruce F. *The Mind of the Novel: Reflexive Fiction and the Ineffable*. Princeton: Princeton University Press, 1982.

Kearney, Richard. *The Wake of Imagination: Toward a Postmodern Culture*. Minneapolis: University of Minnesota Press, 1988.

Kenner, Hugh. "The Next Hundred Years." In *The Horizon of Literature*, edited by Paul Hernadi, 199–210. Lincoln: University of Nebraska Press, 1982.

———. "The Traffic in Words: No place for the avant-garde." Review of *Mulligan Stew*, by Gilbert Sorrentino. *Harper's* (June 1979): 83–84, 88–90.

Kermode, Frank. "The Model of a Modern Modernist." *New York Review of Books* (1 May 1975): 20–23.

Klinkowitz, Jerome. "Aspects of Handke: Fiction." *Partisan Review* 45 (1978): 416–24.

———. *Literary Disruptions: The Making of a Post-Contemporary American Fiction.* 2d ed. Urbana: University of Illinois Press, 1980.

———. *Literary Subversions: New American Fiction and the Practice of Criticism.* Carbondale: Southern Illinois University Press, 1985.

———. *The Self-Apparent Word: Fiction as Language/Language as Fiction.* Carbondale: Southern Illinois University Press, 1984.

———. "Walter Abish: An Interview." *fiction international* 4/5 (1975): 93–100.

———. "Walter Abish and the Surfaces of Life." Review of *How German Is It. The Georgia Review* 35 (1981): 416–20.

Klinkowitz, Jerome, and Roy R. Behrens. *The Life of Fiction.* Urbana: University of Illinois Press, 1977.

Kostelanetz, Richard. "An ABC of Contemporary Reading." In *Esthetics Contemporary*, edited by Richard Kostelanetz, 339–76. Buffalo: Prometheus Books, 1978.

———. *The End of Intelligent Writing: Literary Politics in America.* New York: Sheed and Ward, 1973.

Kowinski, William Severini. *The Malling of America: An Inside Look at the Great Consumer Paradise.* New York: Morrow, 1985.

Kristeva, Julia. "Postmodernism?" In *Romanticism, Modernism, Postmodernism*, edited by Harry R. Garvin, 36–41. Lewisberg: Bucknell University Press, 1980.

———. *Le texte du roman: approche semiologique d'une structure discursive transformationelle.* The Hague: Mouton, 1970.

Kuhn, Thomas S. *The Structure of Scientific Revolutions.* 2d ed. Chicago: University of Chicago Press, 1974.

Laclau, Ernesto. "Politics and the Limits of Modernity." In *Universal Abandon? The Politics of Postmodernism*, edited by Andrew Ross, 63–82. Minneapolis: University of Minnesota Press, 1989.

Laclau, Ernesto, and Chantal Mouffe. *Hegemony and Socialist Strategy: Towards a Radical Democratic Politics.* Translated by Winston Moore and Paul Cammack. London: Verso, 1985.

Leaska, Mitchell. *The Novels of Virginia Woolf: From Beginning to End.* New York: John Jay, 1977.

Leavis, F. R. "After *To the Lighthouse*." In *Twentieth-Century Interpretations of* To the Lighthouse, edited by Thomas A. Vogler, 99–100. Englewood Cliffs, N.J.: Prentice-Hall, 1970.

Levin, Harry. "What Was Modernism?" In *Refractions*, 271–95. New York: Oxford University Press, 1966.

Link, Hannelore. *Rezeptionsforschung: Eine Einführung in Methoden und Probleme.* Stuttgart: Kohlhammer, 1980.

Lodge, David. "The Sad Heart at the Carnival." Review of *Aberration of Starlight,* by Gilbert Sorrentino. *TLS* (10 July 1981): 774.

Lotringer, Sylvère. "Wie Deutsch Ist Es." Interview with Walter Abish. *Semiotext(e)* 4 (1982): 160–78.

Love, Ursula. "'Als sei ich . . . ihr GESCHUNDENES HERZ': Identifizierung und negative Kreativität in Peter Handke's *Wunschloses Unglück.*" *Seminar* 17 (1979): 130–46.

Löwith, Karl. "My Last Meeting with Heidegger in Rome, 1936." Translated by Richard Wolin and Melissa J. Cox. *New German Critique* 45 (1988): 115–16.

———. "The Political Implications of Heidegger's Existentialism." Translated by Richard Wolin and Melissa J. Cox. *New German Critique* 45 (1988): 117–34.

Lukács, Georg. *Essays on Realism.* Translated by David Fernbach. Edited by Rodney Livingston. London: Lawrence and Wishart, 1980.

———. "Realism in the Balance." Translated by Rodney Livingstone. In *Aesthetics and Politics,* Ernst Bloch et al., 28–59. London: New Left Books, 1979.

———. *Studies in European Realism.* Translated by E. Bone. London: Merlin Press, 1972.

———. *The Theory of the Novel.* Translated by Anna Bostock. Cambridge, Mass.: MIT Press, 1971.

———. *Writer and Critic and Other Essays.* Translated and edited by Arthur Kahn. London: Merlin, 1970.

Lunn, Eugene. *Marxism and Modernism: A Historical Study of Lukács, Brecht, Benjamin, and Adorno.* Berkeley: University of California Press, 1982.

Lyons, Gene. "Report on the Fiction Collective." *TriQuarterly* 43 (1978): 635–47.

Lyotard, Jean-François. *The Postmodern Condition: A Report on Knowledge.* Translated by Geoff Bennington and Brian Massumi. Minneapolis: University of Minnesota Press, 1984.

Manger, Philip. "Jurek Becker, *Irreführung des Behörder.*" *Seminar* 17 (1981): 147–63.

Mann, Heinrich. *Der Untertan.* Berlin: Aufbau-Verlag, 1979.

Mann, Thomas. "Germany and the Germans." *The Yale Review* 75 (1986): 181–99.

Martin, Richard. "Walter Abish's Fictions: Perfect Unfamiliarity, Familiar Imperfection." *Journal of American Studies* 17 (1983): 229–41.

Marx, Karl. From *The Critique of Political Economy.* In Adams, *Critical Theory Since Plato,* q.v., 633–34.

McCaffery, Larry. *The Metafictional Muse: The Works of Robert Coover, Donald Barthelme, and William Gass*. Pittsburgh: University of Pittsburgh Press, 1982.

———. "Robert Coover on His Own and Other Fictions: An Interview." *Genre* 14 (1981): 45–63.

McCaffery, Larry, and Sinda Gregory. "An Interview with Walter Abish." In *Alive and Writing: Interviews with American Authors of the 1980s,* edited by Larry McCaffery and Sinda Gregory, 7–25. Urbana: University of Illinois Press, 1987.

McHale, Brian. Review of *In Form: Digressions on the Act of Fiction*, by Ronald Sukenick. *Poetics Today* 6 (1985): 801.

Megill, Allan. *Prophets of Extremity: Nietzsche, Heidegger, Foucault, Derrida.* Berkeley: University of California Press, 1985.

Mellard, James. *The Exploded Form: The Modernist Novel in America.* Urbana: University of Illinois Press, 1980.

Mendelson, Edward. "The Sacred, The Profane and *The Crying of Lot 49*." In *Pynchon: A Collection of Critical Essays*, edited by Edward Mendelson, 112–46. Englewood Cliffs, N.J.: Prentice-Hall, 1978.

Messerli, Douglas. "The Role of Voice in Nonmodernist Fiction." *Contemporary Literature* 25 (1984): 281–304.

Mishan, E. J. *Pornography, Psychedelics and Technology: Essays on the Limits to Freedom.* London: George Allen and Unwin, 1980.

Montaigne, Michel de. "On Custom, and Why We Should Not Easily Change an Accepted Law." In *The Essential Montaigne*, translated and edited by Serge Hughes, 48–63. New York: Mentor, 1970.

Morawski, Stefan. *Inquiries into the Fundamentals of Aesthetics.* Cambridge, Mass.: MIT Press, 1978.

Morrison, Toni. *The Bluest Eye.* New York: Washington Square Press, 1972.

Mouffe, Chantal. "Radical Democracy: Modern or Postmodern?" In *Universal Abandon? The Politics of Postmodernism*, edited by Andrew Ross, 31–45. Minneapolis: University of Minnesota Press, 1989.

Nabokov, Vladimir. *Strong Opinions.* New York: McGraw-Hill, 1973.

Nägele, Rainer. "Modernism and Postmodernism." *Studies in Twentieth-Century Literature* 5 (1980): 5–25.

Nägele, Rainer, and Renate Voris. *Peter Handke.* Munich: Beck, 1978.

Nahm, Milton C. *The Artist as Creator.* Baltimore: Johns Hopkins University Press, 1956.

Newman, Charles. *The Post-Modern Aura: The Act of Fiction in an Age of Inflation.* Evanston: Northwestern University Press, 1985.

Nietzsche, Friedrich. *The Will to Power.* Translated by Walter Kaufmann and R. J. Hollingdale. Edited by Walter Kaufman. New York: Vintage, 1968.

Norris, Christopher. *The Contest of Faculties: Philosophy and Theory after Deconstruction*. London: Methuen, 1985.

O'Brien, Flann. *At-Swim-Two-Birds*. New York: Plume, 1976.

O'Brien, John. "Every Man His Voice." *The Review of Contemporary Fiction* 1 (1981): 62–80.

———. "An Interview with Gilbert Sorrentino." *The Review of Contemporary Fiction* 1 (1981): 5–27.

O'Neil, John. "Power and the Splitting (*Spaltung*) of Language." *New Literary History* 14 (1983): 695–710.

Panofsky, Erwin. *Studies in Iconology: Humanistic Themes in the Art of the Renaissance*. 1939. New York: Harper and Row, 1962.

Pavel, Thomas G. *Fictional Worlds*. Cambridge, Mass.: Harvard University Press, 1986.

Pieiller, Evelyne. "Le derrière blanc de la bonne." Review of *Spanking the Maid*. *La Quinzaine littéraire* (July 16–31, 1984): 20.

Pynchon, Thomas. Introduction to *Slow Learner*, xi–xxxiv. New York: Bantam, 1984.

Quine, W. V. O. "The Ways of Paradox." In *The Ways of Paradox and Other Essays*, rev. ed., 1–18. Cambridge, Mass.: Harvard University Press, 1976.

Quinn, Hal. "The Holocaust Trial." *Maclean's* (11 March 1985): 42–46.

Rentschler, Eric. "New German Film and the Discourse of Bitburg." *New German Critique* 36 (1985): 67–90.

Rich, Adrienne. *Poems: Selected and New, 1950–1974*. New York: Norton, 1974.

Ricoeur, Paul. *Hermeneutics and the Human Sciences*. Translated and edited by John B. Thompson. Cambridge: Cambridge University Press, 1981.

———. "Narrative and Hermeneutics." In *Essays on Aesthetics: Perspectives on the Work of Monroe C. Beardsley*, edited by John Fisher, 149–60. Philadelphia: Temple University Press, 1983.

———. *Time and Narrative*. 2 vols. Translated by Kathleen McLaughlin and David Pellauer. Chicago: University of Chicago Press, 1984; 1985.

Riffaterre, Michael. *Text Production*. Translated by Terese Lyons. New York: Columbia University Press, 1983.

Rigney, Barbara Hill. *Lilith's Daughters: Women and Religion in Contemporary Fiction*. Madison: University of Wisconsin Press, 1982.

Robbe-Grillet, Alain. *For a New Novel: Essays on Fiction*. Translated by Richard Howard. New York: Grove, 1965.

Robinson, Lillian S. "Treason Our Text: Feminist Challenges to the Literary Canon." In Adams and Searle, *Critical Theory Since 1965*, q.v., 572–82.

Rorty, Richard. *Philosophy and the Mirror of Nature*. Princeton: Princeton University Press, 1979.

———. "Postmodernist Bourgeois Liberalism." In *Hermeneutics and Praxis*, edited by Robert Hollinger, 214–21. Notre Dame: University of Notre Dame Press, 1985.

Rousseau, Jean-Jacques. *Les Confessions.* Vol. 1. Edited by Bernard Gagnebin and Marcel Raymond. Paris: Gallimard, 1973.

Russell, Charles. *Poets, Prophets, and Revolutionaries: The Literary Avant-garde from Rimbaud through Postmodernism.* London: Oxford University Press, 1985.

Sade, Marquis de. *La Philosophie dans le boudoir.* Vol. III. *Œuvres completes du Marquis de Sade.* Edited by Gilbert Lely. Paris: Au Circle du Livre Precieux, 1966.

————. *Philosophy in the Bedroom.* In *The Marquis de Sade: The Complete Justine, Philosophy in the Bedroom, and Other Writings,* translated and edited by Richard Seaver and Austyrn Wainhouse, 177–367. New York: Grove, 1966.

Salgas, Jean-Pierre. "Les deux amours de Robert Coover: Cervantes et Beckett." *La Quinzaine littéraire* (July 16–31, 1984): 19–20.

Salzman, Arthur M. *The Fictions of William Gass: The Consolation of Language.* Carbondale: Southern Illinois University Press, 1986.

Sartre, Jean-Paul. *What Is Literature?* Translated by Bernard Frechtman. New York: Harper and Row, 1965.

Sarup, Madan. *An Introductory Guide to Post-Structuralism and Postmodernism.* Athens: University of Georgia Press, 1989.

Schleiermacher, F. D. E. *Hermeneutics: The Handwritten Manuscripts.* Edited by Heinz Kimmerle. Translated by James Duke and Jackson Forstman. Missoula, Mont.: Scholars Press, 1977.

————. "*The Hermeneutics:* Outline of the 1819 Lectures." Translated by Jan Wojcik and Roland Haas. *New Literary History* 10 (1978): 1–16.

Schnabel, Julian. *CVJ: Nicknames of Maitre D's & Other Excerpts from Life.* New York: Random, 1987.

Scholes, Robert. *Fabulation and Metafiction.* Urbana: University of Illinois Press, 1979.

————. *Semiotics and Interpretation.* New Haven: Yale University Press, 1982.

————. *Structural Fabulation: An Essay on Fiction of the Future.* Notre Dame: Notre Dame University Press, 1975.

Schücking, Levin L. "Literarische 'Fehlurteile': Ein Beitrag zur Lehre vom Geschmacksträgertyp." In *Literarische Wertung: Texte zur Entwicklung der Wertungsdiskussion in der Literaturwissenschaften,* edited by Norbert Mecklenburg, 9–24. Tübingen: Deutscher Taschenbuch, 1977.

Schütz, Alfred. *On Phenomenology and Social Relations: Selected Writings.* Edited by Helmut R. Wagner. Chicago: University of Chicago Press, 1970.

Seung, T. K. *Semiotics and Thematics in Hermeneutics.* New York: Columbia University Press, 1982.

Seward, Barbara. *The Symbolic Rose.* New York: Columbia University Press, 1960.

Sherzer, Dina. *Representation in Contemporary French Fiction.* Lincoln: University of Nebraska Press, 1986.

Singer, Alan. *A Metaphorics of Fiction: Discontinuity and Discourse in the Modern Novel.* Tallahassee: Florida State University Press, 1983.

Smith, Amanda. "Robert Coover." Interview. *Publishers Weekly* (26 December 1986): 44–45.

Sontag, Susan. "The Aesthetics of Silence." In *Styles of Radical Will,* 3–34. New York: Delta, 1981.

Sorrentino, Gilbert. *Aberration of Starlight.* Harmondsworth: Penguin, 1981.

———. *Mulligan Stew.* New York: Grove, 1979.

———. *Something Said.* San Francisco: North Point, 1984.

———. *Splendide-Hôtel.* Elmwood Park, Ill.: Dalkey Archive Press, 1984.

———. *Steelwork.* New York: Pantheon, 1970.

Stambrook, F. G. *European Nationalism in the Nineteenth Century.* Melbourne: Cheshire, 1969.

Stephanson, Anders. "Regarding Postmodernism—A Conversation with Fredric Jameson." In *Universal Abandon? The Politics of Postmodernism,* edited by Andrew Ross, 3–30. Minneapolis: University of Minnesota Press, 1989.

Stephens, Michael. *The Dramaturgy of Style: Voice in Short Fiction.* Carbondale: Southern Illinois University Press, 1986.

Sukenick, Ronald. *In Form: Digressions on the Act of Fiction.* Carbondale: Southern Illinois University Press, 1985.

———. *98.6.* New York: Fiction Collective, 1975.

Suvin, Darko. "The Mirror and the Dynamo." In *Radical Perspectives in the Arts,* edited by Lee Baxandall, 68–88. Harmondsworth: Penguin, 1972.

Thielemans, Johan. "The Voice of the Irresponsible: Irresponsible Voices? On Gilbert Sorrentino's *Mulligan Stew.*" In *Representation and Performance in Postmodern Fiction,* edited by Maurice Couturier, 13–29. Montpellier, France: Delta, 1982.

Thiher, Allen. *Words in Reflection: Modern Language Theory and Postmodern Fiction.* Chicago: University of Chicago Press, 1984.

Thuswalder, Werner. *Sprach- und Gattungsexperiment bei Peter Handke: Praxis und Theorie.* Munich: Alfred Winter, 1976.

Tilton, John W. *Cosmic Satire in the Contemporary Novel.* Lewisberg: Bucknell University Press, 1977.

Tocqueville, Alexis de. *Democracy in America.* Vol. 2. Translated by Henry Reeve. New York: Colonial, 1900.

Varsava, Jerry A. "Another Exemplary Fiction: Ambiguity in Coover's *Spanking the Maid.*" *Studies in Short Fiction* 21 (1984): 235–41.

———. "The Last Fictions: Calvino's Borgesian Odyssey." In *Borges and His Successors*, edited by Edna Aizenberg, 183–99. Columbia, Mo.: University of Missouri Press, 1990.

———. Review of *The Philosophy of the Novel: Lukács, Marxism and the Dialectics of Form*, by J. M. Bernstein. *Modern Fiction Studies* 31 (1985): 455–56.

———. "Walter Abish." *Post-War Literatures in English* (December 1989): 1–8.

Vlastos, Gregory. "Zeno of Elea." *The Encyclopedia of Philosophy*. 1967; rpt. 1972.

Warner, Marina. *Alone of All Her Sex: The Myth and the Cult of the Virgin Mary*. New York: Pocket Books, 1976.

Wellek, René. "Poetics, Interpretation, and Criticism." In *The Attack on Literature*, 33–47. Chapel Hill: University of North Carolina Press, 1982.

White, Hayden. "The Fictions of Factual Representation." In *The Literature of Fact*, edited by Angus Fletcher, 21–44. Baltimore: Johns Hopkins University Press, 1973.

———. *Metahistory: The Historical Imagination in the Nineteenth Century*. Baltimore: Johns Hopkins University Press, 1973.

———. *Tropics of Discourse: Essays in Cultural Criticism*. Baltimore: Johns Hopkins University Press, 1978.

———. "The Value of Narrativity in the Representation of Reality." *Critical Inquiry* 7 (1980): 5–27.

Wiener, Jon. "Deconstructing de Man." *The Nation* (9 January 1988): 22–24.

Winter, Hans-Gerhard. "Von der Dokumentarliteratur zur 'neuen Subjectivität': Anmerkungen zur westdeutschen Literatur zur siebziger Jahre." *Seminar* 17 (1981): 95–113.

Wolin, Richard. "The French Heidegger Debate." *New German Critique* 45 (1988): 135–61.

Woolf, Virginia. "Modern Fiction." In *Virginia Woolf: Selections from Her Essays*, edited by Walter James, 116–23. London: Chatto and Windus, 1966.

———. *To the Lighthouse*. New York: Harcourt, 1955.

"Yale Scholar's Articles Found in Nazi Paper." *New York Times* (2 December 1987): B1, B6.

Zamora, Lois. "Clichés and Defamiliarization in the Fiction of Manuel Puig and Luis Rafael Sanchez." *The Journal of Aesthetics and Art Criticism* 41 (1983) 420–36.

Zeraffa, Michel. *Fictions: The Novel and Social Reality*. Translated by Catherine Burns and Tom Burns. Harmondsworth: Penguin, 1976.

Zima, Peter. *Textsoziologie: Eine kritische Einführung*. Stuttgart: J. B. Metzler, 1980.

Index

Abish, Walter, 31, 34, 82–108
—works: *Alphabetical Africa,* 84, 198n.1;
  How German Is It, 22, 77–78, 82–86,
  95–108, 180; *In the Future Perfect,* 86,
  93–96; *Minds Meet,* 84–85, 86–93
Ada (Nabokov), 21, 59, 160
Adorno, Theodor, 60, 76, 102–3, 172,
  200n.13
The Adventures of Huckleberry Finn
  (Twain), 72
Aldridge, John, ix–x, 7–10, 19, 41, 65–
  66, 70, 73, 79
Alighieri, Dante, 44, 131–34, 171
Alter, Robert, 176
Althusser, Louis, 53
Aristotle, ix–x, 2–5, 42, 53, 54
Arnold, Matthew, 14, 20–21
Aronowitz, Stanley, 186
Ashberry, John, 96, 98
At-Swim-Two-Birds (O'Brien), 170–71, 173
Auden, W. H., 153
Auerbach, Erich, x, 42–47, 53, 64
Augustine, 67
author, the: Barthes on, 49–50; Foucault
  on, 50–51; Hirsch on, 47–48, 51; and
  the reader, 46–51; Ricoeur on, 48, 56

Bakhtin, Mikhail, xii, 5, 76, 102, 114,
  166–73 (passim), 208–9n.10

Baldwin, James, 161
Balzac, Honoré de, 5, 45, 67
Barth, John, 8, 17, 19, 72–73, 110
Barthelme, Donald, 16–17, 24, 27,
  31, 65
Barthes, Roland, 49–50, 67, 88, 136, 160
Baudrillard, Jean, 107
Beauvoir, Simone de, 123
Becker, Jurek, 148
Beckett, Samuel, 29, 59, 60, 112
Bellow, Saul, 8, 19, 66, 200–1n.13
Benjamin, Walter, 152
Bennett, Arnold, 11
Bernard, Thomas, 85
Bloom, Harold, 160
Boccaccio, Giovanni, 128
Booth, Wayne, 70
Borges, Jorge Luis, 10, 200n.13
Bowering, George, 111
Bradbury, Malcolm, 180
Brecht, Bertolt, 4–5, 23, 147
Brenkman, John, 51
Britton, Andrew, 186–87
Bronowski, Joseph, 55
Bruss, Elizabeth, 36–37, 38
Burgess, Anthony, 24
Burke, Kenneth, 172, 175
Burroughs, William, 14, 31, 146
Butler, Christopher, 108

229